D0432600

# After the Crisis

# After the Crisis

## Reform, Recovery, and Growth in Europe

EDITED BY

Francesco Caselli, Mário Centeno, and José Tavares

UNIVERSITY PRESS

OXFORD
UNIVERSITY PRESS

Great Clarendon Street, Oxford, OX2 6DP,
United Kingdom

Oxford University Press is a department of the University of Oxford. It furthers the University's objective of excellence in research, scholarship, and education by publishing worldwide. Oxford is a registered trade mark of Oxford University Press in the UK and in certain other countries



First Edition published in 2016

Impression: 1



Published in the United States of America by Oxford University Press
198 Madison Avenue, New York, NY 10016, United States of America

British Library Cataloguing in Publication Data
Data available

Library of Congress Control Number: 2015957297

ISBN 978–0–19–875468–8

Printed in Great Britain by
Clays Ltd, St Ives plc

# Foreword

*Carlos da Silva Costa, Governor of Banco de Portugal*

'If one does not know to which port one is sailing, no wind is favourable.'
*Lucius Annaeus Seneca*

In January 2014 I invited Prof. Mário Centeno to organize a debate and carry out an in-depth study on structural reform and macroeconomic adjustment processes in the context of an Economic and Monetary Union, the only restriction being to ensure the project's scientific quality. Prof. Mário Centeno has worked intensively since then, together with renowned scholars. To this end, Banco de Portugal held a Workshop on 16 January 2015[1] and the 'Growth and Reform in Europe in the Wake of Economic Crisis' conference on 9 May 2015.[2] Important contributions were presented—some of which are compiled in this book—that define the challenges facing Europe in the near future to ensure the prosperity of each member and the union as a whole.

This project is part of Banco de Portugal's express concern to contribute to the creation of wide scientific debate on the causes of current macroeconomic imbalances, the operational rules in a monetary union, and the requirements for the successful participation of member states. These are key elements for defining the areas of consensus and of compromise to underpin the discussion of economic policy guidelines, within a framework of reconciliation of short-term, long-term, and inter-generational interests.

Europe is at the start of an economic recovery process, after more than eight years since the outset of the international financial crisis. At this stage, it is essential to reflect on the economic growth model we want for Europe and, in that context, define objectives, identify constraints, and establish a strategy to achieve those objectives. In addition, reforms must be identified that need to be introduced into the European institutional model for the strategy to work.

[1] Adjustment in European Economies in the Wake of the Economic Crisis' Workshop, https://www.bportugal.pt/en-US/OBancoeoEurosistema/Eventos/Pages/WorkshopAdjustmentinEuropeanEconomiesintheWakeoftheEconomicCrisis.aspx.

[2] http://confeuroeconomy.bportugal.pt/en-US/Home/Pages/default.aspx.

## I. What Type of Economic Growth Model for Europe?

The reflection on the type of economic growth model for Europe must necessarily take into account European citizens' income aspirations and the existing capacity to fulfil such aspirations. We know that there is currently a gap between European society's aspirations and the production capacity to fulfil them. To prolong this situation will place pressure on member states' fiscal policies to raise expenditure and may also lead to an increase in emigration and household indebtedness. Hence, the priority is to identify and put into practice conditions that promote sustainable potential output growth in Europe as a whole and in every member country.

### *What Should Be Our Goal?*

Europe must aim to pave the way for a rise in the per capita income of Europeans, in a context of achieving an unemployment rate close to the natural rate and of safeguarding fundamental macroeconomic balances. In fact, an increase in per capita income with high unemployment gives rise to social cohesion problems, which will be all the more serious the more unequal is the territorial distribution of unemployment. In turn, an increase in per capita income based on the activity of sectors fed by demand that is not sustainable in the long term—supported, for example, by the growing indebtedness of economic agents—will prove unsustainable and hence temporary. One cannot forget that the processes to correct this type of situation involve high macroeconomic, social, and personal costs.

The increase in per capita income does not mean that sustainable prosperity has been achieved in Europe, as it could be temporary. The unemployment rate must be considered simultaneously with the sustainability of economic agents' indebtedness levels and their implications for society's cohesion must be assessed.

### *What Are the Constraints on Achieving this Goal?*

In the pursuit of the goal of increasing per capita income,the euro area currently faces a series of constraints, caused by an accumulation of imbalances in the past.

First, the economic agents' indebtedness levels are different across member states and often quite high, which limits policies (in terms of their nature and sustainability) as well as the initiatives of the economic agents in question.

Second, long-term unemployment levels are very high. This means that jobs must be created not only to absorb unemployment resulting from the

Schumpeterian process and the increment of productivity, but also to absorb this stock of long-term unemployed.

Third, restrictions resulting from demographic trends, with the progressive ageing of the population (associated with a higher life expectancy and a lower birth rate) and the consequent decline in the proportion of the labour force.

### *Which Strategy Should we Adopt?*

The increase in the rate of return on new investment is instrumental to optimizing saving allocation, achieving an increase in potential output, and ensuring the sustainability of the European social model. This means that value added per asset in Europe will have to grow more than would be necessary with a younger population and a less inclusive social model. It is therefore crucial to allocate resources efficiently and, at this level, the financial system plays a key role.

The strategy to achieve this result includes a considerable investment in radical innovation. Growth in European countries has been driven by incremental innovation, whereas in the USA radical innovation assumes a major role. The available studies on this issue suggest that the most innovative economies have four fundamental features:

1. High competition. Innovation is an effective way for enterprises to deal with competition;
2. High quality of education and universities and predominance of a culture of merit and entrepreneurship;
3. Flexible labour market;
4. Significant share of capital markets in corporate finance.

In addition to these four features, there are two other conditions that I deem important so that economies retain the ideas they produce:

5. The existence of a large market (in contrast to small, fragmented markets or autarky regimes);
6. Society's ability to deal with failure.

Europe presents limitations as regards some of these features that need to be solved to fully benefit from the potential of the single market and radical innovation. First of all, strong investment is needed in the field of technological research and development (R&D). In addition, it is important to foster the implementation of the outcome of R&D through close liaison between research centres and the corporate sector. This requires development of an entrepreneurship culture supported by society's ability to deal with failure.

In addition, the quality of human capital should be improved on an ongoing basis through education and vocational training. Education facilitates the transmission of the knowledge necessary for the adoption of new working methods and new technologies—making it possible to adjust labour supply to labour demand—and also increases an economy's capacity for innovation by developing new ideas.

Finally, it is essential to promote and develop alternative financial instruments to bank financing and new types of financing, including seed and risk capital. The deepening of financial integration in Europe, including the creation of a single capital market, is key to facilitating European enterprises' access to innovative financial instruments. Corporate self-financing is another dimension that cannot be overlooked. Strategies relying on extremely high leverage make enterprises more vulnerable to slowing demand and often incapable of responding to new market challenges. Self-financing must be reinforced so that enterprises become more resilient and capable of making a stronger contribution to growth.

## II. Which Reforms to the European Governance Model are Necessary?

To address these challenges, the European governance model requires changes. Specifically, an approach from the general to the particular should be adopted—an overall view—to complement the traditional approach from the particular to the general.

It must be assumed that the whole is greater than the sum of its parts. Therefore, the whole must have its own governance model ensuring the reconciliation of the parts and the consistency and compatibility of the respective actions with the optimization of the whole. Therefore, the following should be taken into account:

- spillover effects from each member state's actions on the other countries;
- central coordination of the member states' policies.

The body responsible for the economic policy of the whole and its consistency with national policies in the euro area should be the Eurogroup, which would have a permanent and independent government body. In addition, an independent European 'Public Finance Council' should be set up, responsible for issuing duly founded opinions on fiscal adjustment trends of the member states and the euro area as a whole.

Europe should also be equipped with mechanisms to safeguard the cohesion of the group in response to disruptive factors, such as: idiosyncratic shocks exogenous to policy; common shocks but with asymmetric effects; and specific shocks resulting from poor policies by member states. The first two types of shocks require an attitude of collective responsibility within the group. The shocks resulting from poor policies by member states require financial support mechanisms with inherent conditionality. For this case, it is vital that there is an institution, independent from the member states, empowered and resourced to negotiate the financial support and associated conditions with the country in question—a European Monetary Fund. An empowered institution, in the sense that it must not require approval by national parliaments of the conditions and the amounts required for the purpose; and resourced, in the sense that it should be equipped with technological and technical means allowing for prompt and informed action.

The strengthening of the integration process will naturally be accompanied by a democratic legitimization and accountability process. In this context, the great challenge is to ensure that the European Parliament is able to organize itself in line with two groups: the European Union and the euro area, creating a sub-Chamber that ensures control and political legitimization of all decisions taken at Eurogroup level.

In parallel, it is fundamental to optimize the operation of the European Commission, an entity that is critical for ensuring the existence and operation of the European Union as a whole, and vital for contemplating the future of that same whole. Therefore, in the long run, the Commission should transition to an internal organization model similar to the European Central Bank's: a Board of Commissioners formed by a commissioner from each member state who, in the framework of a collegiate body, participates in policy stance decisions and the resulting legislative proposals; and an Executive Board responsible for day-to-day management and implementation of the policies defined by the Board of Commissioners. The Executive Board would comprise a small group of commissioners, appointed on a rotating basis among the member states.

Finally, I would like to highlight a subject that I think is very important and that must be taken into account at both the European and national levels. There is no economic policy without political leadership conferring legitimacy and meaning unto it. It shall be the responsibility of the political agents to decipher the proposals advanced by the economists, giving them sense and logic as responses to economic growth sustainability and people's aspirations, that is, by legitimizing them and making them possible. The dialogue between economists and politicians, while respecting their specific fields (scientific versus social mobilization), is crucial and should go hand in hand, to produce sound economic policy. A good technical solution is not enough for it to be transformed into a successful or a viable policy. Likewise, a political message is not enough for it to be technically feasible.

The structural reform case illustrates the importance of this subject. Very frequently, structural reforms are presented as objectives per se, without any regard for explaining the purpose to be achieved, making them more difficult to be accepted by the public. Reforms must be presented according to the ultimate objective to be achieved, namely the sustainable increase in per capita income in Europe and its members, to put into perspective possible short-term costs for future benefits.

# Contents

# CONTENTS

# List of Figures

# List of Tables

# List of Contributors

**Francesco Caselli**, Norman Sosnow Professor of Economics, London School of Economics

**Mário Centeno**, Advisor of the Board, Banco de Portugal and Professor of Economics, Lisbon University

**Antonio Fatás**, Professor of Economics, INSEAD

**Carlo A. Favero**, Deutsche Bank Chair in Asset Pricing and Quantitative Finance, Università Bocconi and Research Fellow, Centre for Economic Policy Research (CEPR)

**Jeffry Frieden**, Professor of Government, Harvard University

**Vincenzo Galasso**, Professor of Economics, Università Bocconi Research Fellow, Centre for Economic Policy Research (CEPR)

**Paul De Grauwe**, John Paulson Chair in European Political Economy, European Institute, London School of Economics

**Yuemei Ji**, Lecturer in Economics, University College London

**Philip R. Lane**, Whately Professor of Political Economy, Trinity College Dublin and Research Fellow, Centre for Economic Policy Research (CEPR)

**Álvaro Novo**, Banco de Portugal

**André Sapir**, University Professor, Université libre de Bruxelles and Senior Fellow, Bruegel

**Carlos da Silva Costa**, Governor of Banco de Portugal

**José Tavares**, Professor of Economics, Nova School of Business and Economics

# List of Contributors

# Introduction

## Structural Reform and European Integration After the Crisis

*Francesco Caselli, Mário Centeno, and José Tavares*

### A Crisis Too Many?

When the global financial crisis struck, European countries were collectively engaged in two long-term projects. The first project was one of supply side economic reform to boost long-term economic growth. The need for reform was underscored by the apparent slowdown, if not reversal, in the process of catching up to US productivity levels, a concern with the impact of adverse demographic trends, and perceived threats to competitiveness from fast-growing emerging economies. As a result, most European countries had initiated reforms to make labour markets more flexible, product markets more competitive, and capital markets more open and efficient.

As documented by Antonio Fatás in the first chapter of this book, progress had been very uneven across countries, and much was left to be done in the areas of labour market flexibility, product market competitiveness, and capital market openness and efficiency, as well as in public sector reforms, including tax, privatization, pensions, and so forth. There was, nonetheless, a fundamental consensus among policymakers, economists, mainstream politicians, and perhaps even a majority of public opinion, that the direction of travel was towards further reform. Difficulties and delays in implementing this agenda were attributed to the selfish defence of privileges by powerful and entrenched special interests, rather than fundamental differences of opinion as to the need for reform.

The second long-term project that occupied Europe was the deepening of economic, financial, and political integration. 'Europe' had, of course, already come a long way with the creation of a common market, as well as a variety of executive, legislative, and judicial bodies to which member countries had transferred significant powers. Perhaps most dramatically, a large majority of countries now shared a common currency.

However, the integration project was believed by many to be unfinished. Admittedly, there were large differences between countries as to how much further integration was desirable, and how political it should be. Some preferred a minimalist interpretation that limited integration to a deepening of the European common market. Others favoured broader interpretations that would point, sooner or later, to a political union. Such differences were the cause of divisions and mutual suspicions, for example between countries perceived as 'compliers' and countries perceived as 'defiers'. Yet, most observers would have assumed that, while there was disagreement as to what Europe should mean, there was going to be more of it.

The projects of supply side economic reform and European integration were intimately connected. The European Union had long drawn its legitimacy and promise from its ability to associate itself with favourable economic outcomes, most notably in the wake of the drive for a common market. The realities of slowing economic growth and the uneven pace of reforms across countries made some economies visibly more competitive than others, and these disparities made further integration a harder goal to pursue. Growth-enhancing reforms in the less strongly performing economies were thus seen as critical for progress on integration. At the same time, closer integration could add pressure to reform-laggards, via increased competition as well as by example.

The recognition of the need for a new impulse in both integration and reform was embodied in the 'Lisbon Agenda', a masterplan for supply side reform, a guide for the European Commission's actions to make the European Union the most competitive economic area on the planet. Europe was to wield both sticks and carrots for would-be reformers. Furthermore, by making the reform process a common endeavour, Europe could cement a greater sense of cooperation and common governance.

Thus, economic reform and deepening integration were responses in the making for two slow-moving crises. On the one hand, the perceived crisis of European productivity, threatening long-term prosperity. On the other, the difficulties of integrating economic policies in a European Union whose successive enlargements produced an economy of daunting size and diversity. The financial and later sovereign-debt crisis may have been a crisis too many. It shifted the focus to the fiscal and immediate needs of a subset of European debtor economies, whose interests were at odds with those of fellow European, creditor nations.

## Threats to Further Structural Reform

It is too early to tell whether the financial-cum-sovereign crisis that hit the continent from 2007 onwards will have long-term effects on the dual project of economic reform and integration in Europe, much less what such effects might be. On the face of it, some of the hardest-hit Eurozone countries, which, perhaps not coincidentally, also happened to be among the most egregious reform laggards, appear to have accelerated the pace of reform. Greece has implemented an array of reforms that, in just a few years, have moved it from 109th to 61st in the World Bank's Doing Business ranking. Italy, Spain, Portugal, and others also made changes in market regulations.

However, it is far from clear that the pace of reform and integration will be sustained. Indeed, the possibility that those reforms are reversed is both real and worrisome. Two related sets of issues have fed the complexity of the current situation in Europe. Policy and performance in the short and the long run, on the one hand. And technical and external versus political and internal sources of legitimacy, on the other.

First, the issue of fiscal and economic performance and the conflict between the short-run and the long-term. There has been an unfortunate 'bundling' of supply side structural reforms with measures to reduce public spending and increase taxes—measures now commonly referred to as 'austerity'. There is no logical reason why supply side reform and austerity should be implemented together. The bundling of structural reforms with fiscal austerity can prevent the public from distinguishing the nature and timing of their consequences. Timing here is of the essence: the coincidence in the public debate of austerity, with clear immediate contractionary effects, blurs the potential long-term growth benefits of supply side measures.

This problem was made worse by a tendency to present supply side reforms as a policy response to the recession that hit European economies. Clearly the recession was caused by a collapse of internal and external aggregate demand, and, as pointed out by De Grauwe and Ji in the second chapter of this volume, by definition supply side reforms cannot fix a problem of insufficient demand. What they can at best do is to increase the long-run trend growth rate (a goal that Europe will need to return to when the crisis abates). By inappropriately presenting supply side reforms as counter-cyclical policy tools, policymakers may have made political support for reforms hostage to a prompt and successful exit from the recession (which for some countries is proving an elusive outcome).

The second set of issues relates to the legitimacy of both the austerity and the reform measures. Both have been perceived, often not unreasonably, as being imposed by outside players, rather than freely chosen by the countries implementing them. European institutions, and sometimes even individual countries, were seen as the originators of the economic reform initiatives (and as instigators of harsh austerity measures). Technical arguments and democratic accountability have sometimes come head to head. Complex technical arguments were received by national audiences with caution and scepticism; and technocratic governments dangerously ignored the need to build democratic legitimacy. This lack of 'domestic ownership' by citizens and voters makes policy reversals more likely, adding to uncertainty and making the fiscal and economic transition more costly.

To these crisis-induced threats to the structural reform process, we should add the issue of the changing demographic structure of the electorate. As pointed out by Favero and Galasso in their chapter, old and ageing populations may naturally resist important structural changes.

## European Integration: Deeper, Unravelling, Political?

What about European integration? Again, the early response is ambiguous. The Eurozone crisis exposed a wealth of elements of incompleteness, certainly in the architecture of the common currency, but perhaps also in the European Union as an economic and political space. For example, in his chapter André Sapir points to the lack of adequate federal level institutions to deal with asymmetric shocks, especially given the restrictions imposed on country level fiscal policies of debtor countries in another chapter. Philip Lane emphasizes the absence of effective area-wide institutions of macrofinancial management.

Advocates of further integration hope the problems uncovered by the crisis will spur further steps towards a more interdependent continent, and, indeed, take comfort in tentative moves towards a banking union, as well as the introduction of modest signs of an embryonic common fiscal policy. In taking this stance, 'Europhiles' play by the book, remaining true to the idea that each further step toward integration raises issues and problems whose 'solution' leads to a further deepening of the union.

But this integrationist tendency, which dominated the political and economic debate before the crisis, is now open to challenge as never before. Large sectors of public opinion in the countries worst afflicted by the crisis raise at least two distinct complaints against 'Europe'. First, many believe that the lack of country-specific monetary tools has exacerbated the severity of the crisis. In short, many regret their country's participation in the common currency area. Second, there is widespread discontent at the European response to the crisis, which is felt by many as having exacerbated it (particularly due to the insistence on austerity, as discussed above).

There are similar gripes in creditor countries, although working in opposite directions. In these countries, the existence of the Union and of the euro are believed by many to have facilitated excessive borrowing; more alarmingly, many citizens of creditor countries fear that further integration will lead to permanent international fiscal transfers.

Even neutral observers have been taken aback by the haphazard handling of the crisis, and many also by what they perceive as misguided institutional and economic responses.

In light of these critical attitudes it seems likely that further steps towards integration will encounter more vocal opposition, or at least, more stringent scrutiny. The stark changes in public opinion outlined in Jeff Frieden's chapter are testimonies to coming difficulties.

An additional emerging obstacle to further integration is represented by the wild disparities in income distribution among European countries. As shown by Caselli, Centeno, Novo, and Tavares in their chapter, the income distributions of European countries overlap to a much lesser extent than, for example, those of US regions; and country attitudes towards redistribution vary markedly. Both these features will make it harder to design federal fiscal institutions.

## One Or The Other?

The crisis has therefore had a major, although as yet ambiguous, impact on both the structural-reform project and the project of European integration. It may also have had an impact on how one related to the other.

As mentioned, the two projects had historically been complementary, with European integration a spur for reform and reform seen as a prerequisite for further integration. The reflections above suggest that the crisis may have broken this complementarity, and perhaps turned it into substitutability.

In particular, our reflections lead us to conclude that we may have come to a juncture where the projects of structural reform can only survive at the expense of advances on the path of European integration. Public-opinion support for supply side reform is at a low ebb, and further reform is unlikely to happen without outside pressure. Yet, the more 'Europe' pushes for reform, the more public opinion is likely to direct the despondency generated by the reform process to its perceived instigator—and resist further transfers of sovereignty to 'Europe'.

It is clear that Europe, collectively and as a collection of countries, faces momentous decisions on the direction, intensity, and pace of the (hitherto) twin programmes of structural reform and economic-political integration. Our hope is that this book will play a role, however modest, in informing these future decisions.

# 1

# The Agenda for Structural Reform in Europe

*Antonio Fatás*

## 1.1. Introduction

The need for structural reforms in Europe has been at the centre of the economic policy debate in recent decades. Structural reforms are seen as a set of necessary policies to improve both the growth and employment outcomes of European economies that are seen as performing below their potential and lagging relative to other advanced economies.

The task of designing optimal policies to increase growth is always relevant for the strategy of any government, advanced or emerging. In the case of Europe, the focus has been on the need to remove barriers to innovation and business creation, reduce regulation, and promote flexibility to strengthen economic performance. This discussion became prominent after the 1970s in which Europe did not adapt well to the global recessions associated with the oil price shocks. Unemployment remained elevated and the convergence process that Europe had started after World War II slowed down or stopped. As a result, the term *Eurosclerosis* was used to describe the lack of dynamism of Europe relative to other advanced economies, in particular the USA.

The years that followed saw some European economies growing at rates similar to that of the USA, but leaving a significant gap in terms of Gross Domestic Product (GDP) per capita. In addition, during the 1990s US productivity rate increased faster than in most European countries. This combined with another disappointing performance in terms of the labour market created a sense of urgency in the need to implement a broad set of European reforms.

The Lisbon Strategy launched in 2000 was an inflection point that reflected on the urgency with which policymakers saw the need for these reforms. The initiative was an attempt 'to agree on a new strategic goal for the Union in order to strengthen employment, economic reform and social cohesion as part of a knowledge-based economy'.[1] Since then, reforms have been a key

[1] European Council (2000).

priority in any economic policy discussions either at the country or at the supranational (EU) level.

In the last fifteen years very few European countries have managed to close the gap relative to the USA in terms of productivity and employment, and for some countries the gap is increasing. In fact, the recent global financial crisis has been another reminder of the weaknesses of the European economic model, reinforcing the perception that the growth engine in Europe is not working at its potential speed.

This chapter looks at the state of the debate around structural reforms in Europe by providing first a macroeconomic diagnosis of the performance gap of these countries relative to the other advanced economies. We then assess several measures of structural weaknesses and policies in Europe and how they relate to economic outcomes. From here we review the evidence on the effects of past economic reforms and finish with a reflection on how to move the reform agenda going forward.

## 1.2. How Far is Europe from Its Potential?

### 1.2.1. *Distance to the Frontier*

Structural reforms are about improving economic policies to let an economy reach its potential. European countries have levels of activity per capita that are substantially higher than most other countries in the world but the right benchmark of comparison should be the other advanced economies. How does Europe compare with other advanced economies?

To set a benchmark for European economic performance, we can think about the traditional Solow model that views growth as a combination of an exogenous component (technological progress) representing the technology frontier of the world and the dynamics of convergence to that frontier for countries that are below it. The data show that while most European economies are very close to the technology frontier, in some cases they have stopped converging at a level of GDP per capita that is still significantly below that of the frontier. How do we interpret a constant gap to the frontier? We typically think about these economies as having reached a steady-state level of GDP per capita that is lower than that of the best performing countries.

In the traditional Solow model, differences in steady states are the result of differences in technology, saving rate, or population growth rates. Moving beyond the Solow model we can think of some of these variables (saving rate or technology) as endogenous. In particular, they might depend on factors that can be affected by structural barriers or bad policies. In that context, structural reforms can be seen as removing those barriers and improving policies to increase the steady-state level of output.

Estimating the steady state for each European economy requires strong assumptions about the dynamics of growth. Here we take a much simpler view of these gaps and we use the USA as an indicator of the technology frontier and the potential steady state that could be achieved in the absence of distortions of inefficiencies. This is, of course, a simplification for several reasons. First, there could be room for structural reforms in the USA as well, so the true potential might be even higher. And, second, not all differences in steady states need to be related to deficiencies to be addressed by structural reforms. Some might reflect differences in preferences, geography, or demographics that cannot be changed.

That we are framing our analysis in terms of the gap to the frontier means that it is most appropriate for European countries that are closer to the frontier. Some European economies are still in the convergence phase and for them economic performance is about the speed of convergence. But even in these cases, their projected steady-state level of GDP per capita also matters, as convergence is relative to this level. If they are heading towards a level of income per capita that is significantly lower than that of the frontier, we expect them to grow at a lower rate.

### 1.2.2. *Living Standards (GDP per Capita)*

We start by comparing GDP per capita in a sample that includes all EU and Organization for Economic Co-operation and Development (OECD) members. We make the US level in 2013 equal to 100 and compute the relative GDP per capita of all the other countries.

The US economy is only surpassed by three OECD economies: Luxembourg, Switzerland, and Norway. As the GDPs of these three countries are influenced by special conditions (size or natural resources), we will treat them as 'exceptions' and maintain the logic that the USA is the frontier in our analysis.[2] Having the USA as the benchmark, we can see in Figure 1.1 that there is a significant gap in European GDP per capita relative to the USA. The GDPs of Germany, the UK, and France are 20–32% lower than that of the USA. The gap for some other European countries (Netherlands, Sweden, or Austria) is closer (within 20%), but many others, in particular Eastern Europe, have much wider gaps.

As mentioned earlier, we cannot interpret all these numbers as a static gap. It is clear that among the EU countries some can be seen as being in the convergence phase towards steady state, such as Eastern Europe. In this case

[2] Of course, the true frontier is likely to be a combination of features and industries that spread across this group of countries. The USA is not the reference for every aspect of economic performance or any diagnosis of potential institutional failures. An alternative (used by the OECD) would be to use the best three countries in a particular dimension as the frontier.

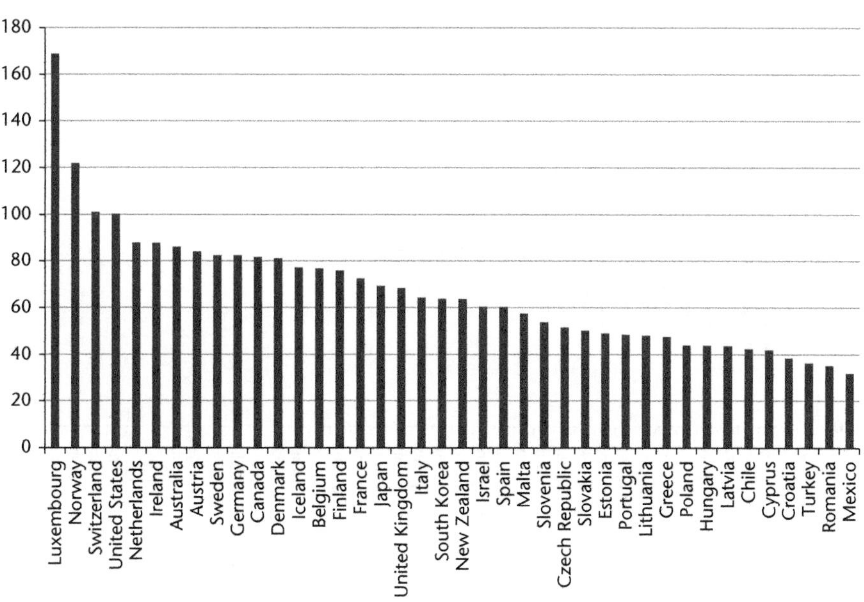


**Figure 1.1.** GDP per Capita Relative to USA (2013).

we need to think about this gap in terms of the speed of converging. But we cannot forget that other countries, such as Italy, not only display a very large gap (for Italy, close to 40%) but also stopped converging some time ago, and have been on a diverging trajectory for years, indicating the existence of a very low (and possibly decreasing) steady state.

Figure 1.1 includes all OECD economies as well as all EU members. When comparing the EU with other advanced countries such as Canada, Australia, or South Korea, we can see that these three countries have levels between 15% and 36% below that of the USA, similar to the gap of the most advanced EU members. In the case of South Korea one can make the argument that it is still on a convergence path; however, the same cannot be said about the other countries, as we will show later.

GDP per capita offers a view of economic performance that includes both an element of technology and one of labour utilization. We can decompose GDP per capita into GDP per hour worked and hours to population as indicators of each of these two dimensions.

### 1.2.3. *Productivity (GDP per Hour)*

Figure 1.2 displays GDP per hour relative to the US level. Overall we see a similar pattern to that shown in Figure 1.1, that is a gap between European countries and the USA, but we also notice two significant differences. The gap

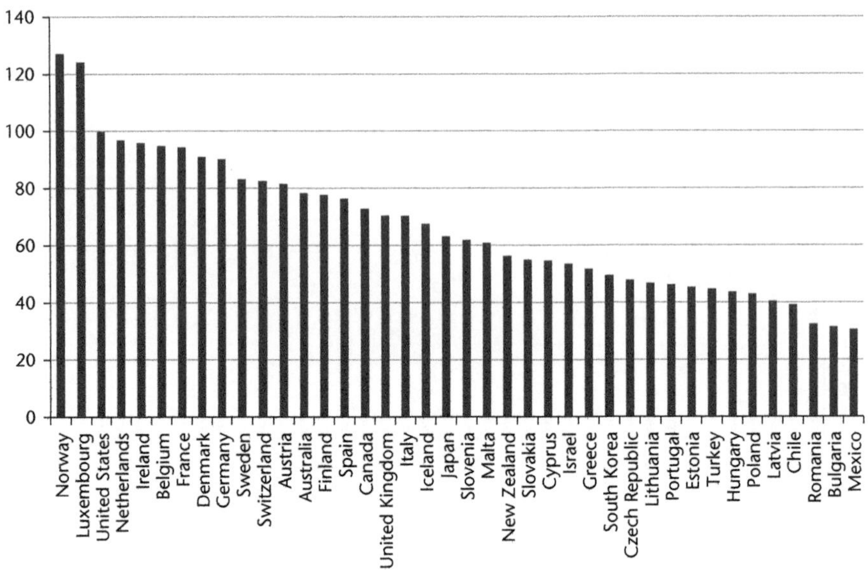


**Figure 1.2.** GDP per Hour Relative to the USA (2013).

tends to be smaller than in the case of GDP per capita. France and Germany are now as close as 5–10%. And when compared with the other non-European countries, we can see that Europe does a lot better in this dimension than in GDP per capita.

As an example, Spain or Italy's GDP per hour is very similar to that of Canada and higher than that of Japan, New Zealand, or South Korea, but these countries remain at a much lower level in terms of income per capita.

### 1.2.4. *Labour Market and Demographics*

The fact that for some of the large European countries (Germany, France, Italy, or Spain) the gap in GDP per hour is smaller than the gap in GDP per capita means that there is a gap in the utilization of labour resources relative to the USA. On the other hand, for some of the Scandinavian economies as well as some of the Eastern European ones the pattern is reversed, signalling that they make more intensive use of their population relative to the USA.

To capture the intensity with which population resources are being utilized, we start with an aggregate view on labour resources and calculate the ratio of total hours worked to population (Figure 1.3).

What is interesting in this figure is the leading position of non-EU countries (South Korea, New Zealand, Israel, Canada, Australia, and Japan) as well as some of the Eastern European economies. At the bottom of the list we

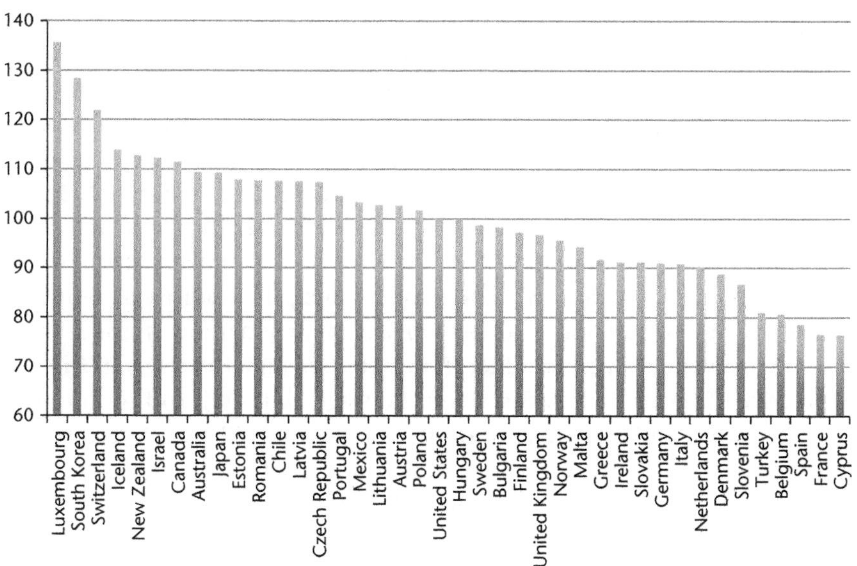


**Figure 1.3.** Hours per Capita Relative to the USA (2013).

find some of the most advanced EU countries (such as France, Belgium, and Denmark) with very low hours relative to population.

The ratio of hours to population hides several distinct dimensions. First, demographics, as the age profile of the population will have an effect on the working-age population; second, the willingness to participate in the labour force; third, the ability of those in the labour force to find a job; and, finally, the number of hours worked by those who are employed.

We certainly want to remove from our analysis the demographic dimension, given that it will be unrelated to labour market policies. The best way to do so is to distinguish between total population and working-age population. To do this, we decompose GDP per capita into three ratios:

$$\frac{GDP}{Population} = \frac{GDP}{Hours} \frac{Hours}{WA\ Population} \frac{WA\ Population}{Population}$$

where WA Population is the working-age population (defined as fifteen to sixty-four years old).[3] The three terms in the equation capture labour productivity, the performance of the labour market, and demographic considerations, respectively.

[3] The definition of the working-age population is a difficult one. The traditional definition of 15–64 years old ignores that in some countries a significant percentage of the population aged over 64 is still engaged in the labour market. The alternative is to define working-age population as adult population (over 15 years old).

Figure 1.4 decomposes the gap with the US economy in terms of each of these three factors by taking natural logarithms in the above expression. The figure shows that although productivity remains the largest factor, there are many interesting differences across countries. Typically demographics play a small role in the gap but the employment performance can be significant for some countries.[4] In particular, in countries such as Spain, France, or Belgium, the employment underperformance is as large or larger than productivity.

But this decomposition still does not provide a complete picture of the labour market and the role of demographics. First, the traditional definition of working-age population as fifteen to sixty-four years old is not relevant in some countries as workers older than sixty-five remain active. In the USA about 30% of individuals whose age is between sixty-five and seventy-four years are active, and this segment of the population is likely to increase over time on most OECD countries. In addition, activity rates across different age groups vary enormously across countries so treating all the working-age population as a homogenous group can be misleading.

As an illustration of this pattern, Figure 1.5 compares a selected group of countries by their employment rate across different age groups. Countries are ordered according to their overall employment rate (in increasing order).

All European countries except for Spain have higher employment to population ratios than the USA for the group between twenty-five and fifty-four years old. This is even true for countries like France in which the overall employment rate is much lower than in the USA. But the USA is almost at the top when ranking employment rate for those below twenty-five and above fifty-five.[5] This means that the low use of labour resources heavily depends on policies or norms that affect different age groups differently. And, as the case of France shows, there tends to be a correlation between low employment rates among younger and older workers.[6]

What is interesting is that this pattern is common among many countries. We plot in Figure 1.6 the overall employment rate (relative to the USA) against the dispersion of employment rates across the three age groups we

[4] Demographics play a small role because we are looking at the level GDP per capita. If we were to think in terms of GDP and its growth rate, the fact that some European countries are likely to see a decline in population, in addition to a worsening of the ageing structure, will make demographics a much larger factor.

[5] This comparison would be much more dramatic if we were to include those above sixty-five years old. In the USA more than a quarter of those above sixty-five years old are still active, a much higher number than in any European country.

[6] Why the number of hours is so low in some countries is an open question. It might be that this is driven by preferences for leisure and these preferences affect key parameters in the labour market, including taxation (see Ek, 2015). However, as the disaggregated data by age groups shows that these preferences do not occur in all age groups, this suggests that there could be some other factors that play a role and that cannot be fully understood in the context of the representative agent model.

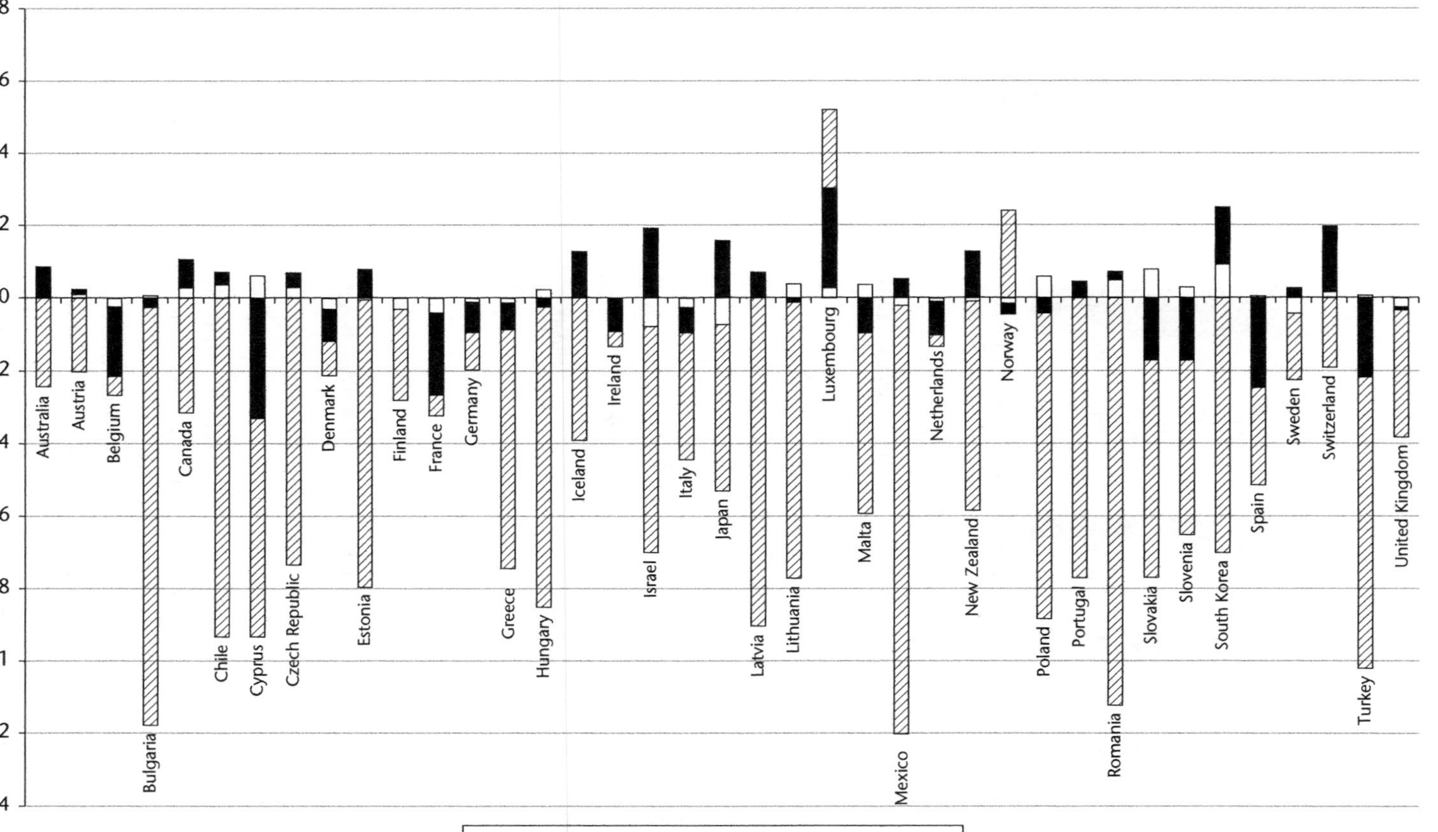


**Figure 1.4.** Decomposition of Differences in GDP per Capita.

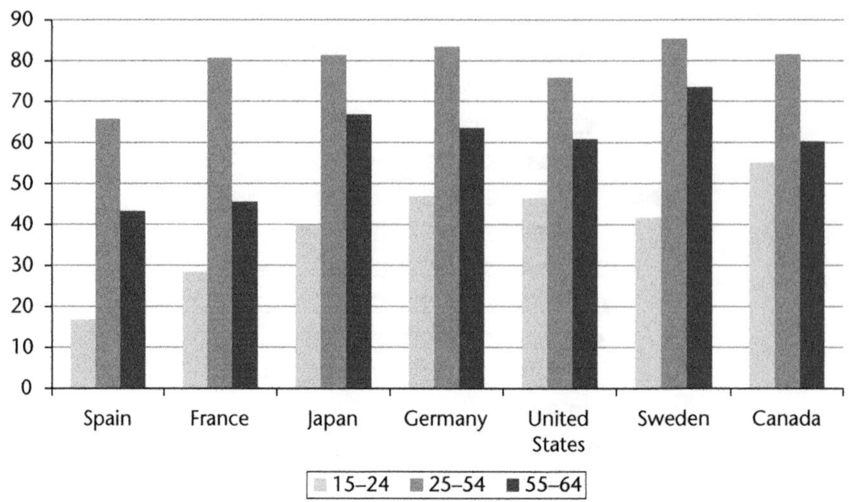


**Figure 1.5.** Employment Rates by Age Group.

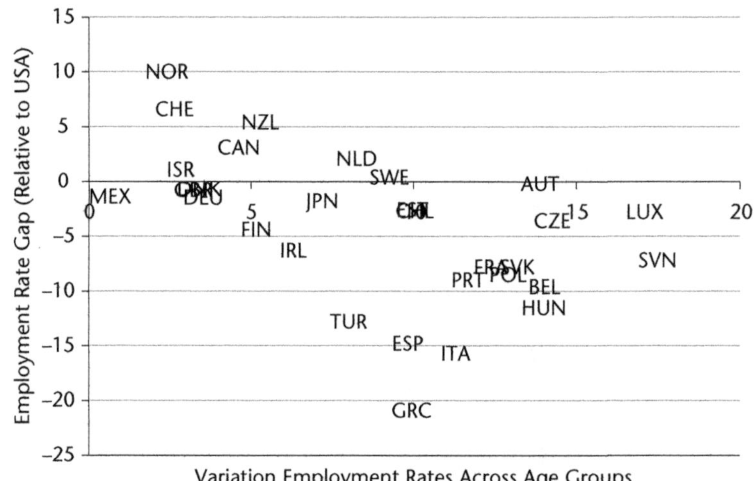


**Figure 1.6.** Average and Dispersion Employment Rate.

identified earlier.[7] There is an inverse relationship that suggests the overall low employment rates are related to the differences in employment rates between prime-age workers and the rest.

A second interesting question is whether there is any pattern between labour productivity and intensity of use of labour resources. Do we see a

[7] Where employment rates are also measured against the USA figure and dispersion is simply measured as the standard deviation of the three indicators.

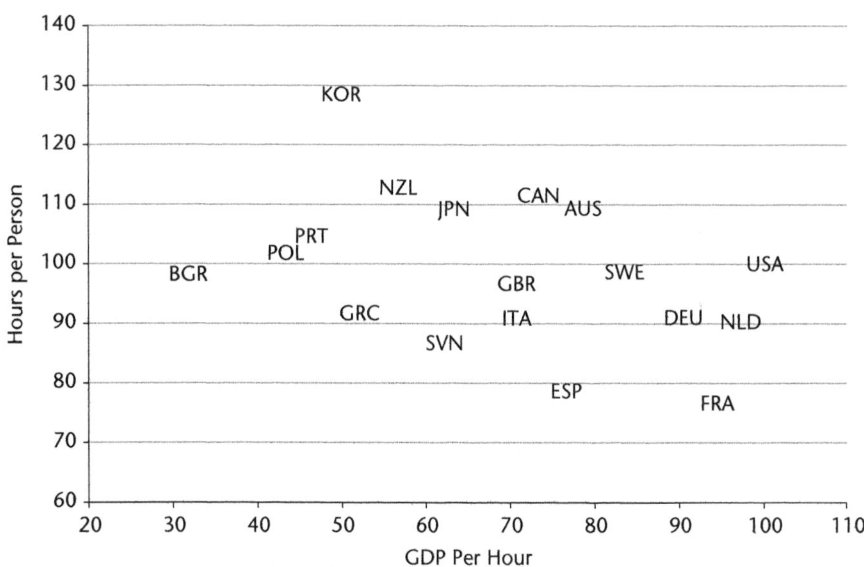


**Figure 1.7.** Labour Productivity and Hours per Person (2013).

positive correlation between the two gaps, signalling underperformance on both dimensions? Figure 1.7 shows that this is not the case. If anything, there is a mild negative pattern.

France and Spain display relatively high GDP per hour but very low hours per capita. On the other side, New Zealand or South Korea have very high hours per person but very low GDP per hour. This negative correlation suggests that for some countries progress in one of these indicators could come at the expense of deterioration in the other one. If productivity is high because of the low activity of the least productive workers, efforts to increase their participation will result in lower GDP per hour. There are also countries with underperformance on both dimensions such as Turkey or Cyprus and some that perform better than most on both dimensions (Luxembourg) where the trade off seems less relevant.[8]

As a summary, we have found that the gap in GDP per capita between Europe and the USA varies across different European economies. It varies in size but also in terms of its origin. While labour productivity is a large factor for most countries, for a few of the European economies the labour market gap is as large or larger. This group includes both periphery countries (such as Spain or Cyprus) and core economies (such as Denmark or France), so the traditional groupings of countries across standard labels (high and low

[8] De Michelis et al. (2013) provide a deeper analysis of the trade off between productivity and labour market intensity.

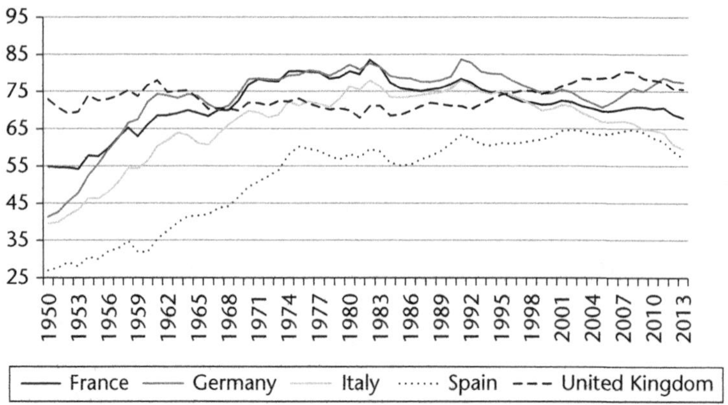


**Figure 1.8.** Convergence in GDP per Capita (USA=100).

GDP per capita) do not correlate well with the relative importance of the labour market. In addition, the labour market outcomes are mainly driven by low employment rates in young and old workers. Finally, it seems that for some of these countries there is a trade off between employment rates and productivity; by employing only the most productive countries they have high labour productivity.

### 1.2.5. *Long-term Trends*

So far our analysis has looked only at the current gaps in terms of productivity and labour markets. To get a broader perspective on the origin and evolution of these gaps, we now look at how they have been changing over recent decades. We will once again look at the gap relative to the frontier, where we maintain the USA as a benchmark.[9]

Figure 1.8 shows the evolution of GDP per capita since 1950 for some of the largest EU economies, always relative to the USA. There are two distinct patterns. The UK has maintained a gap of about 25% for the last five decades. The other four countries (France, Germany, Spain, and Italy) embarked on a very fast convergence process in the early years but this process stopped during the 1970s (with the exception of Spain where if continued until the year 2000) around a gap level of 25–35%. Since then the convergence has been reversed, in particular in Italy and Spain but also to a lesser extent in France and Germany.

[9] For our analysis of long-term trends we make use of the total economy database from the conference board. The data make use of Public-Private Partnership (PPP) adjustment based on the 2005 OECD calculations and do not include the recent revisions to national accounts. For this reason, the 2013 level does not always coincide with the figures we have shown earlier. But because we are trying to understand long-term trends we prefer to use data that come from a single source.

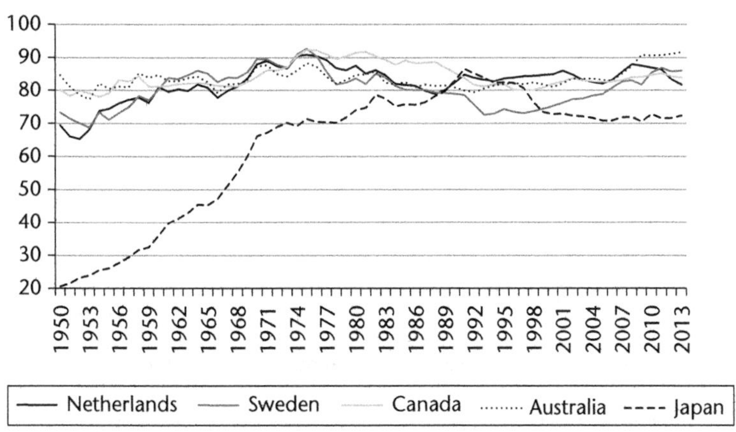


**Figure 1.9.** Convergence in GDP per Capita (USA=100).

The convergence that took place during the early years is consistent with the international evidence in favour of the Solow (convergence) model. Within that framework, the stable gap that remains could be seen as a difference in steady states, possibly driven by barriers that can be the target of structural reforms. That the gap increases during the most recent decades can be a sign of either an increase in these structural barriers or an increase in their negative effects.

To get a perspective on how different the behaviour of European countries is relative to other advanced economies, we reproduce in Figure 1.9 the same analysis for an additional set of OECD countries.

What we see is that some of these economies are more similar to the UK in terms of the evolution of their gaps to the USA (in particular Canada and Australia). Gaps are fairly stable over time with GDP per capita around 75–80% of the USA level. Sweden and the Netherlands display earlier convergence but then stagnation more recently (Sweden has a specific U-shape pattern since the end of the 1970s). In the case of Japan we see a phenomenon similar to that of the large European countries but more dramatic, with very fast convergence followed by divergence since 1990.

So far we have only looked at the most advanced economies in our sample. In Figure 1.10 we show the behaviour of some EU countries with the lowest GDP per capita. Their behaviour is driven by their specific circumstances of transitioning from planned economies to market economies during the last two decades. A collapse of their economies is followed by a persistent pattern of convergence more visible in countries such as Estonia or Poland than in Hungary or Romania.

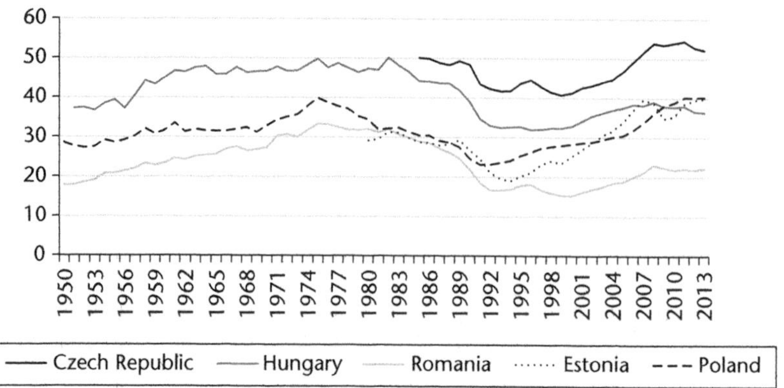


**Figure 1.10.** Convergence in GDP per Capita (USA=100).

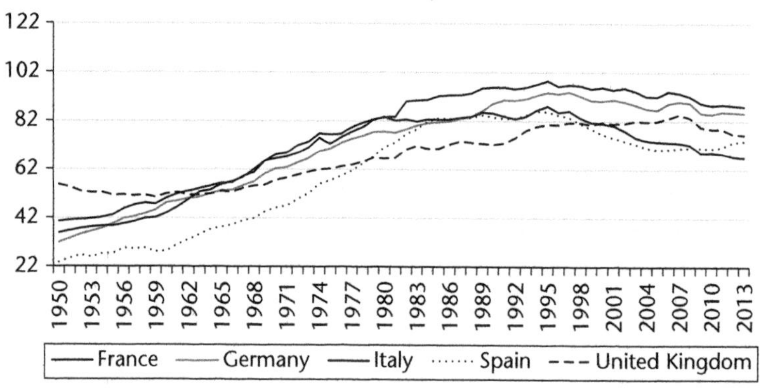


**Figure 1.11.** Convergence in GDP per Hour (USA=100).

As argued earlier, GDP per capita has both an element of technology and one of labour market performance that are interesting to understand separately. Also, the logic of convergence under the Solow model is not one that applies to GDP per capita but to productivity. We now replicate the above charts but using GDP per hour as a proxy for labour productivity.

Figures 1.11 and 1.12 show that among the large European countries, convergence in GDP per hour is stronger than in GDP per capita. The gap remains smaller in the later years and the convergence continues until the year 2000 in France and Germany and until the 1990s for the other three countries. We do see, however, that there is also a slowing of convergence or even a reversal in Italy or Spain in the last 10 years.

One final comparison using some other OECD countries (Figure 1.13): the convergence in labour productivity of the five largest EU countries (EU5) is similar or stronger to that of other advanced economies. In particular,

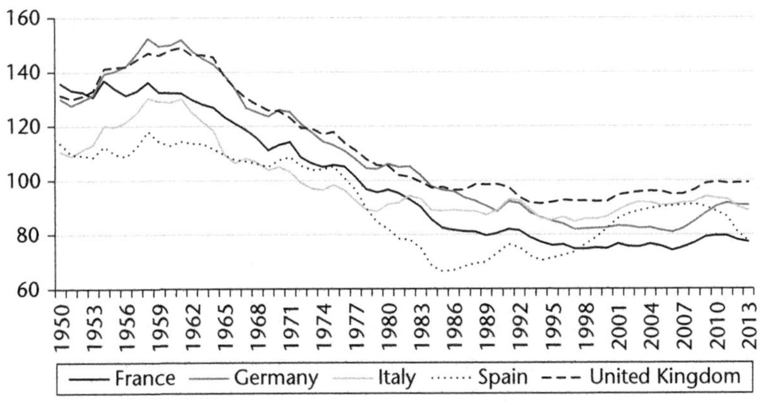


**Figure 1.12.** Convergence in Hours per Capita (USA=100).

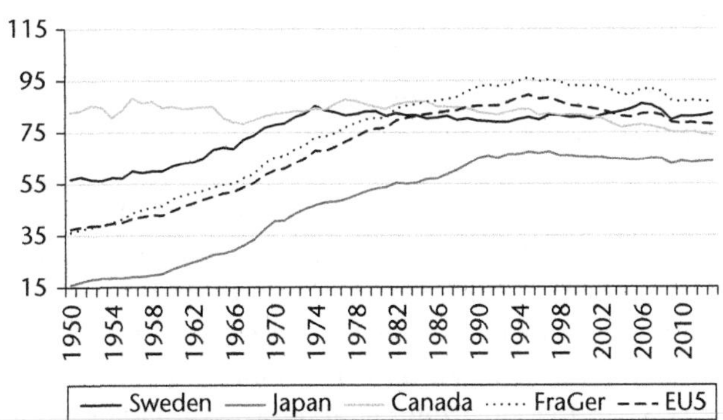


**Figure 1.13.** Convergence in GDP per Hour (USA=100).

productivity levels catch up with those of Canada and Sweden by the early 1980s and have remained at a similar level since then. In the case of France and Germany (*FraGer*) the productivity remains higher, although we observe again a slight reversal since the mid-1990s.

The evidence shown so far portrays a consistent picture of a persistent and in some cases increasing gap of European economies with the USA since the 1970s. This pattern is not too different from the other advanced economies that are also stuck at a level of GDP per capita or productivity that is below that of the USA. This could be signalling that the dynamics of the last decades are driven more by the ability of the USA to innovate and distance itself from the other advanced economies, including Europe. There is, however, some evidence of lower performance among a few of the European countries in the last fifteen years, driven in some cases by the effects of the global financial crisis that started in 2008.

## 1.3. Convergence, Steady State, and Structural Reforms

How can structural reforms help to close the gaps that we identified in Section 1.2? We frame this question within the academic literature on understanding the institutional and policy determinants of long-term growth. The literature was originally built around the Solow (1956) model in which countries are seen as converging to a steady state that is affected by technology, population growth rates, and saving rates, as well as the depreciation rate. Originally, long-term growth rates were considered to be exogenous or driven by the technology frontier, but later a second wave in the literature took on the tasks of understanding what drives long-term growth by understanding the determinants of technological progress.[10]

From an empirical point of view, most of the literature is focused on the notion of convergence and the determinants of the steady state. This is partly driven by early tests of the Solow model providing a good description of the cross-country and cross-regional growth dynamics.[11] On the other hand, endogenous growth models are much less successful, establishing a set of empirical facts matched by a stylized model that includes the factors driving innovation and long-term growth rates.

The empirical literature developed beyond the traditional factors of the original Solow model and became an open exploration of variables that could potentially drive growth or differences in steady states in a cross-section of countries. Many papers provide a good assessment of the key variables that seem to be robust to different empirical specification. For example, Easterly and Levine (2001) and Doppelhofer et al. (2004) provide such analysis, and Barro (2012) presents a recent update on how the standard Solow model fits the cross-country data.

In all these studies a few variables appear as consistent determinants of economic growth or differences in steady states. In particular, investment in physical and human capital appears as a very strong and robust determinant of long-term growth rates.[12]

When it comes to variables that are affected directly by policies or institutions, the most robust ones tend to be broad indicators of either macroeconomic policy (inflation and its volatility, size of government, openness, the black market exchange rate premium) or fundamental institutions such as democracy, rule of law, or constraints on the executive (as in, e.g., Hall and Jones, 1999; Rodrik et al., 2004; Barro, 1996; Glaeser et al., 2004; Acemoglu et al., 2001).

[10] See Romer (1986) or Romer (1990).

[11] See Barro and Sala-i-Martin (1992), Mankiw et al. (1992), or Barro et al. (1991).

[12] In addition, and from Doppelhofer et al. (2004), variables such as fraction of tropical area and population density are also robust.

Most of these policies are relevant when looking at a large sample of countries that includes advanced and emerging markets, but less so when focusing on advanced economies, and Europe in particular. The variation in many of these variables (e.g. democracy or rule of law) is too small to become a significant determinant of economic performance.

In recent years, there has been an effort to provide much more granular measures of institutions and policies through, for example, the Governance Indicators or the Doing Business database produced by the World Bank. Because of their short length (starting in the late 1990s or early 2000s), empirical studies using these variables are less comprehensive, although there is evidence that these variables matter when looking at growth differences. For example Djankov et al. (2006) present evidence of the growth effects of indicators of Doing Business, and Kaufmann et al. (2009) discuss how governance matters.

Although policy and institutional indicators are important for growth, the academic literature provides limited help in the design of reforms, especially for OECD economies. First, there is the issue of data quality and having enough detailed indicators capable of informing policy design. Second, and more importantly, the growth literature does not provide a clear framework to identify what matters for countries that are close to the frontier. For some of these countries, the issue of convergence is not relevant; the real issue is the difference in steady-state levels. Although this is explicitly included in the empirical analysis, the specifications are not always consistent or insightful. It is quite common that the same sample of countries is used to run regressions both for convergence dynamics and to study steady-state differences (as in the seminal work of Mankiw et al. 1992, or Gillanders and Whelan, 2014 more recently in the context of reforms).

Convergence and differences in steady states are analysed together because within the framework of the Solow growth model some variables matter for both, such as the saving rate. When it comes to policy and institutional variables the logic is similar. They are likely to matter for both convergence and steady states. But because there is no accepted conceptual framework to test these hypotheses, the empirical analysis just looks at the data in an unstructured manner. In addition, our understanding of what drives the frontier and how countries manage to follow closely the technology leaders is also very limited, and this is yet another handicap on our ability to understand what matters for growth in these economies.

Most of the recent work targeted towards designing economic reform agendas is driven by the efforts of the OECD to create a set of variables that capture at a much more microeconomic level the potential bottlenecks created in product and labour markets. Typically, the framework used within these studies is similar to that of the convergence literature in which structural reform indicators are seen as a way to close the gap with the frontier. In some of the empirical analysis these indicators themselves are shown to have a different impact depending on the relative position to the frontier. But whether these indicators are affecting innovation, adoption of other countries' innovations, or a static concept of efficiency is not always made precise in the analysis.

Because of all these conceptual and empirical difficulties, most of the policy recipes about structural reforms are not based on empirical assessments of what are proven to be strong determinants of differences in economic performance. Instead, they are typically based on the premise that more competition, fewer barriers to innovation, a more flexible labour market, or smaller tax inefficiencies should lead to higher employment as well as productivity. From here we build a set of specific indicators that can capture all those microeconomic dimensions.

In summary, the notion of structural reforms fits well with the idea that policies and institutions matter for growth. The assumption is that these variables affect the transition to the frontier, the steady state as well as the speed at which the frontier grows. However, our understanding of how structural reforms can affect each of these dynamics separately is very limited. As a result, the design of reforms is not based on concrete empirical results of what makes a certain policy work but rather on the assumption that flexibility and letting markets work should lead to better economic performance at all levels for all countries.

## 1.4. Measuring Structural Gaps in Policies

We now look at several different sets of indicators of policies and institutions and we compare the gap in these indicators with the productivity and employment gaps identified in Section 1.2. There are two main sets of indicators we consider: Doing Business (World Bank) and Product and Labour Market Regulations (OECD). These are the most detailed indicators about policies, regulations, and institutions that can help us think about reform.[13]

### 1.4.1. *Doing Business (World Bank)*

The Doing Business (DB) database contains a very large collection of indicators covering many aspects of the easiness of doing business. The indicators include variables related to how difficult or costly is to start up a business or

[13] There is a third set of indicators that provide a much broader view on these issues: Governance Indicators (World Bank). We have reproduced most of the results in the chapter using these indicators. The results are available on request or in an appendix available at the author's website.

get a set of regulatory processes done, or indicators of enforcing contracts. There is also a set of indicators regarding labour market flexibility although they are not included in their main index and ranking. This set of indicators possibly might be better suited to emerging markets but there are also interesting and large differences across OECD countries.

We first check how the DB indicators can help us to understand the income and employment gaps of our sample. We use as the main variable the distance to the frontier index as opposed to the ordinal ranking. The distance to the frontier index is designed to 'assess the absolute level of regulatory performance and how it improves over time. This measure shows the distance of each economy to the "frontier", which represents the best performance observed on each of the indicators (...) An economy's distance to frontier is reflected on a scale from 0 to 100, where 0 represents the lowest performance and 100 represents the frontier'.

Table 1.1 shows that there is a positive and significant correlation between measures of policies and GDP per capita or GDP per hour.[14] The explanatory power of this variable is very high and the coefficient is highly significant. The structural indicator is also significantly correlated with the labour performance as measured by hours per capita, although the fit is much weaker than for measures of productivity.[15] Figure 1.14 shows the correlation with GDP per capita and we can see that European countries display a very similar pattern from the other OECD countries.

We can decompose the general DB index into ten categories that cover specific aspects of the ease of doing business. In each of these categories there are a number of individual indicators that provide more detailed information on the distance to the institutional frontier for each of these countries.

There is a high collinearity between each of the indicators so separating the individual effects is not an easy task. A simple linear regression on each of

**Table 1.1.** DB Distance to the Frontier and Economic Performance

| Variables | GDP Per Capita | GDP Per Hour | Hours Per Capita |
|---|---|---|---|
| Doing Business | 2.026*** | 1.727*** | 0.558** |
| | (0.380) | (0.482) | (0.242) |
| Constant | −88.58*** | −64.72* | 57.10*** |
| | (27.90) | (35.70) | (18.24) |
| Observations | 40 | 39 | 39 |
| R-squared | 0.462 | 0.276 | 0.103 |

Robust standard errors in parentheses.
*** $p<0.01$, ** $p<0.05$, * $p<0.1$.

14 Luxembourg is removed from the regressions, as it is a clear outlier.

15 This should not be a surprise because some of the labour market indicators are not included in the general ranking.

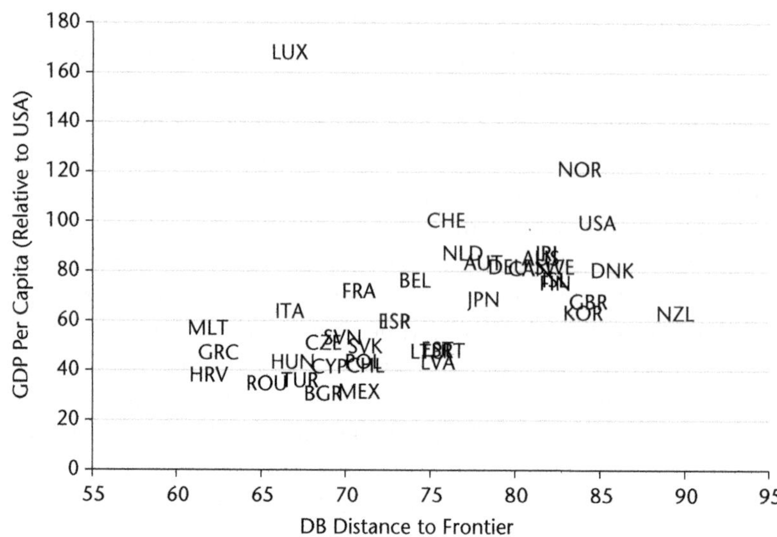


**Figure 1.14.** DB Distance to Frontier and GDP per Capita.

the ten indicators and a process of eliminating every indicator that is not significant at a 10% level leaves very few indicators as relevant. In particular, for GDP per capita or per hour the three that matter are Getting Electricity, which is likely to be a proxy for bureaucratic barriers, Paying Taxes (only marginally from a statistical point of view), and Resolving Insolvency (Table 1.2).

This empirical analysis highlights the positive and strong correlation between measures of institutions, regulatory processes and policies with productivity and employment, supporting the view that gains from reform can be large. But we can also see the difficulties in translating this result into concrete proposals given the strong correlation between all indicators and the difficulty of ruling out the influence of omitted variables.

## 1.4.2. *Product and Labour Market Indicators (OECD)*

In 2005 the OECD first published a report called *Going for Growth* to generate a consistent reform agenda across advanced economies.[16] The goal of the initiative was to create measures of progress that provided accountability and also to generate peer pressure among governments of member countries. The OECD project involved the definition of measures of structural weaknesses as well as setting up a strategy based on priorities to be renewed or updated on a regular basis.

[16] OECD (2005).

**Table 1.2.** DB Indicators and Economic Performance

| Variables | GDP Per Capita | | GDP Per Hour | | Hours Per Capita | |
|---|---|---|---|---|---|---|
| Starting Business | −0.0146 | | 0.0717 | | 0.0244 | |
| | (0.460) | | (0.516) | | (0.426) | |
| Construction Permits | −0.132 | | −0.495 | | 0.0600 | |
| | (0.203) | | (0.407) | | (0.349) | |
| Getting Electricity | 0.365* | 0.492** | 0.369 | 0.431* | 0.166 | |
| | (0.211) | (0.203) | (0.297) | (0.224) | (0.263) | |
| Registering Property | 0.138 | | −0.0720 | | 0.232 | 0.273* |
| | (0.215) | | (0.297) | | (0.175) | (0.135) |
| Getting Credit | −0.0622 | | −0.208 | | 0.229 | 0.226** |
| | (0.202) | | (0.235) | | (0.141) | (0.0905) |
| Protecting Investors | −0.133 | | −0.206 | | 0.108 | |
| | (0.303) | | (0.246) | | (0.197) | |
| Paying Taxes | 0.402 | 0.478 | 0.519 | | −0.230 | |
| | (0.334) | (0.301) | (0.372) | | (0.270) | |
| International Trading | 0.609 | | 0.709 | | 0.178 | |
| | (0.601) | | (0.748) | | (0.547) | |
| Enforcing Contracts | 0.197 | | 0.273 | | 0.107 | |
| | (0.326) | | (0.421) | | (0.295) | |
| Resolving Insolvency | 0.452*** | 0.480*** | 0.507*** | 0.558*** | −0.114 | |
| | (0.139) | (0.102) | (0.178) | (0.116) | (0.124) | |
| Constant | −79.70 | −45.73 | −55.06 | −6.783 | 42.87 | 61.97*** |
| | (54.35) | (27.29) | (68.43) | (15.69) | (54.28) | (10.41) |
| Observations | 40 | 40 | 39 | 39 | 39 | 39 |
| R-squared | 0.635 | 0.607 | 0.558 | 0.471 | 0.291 | 0.221 |

Robust standard errors in parentheses.
*** $p<0.01$, ** $p<0.05$, * $p<0.1$.

Although there have been changes to the process, the basic structure of indicators remains unchanged. The focus of the indicators covers several areas:

1. Maximizing the use of the labour resources:
   a. Labour market indicators in particular related to the cost of labour, unemployment benefits as well as active labour market policies.
   b. Taxation of labour with the perspective of encouraging participation.
2. Maximizing the contribution of the labour force through improvements in the quality of education.
3. Eliminating inefficiencies and fostering competition through
   a. High quality regulation, market openness, and ensuring competition in product markets.
   b. Rationalizing support to agriculture.
4. Policies geared towards innovation.

When it comes to the indicator on policies that promote competition, the main index is the product market regulation index (PMR). We now use this indicator as an explanatory variable of the productivity and labour market gaps as we did with the World Bank measures. Regression results are included in Table 1.3.

The fit of the regression is high, although not as high as in previous specifications. The best fit is with measures of productivity (such as GDP per hour). When using labour market indicators (Hours per Capita) the coefficient is not significant. This is expected, as the PMR indicators do not include a labour market dimension.

Figure 1.15 shows the correlation between PMR and GDP per capita. The correlation is again strong and Europe fits the same pattern as the other OECD members (Luxembourg is an outlier and is excluded from the regressions).

**Table 1.3.** Product Market Regulation and Economic Performance (2013)

| Variables | GDP Per Capita | GDP Per Hour | Hours Per Capita |
|---|---|---|---|
| Product Market Regulation | −35.57*** | −37.46*** | 1.792 |
| | (7.014) | (8.630) | (8.476) |
| Constant | 116.6*** | 120.9*** | 96.53*** |
| | (11.05) | (13.38) | (11.92) |
| Observations | 40 | 39 | 39 |
| R-squared | 0.247 | 0.222 | 0.002 |

Robust standard errors in parentheses.
*** $p<0.01$, ** $p<0.05$, * $p<0.1$.

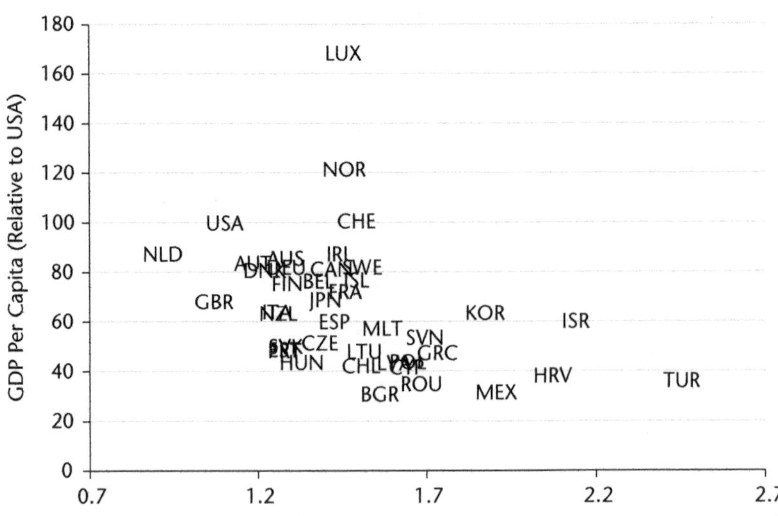


**Figure 1.15.** Product Market Regulation and Economic Performance (2013).

**Table 1.4.** PMR Indicators and Economic Performance

| Variables | GDP Per Capita | GDP Per Capita | GDP Per Capita | GDP Per Capita |
|---|---|---|---|---|
| State Control | −20.64*** | | | −13.61 |
| | (5.649) | | | (8.120) |
| Barriers to Entrepreneurship | | −24.04*** | | −12.05 |
| | | (6.689) | | (8.820) |
| Barriers to Trade and Inv. | | | −17.17** | −9.335 |
| | | | (6.940) | (7.495) |
| Constant | 108.6*** | 105.1*** | 73.15*** | 119.3*** |
| | (12.76) | (12.45) | (5.710) | (13.82) |
| Observations | 40 | 40 | 40 | 40 |
| R-squared | 0.175 | 0.172 | 0.089 | 0.250 |

Robust standard errors in parentheses.
*** p<0.01, ** p<0.05, * p<0.1.

The index of product market regulation is divided into three categories: state control, barriers to entrepreneurship, and barriers to trade and investment. The three indicators are highly correlated with each other. Each is significant as an explanatory variable for GDP per capita differences, but when included together in a regression none of them are significant because of the strong multicollinearity (Table 1.4).

When it comes to labour market indicators, the OECD considers many dimensions. One is the protection of employment as a barrier to a dynamic labour market. It captures the 'strictness of regulations on dismissals and the use of temporary contracts'. The second set of variables that is considered are those measuring the incentives for participation in the labour force as well as the incentives for searching for a job when unemployed. It can include measures of the tax wedge on labour market, generosity of unemployment benefits, spending on active labour market policies as well as the rules of pension reforms that might keep older works away from the labour force.

We concentrate here on three of these indicators: an index of employment protection, a measure of the tax wedge in labour markets, as well as the importance of taxes on labour (social security charges as percentage of GDP).[17] We first check whether these three indicators are correlated with standard measures of labour market performance.

As we did earlier we consider the role of different age groups when measuring labour market outcomes. In particular, we first consider three definitions of labour resources: total population, working age (fifteen to sixty-four), and

[17] For employment protection we use the 'version 2' of the indicator, which incorporates twelve items related to regulations for individual and collective dismissals. As a measure of the tax wedge, we use the average tax wedge for one earner couples at 100% of average earnings with two children.

**Table 1.5.** Hours per Person and Labour Market Policies

| Variables | Hours per Capita | | | |
|---|---|---|---|---|
| Employment Protection | −7.328** | | | 0.400 |
| | (3.388) | | | (3.712) |
| Tax Wedge | | −0.738*** | | −0.819** |
| | | (0.188) | | (0.335) |
| Social Security Taxes | | | −1.021** | 0.301 |
| | | | (0.448) | (0.611) |
| Constant | 117.6*** | 119.3*** | 108.5*** | 117.4*** |
| | (7.322) | (5.835) | (4.436) | (5.797) |
| Observations | 35 | 33 | 29 | 29 |
| R-squared | 0.076 | 0.399 | 0.132 | 0.404 |

Robust standard errors in parentheses.
*** p<0.01, ** p<0.05, * p<0.1.

**Table 1.6.** Hours per Adult and Labour Market Policies

| Variables | Hours per Adult Population | | | |
|---|---|---|---|---|
| Employment Protection | −9.732** | | | 1.886 |
| | (3.813) | | | (4.474) |
| Tax Wedge | | −0.897*** | | −0.808** |
| | | (0.186) | | (0.353) |
| Social Security Taxes | | | −1.651*** | −0.445 |
| | | | (0.493) | (0.750) |
| Constant | 122.1*** | 122.7*** | 113.8*** | 120.0*** |
| | (8.502) | (6.113) | (5.349) | (6.864) |
| Observations | 35 | 33 | 29 | 29 |
| R-squared | 0.110 | 0.456 | 0.260 | 0.456 |

Robust standard errors in parentheses.
*** p<0.01, ** p<0.05, * p<0.1.

adult population (fifteen and over). Tables 1.5 and 1.6 show the results for two of these measures (we do not report results using working-age-population but they are in line with those of the other two variables). There is a strong correlation between our three indicators of labour market policies and labour market outcomes. The fit is larger for hours per adult population (which removes some of the demographic differences), with an R-squared of 45%. The three variables are significant when introduced individually, but only the tax wedge is significant when introduced at the same time.

As we know from our early discussion, the performance of the labour market can be very different across different population groups. We repeat the regression above by age group. In particular we check how labour market policies affect prime-age workers versus those below twenty-five and those above fifty-five. For the sake of space we only include as explanatory variables two of the labour market policies: employment protection and social security taxes as percentage of GDP.

**Table 1.7.** Employment Rate and Labour Market Policies

| Variables | Employment Rate | | Employment Rate | |
|---|---|---|---|---|
| | 15+ | | 15–24 | |
| Employment Protection | −4.844*** | | −8.406** | |
| | (1.508) | | (3.837) | |
| Social Security Taxes | | −0.779*** | | −1.598*** |
| | | (0.228) | | (0.491) |
| Constant | 66.60*** | 62.35*** | 56.48*** | 51.19*** |
| | (3.254) | (2.614) | (8.029) | (5.103) |
| Observations | 33 | 29 | 32 | 29 |
| R-squared | 0.103 | 0.215 | 0.079 | 0.250 |

Robust standard errors in parentheses.
*** $p<0.01$, ** $p<0.05$, * $p<0.1$.

**Table 1.8.** Employment Rate and Labour Market Policies

| Variables | Employment Rate | | Employment Rate | |
|---|---|---|---|---|
| | 25–54 | | 55–64 | |
| Employment Protection | −0.552 | | −11.21*** | |
| | (1.602) | | (3.196) | |
| Social Security Taxes | | 0.0975 | | −1.596*** |
| | | (0.202) | | (0.334) |
| Constant | 79.28*** | 76.85*** | 80.34*** | 68.83*** |
| | (3.190) | (2.258) | (6.834) | (3.651) |
| Observations | 33 | 29 | 33 | 29 |
| R-squared | 0.002 | 0.004 | 0.188 | 0.318 |

Robust standard errors in parentheses.
*** $p<0.01$, ** $p<0.05$, * $p<0.1$.

The dependent variable is always employment as a ratio to population in a given age range. The results confirm that labour market policies discourage employment but we can see that this is concentrated into two age groups, those below twenty-five and those above fifty-five (Tables 1.7 and 1.8). When using the twenty-five to fifty-four age range, none of the labour market policies seem to be significantly correlated with the employment levels of this group.

This is an interesting result as it confirms the importance of how fragmented labour markets explain not only the low level of employment activity in some economies but also how policies are responsible for the fragmentation of the labour market. Reform design should take these differences into account.

### 1.4.3. *Additional Policies and Potential Reforms*

We have discussed so far two sets of alternative indicators that are commonly used to look at the policies, regulations, and institutions that can support growth. While the detailed information contained in each of the individual indicators is vast, there are many other policies that can be considered as determinants of growth and potentially target of reforms. We briefly mention some of them in this section.

As mentioned earlier, human capital is one of the key determinants of growth performance. Human capital is influenced by both the number of years of formal training and the quality of the education system. This is one of the areas of focus for reforms in some of the countries in our sample.

Innovation and research and development (R&D) activities are necessary for countries that are close enough to the technology frontier. Having support for these activities via fiscal policy or availability of financing or having an ecosystem that allows the translation of basic research into applied innovations are all policies that can potentially lead to higher productivity and faster growth.

Finally, there are sectors that can be enablers of other activities and be responsible for improvements in economic performance. Energy costs can have an effect on investment or growth in manufacturing and the financial sector and its ability to channel capital to its best use, and in particular towards riskier innovative activities, is an engine of growth.[18]

These are all dimensions that are relevant for the analysis of structural policies but, for the sake of space, we do not analyse them in detail in this chapter. What we know from cross-country comparisons is that they tend to be correlated with both the macro and the more disaggregated indicators we reviewed earlier. As an example, information and communication technology (ICT) is seen as one of the key factors explaining differences in productivity among advanced economies and also the gap that exists between many of these countries and the USA (Ark, 2002). At the same time, the diffusion of ICT seems to be related to market rigidities. Countries with lower flexibility in labour and product markets, as measured by the OECD indicators, have a lower speed of ICT diffusion (Cette and Lopez, 2008).

## 1.5. The Pace of Reform

Section 1.4 documented an important stylized fact: there is a strong correlation between structural weaknesses, policies, and macroeconomic performance. We now ask whether we have we seen any improvement in the indicators in recent years or decades. Are countries reforming? And, if so, at which pace?

[18] See Petersen Institute of International Economics (PIIE) (2014) for some ideas on reform in the financial sector in Europe.

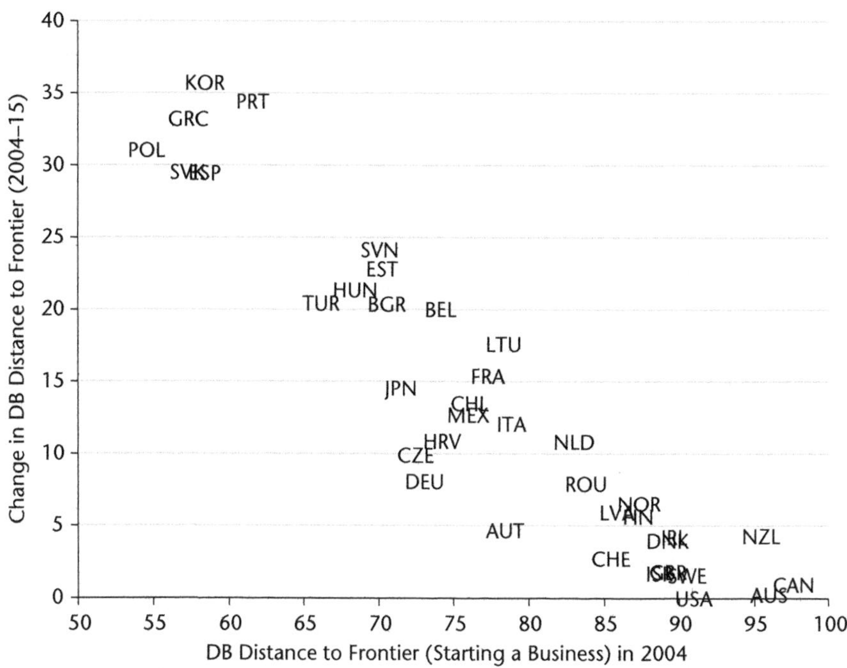


**Figure 1.16.** DB Starting a Business Reforms.

We start measuring improvements using the Doing Business indicators. Because of lack of data availability for many years we cannot use the main index, instead we use an indicator that was available for more years: the easiness of starting a business. We use again the distance to the frontier and we check whether there is any convergence among countries in our sample during the years 2004–15.

The results are captured in Figure 1.16. Here we see a very strong pattern of convergence. Countries that were further away from the frontier have seen significantly larger progress during the past decade. And the European countries follow the same strong pattern as the other advanced economies.[19]

It is important to see that the magnitude of convergence is very strong. Take Portugal or Greece as examples. Back in 2004 these countries were at a level of around 60 relative to the frontier (the frontier takes value of 100 and it represents the best practice). By 2015 their index had climbed all the way up to 90. But despite this convergence we need to remember that the current

[19] The same convergence result is found when using Enforcing Contracts as the indicator of reform.

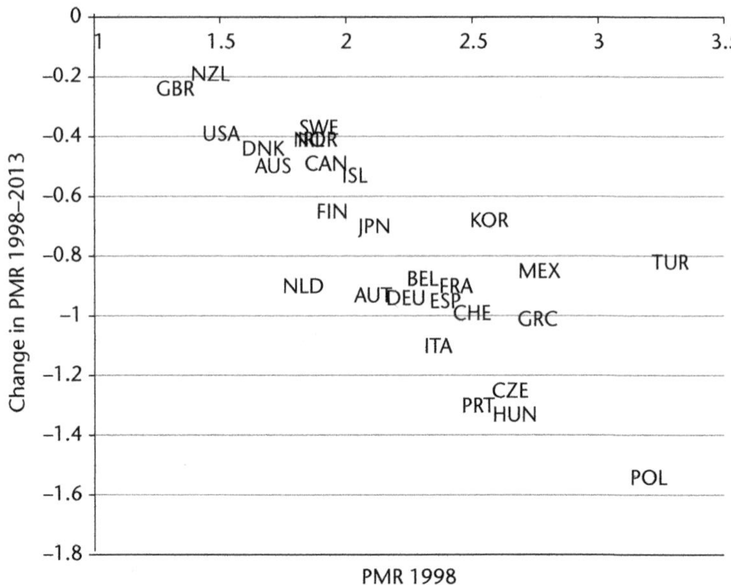


**Figure 1.17.** PMR Reforms.

(small) differences in this indicator matter for the observed differences in GDP per capita and productivity, as shown in Section 1.4.

We now move to the OECD indices of product and labour market regulations. The pattern is also one of strong convergence. Figure 1.17 shows that reforms have been the fastest in countries that started in 1998 with larger barriers in product markets. The pattern of reform is homogenous, as in the case of the Doing Business indicators. Southern Europe sees improvements that are large compared with the countries that started with lower values for the index.

What is again remarkable is that convergence is very strong. The PMR index is an absolute index so the reading of this chart is slightly different from reading of Figure 1.16. In this case we see that all countries are improving their regulations. But those that start with higher values are moving faster and significantly reducing the difference with best practices.

For example, Portugal starts with a value of 2.59 in 1998, much higher than that of Sweden, 1.89. By 2013 the values have almost converged, Portugal is now at 1.29 and Sweden is at 1.52.

The timing of these reforms has not been uniform during these years. In fact, when we break the sample into three subsamples we can see that reforms were larger in the periods 1998–2003 than in any of the next two periods, both for non-EU countries and EU countries (Figure 1.18). Among individual countries the trend towards a slower pace of reform is visible in

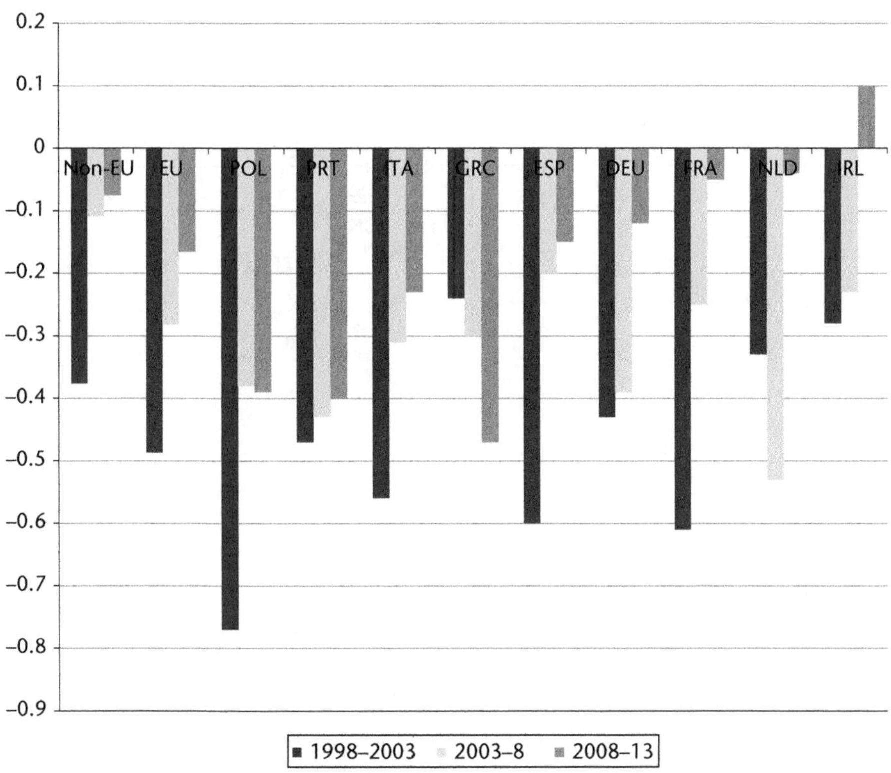


**Figure 1.18.** The Timing of PMR Reforms.

all countries in the figure, with the exception of Greece. Similar evidence of slowing reforms can be found in the 10-year OECD review of the Going for Growth initiative (OECD, 2015). This slowdown could be a sign of fatigue or the fact that reforms get harder as progress takes place and all countries have regulatory frameworks that are much more similar.

When it comes to labour market policies and employment protection in particular, the convergence is less obvious, partly driven by the fact that the estimates for 1998 are very similar across a large number of countries (Figure 1.19). Among EU countries, Portugal has seen the largest reform together with some of the other Southern economies plus Slovakia. For most other countries the change is very close to zero.

A more detailed analysis of the timing of labour reforms for the last decade using the LABREF database can be found in Turrini et al. (2014). Their analysis shows that labour market reforms have remained stable during the last decade, possibly with a peak right before the crisis. The crisis itself has triggered some additional reforms mostly in terms of flexibility and wage setting, but it has also resulted in reversals of previous reforms in the tax

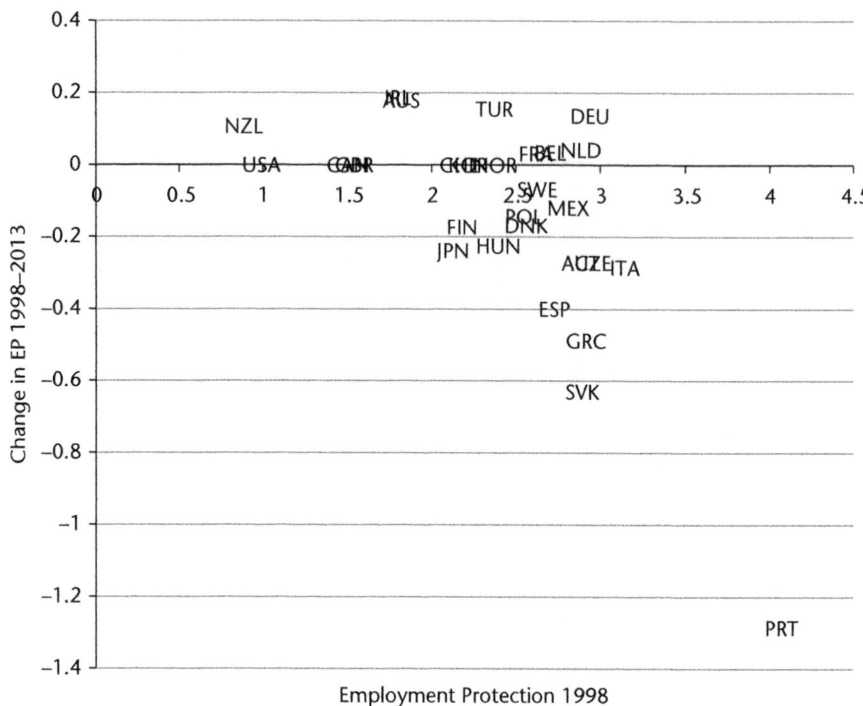


Figure 1.19. Convergence in Employment Protection.

wedge or amount of social security charges, a result of the difficult budgetary situation faced by many governments.

Overall, our analysis of changes in the three indicators of policies and institutions shows that there has been significant convergence over the last 10–15 years. The visibility of these indices and rankings combined with the efforts of supranational organizations such as the EU or the OECD seem to have had an effect on the reform efforts in our sample of countries.

It is interesting to note that despite the strong convergence in these indicators, and as we have shown in Section 1.2, the current (smaller) differences still correlate well with productivity and employment. This means that there is potential room for further convergence to improve performance, even if the distance between countries is much smaller than in the past.

## 1.6. The Benefits of Reform

Our empirical analysis so far has shown two stylized facts. We have first shown that the gaps in policies among advanced economies correlate with measures of economic performance: productivity and employment. In addition we have seen that in the last two decades there has been a reform effort that has resulted in convergence of policies, even if there is room for further convergence.

Have the previous reforms paid off in terms of closing the productivity and labour gap? The evidence provides weak support in favour of positive economic effects. Before we review the actual evidence, it is important to stress that most of the literature on the potential effects of reform is based on indirect evidence. In some cases the benefits of reforms are studied in a context in which countries are assumed to be able to find ways to close their gaps in terms of productivity and labour practices. For example, what would be the GDP per capita of Southern Europe if it could achieve the labour force participation of Switzerland (McQuinn and Whelan, 2015)? This is a useful analysis of the potential for improvement but it does not help us to understand the actual impact or feasibility of different reform strategies.

The second type of analysis is done through simulations of large-scale macroeconomic models. Bouis and Duval (2011) present a very useful summary of the literature (see also Varga and in 't Veld, 2014; Anderson et al., 2014; OECD, 2015; de Bandt and Vigna, 2008). These studies identify large gains coming from reforms that can be as high as 10% of GDP over a five-year horizon for some countries, and as high as 20% of GDP over a ten-year horizon.[20] But these simulations are produced with models that assume the benefits of reducing frictions in product and labour markets. Although the parameters might be estimated from additional empirical work, there is still a feeling that some of these results are 'assumed' from the structure of the models.

minu1.5pt When it comes to the direct empirical analysis of the benefits of reforms, the literature struggles with many challenges. First, it is not always easy to characterize and measure the reforms. Despite all the efforts to quantify policies, there remains much uncertainty about the size and quality of reforms. Second, reforms are likely to have an effect over time, which makes the estimation of its impact more difficult. Third, reforms are likely to have different effects depending on the economic environment as well as whether or not other reforms take place at the same time. In practice, it will be hard to design experiments in which the effects of specific reforms can be isolated. And, finally, measuring the actual effects of reform on productivity or labour market outcomes is also subject to the usual uncertainty in establishing causality when there are many other factors affecting macroeconomic performance.

We start by doing a quick empirical test on how reforms correlate with standard measures of growth and improvements in the labour market. Our approach is to use a very simple specification to see if there is an obvious

[20] See Bouis and Duval (2011) or Anderson et al. (2014).

correlation in the data between the two. One should not attach a causal relationship to the estimates given the (large) number of omitted variables that could be introduced in the regression.

We first regress growth in the period 2000–13 against product market reforms (OECD) during the early years 1998–2003.[21] We include in the regression the initial (log) level of GDP per hour to capture convergence dynamics. In the second specification we include an interaction term between the initial level of GDP per hour and the reform in PMR.

The results from the first column of Table 1.9 show that there is unconditional convergence in GDP per hour during these years and that reform has a positive but non-significant effect. When we introduce the interaction term reforms become significant, as well as the interaction term. This means that the effects of reform are stronger for countries far away from the frontier. Another way of reading the results is that there is no convergence except for countries that have done enough reforms. This second column provides support for the idea that the reforms of the years 1998–2003 are correlated with the growth performance afterwards.

The third column looks at the effects of labour market reforms over the same time horizon.[22] Here the evidence is weak. Although the coefficient is positive, it is not significant and the fit of the regression is very low.

So there is some evidence supporting the idea that the convergence in product market regulations has encouraged stronger convergence in

**Table 1.9.** The Effects of Reforms

| Variables | GDP Per Hour | | Hours per Capita |
|---|---|---|---|
| | Growth 2000–13 | | Growth 2000–13 |
| Initial GDP Per Hour | −0.015*** | 0.009 | |
| | (0.0035) | (0.0058) | |
| PMR Reform 1998–2003 | 0.0051 | 0.178*** | |
| | (0.0060) | (0.040) | |
| Interaction PMRx | | −0.048*** | |
| Initial GDP per Hour | | (0.011) | |
| Labour Market Reform 1998–2003 | | | 0.0452 |
| | | | (0.126) |
| Constant | 0.067*** | −0.023 | −0.0245 |
| | (0.004) | (0.021) | (0.0157) |
| Observations | 27 | 27 | 27 |
| R-squared | 0.554 | 0.676 | 0.003 |

Robust standard errors in parentheses.
*** $p<0.01$, ** $p<0.05$, * $p<0.1$.

[21] The reform period (1998–2003) is chosen because of data availability and it partially overlaps with the period over which we measure growth (2000–13). We have reproduced our regressions using the period 2003–13 to measure growth and the estimates are practically identical.

[22] Labour market reform is measured as the change in the employment protection indicator used in Section 1.4.2.

productivity, but to establish this as a robust result we would need to impose a much richer structure on the regression and introduce a variety of potential control variables. This is what the vast literature on the economic effect of reforms does, from a variety of perspectives and using many different datasets. We quickly review some of the literature to get a sense on what we know and what we do not know about the effect of reforms.

There are more studies in the area of labour market reforms mostly because it is easier to characterize changes in policies and measure their potential effects. The evidence is mixed. In a recent survey by the OECD about the empirical evidence in favour of labour reforms, the results of the literature are shown to vary enormously depending on the particular study (OECD, 2013a). Earlier work on the effects of labour reforms on aggregate employment found limited supporting evidence, as surveyed by Boeri (2011). Studies on more recent reforms show some positive results but with weak statistical significance (Turrini et al., 2014).

Some of the reforms that target a specific group of the population or a very specific policy seem to have a stronger impact on outcomes. For example when it comes to particular labour flows, or on how active labour policies reduce unemployment spells, the evidence seems to support the role of reforms although it is often difficult to see the general equilibrium effects (for example, Estevão, 2007).

Evidence following particular reforms has difficulty isolating the effects of the reforms. As an example, a study of the recent 2012 labour reform in Spain (OECD, 2013b) finds that following the reform we have seen a strong downward adjustment of unit labour costs, but a similar pattern is also observed in several other European economies during the crisis.

When it comes to evidence regarding productivity growth, the results on aggregate data provide support for the hypothesis of faster productivity growth in countries with better policies as in our regression (Nicoletti and Scarpetta, 2003; OECD, 2015). The evidence, however, is based on cross-country analysis and subject to the usual potential causality as well as omitted variables criticism.

One way to identify better the economic effects of reforms on productivity is to look at some microeconomic data at the sectoral level. When looking at disaggregated data at the sectoral or firm level, policies and regulations at the country level matter, but firm or industry characteristics such as attractiveness to Foreign Direct Investment (FDI) or access to credit or spending on ICT might have a much larger and significant effect (Andrea et al., 2013). It is not a surprise that these variables matter, what remains uncertain is the extent to which some of these variables might also be affected by institutions and policies that are not well captured by the traditional indicators. As mentioned earlier, at the aggregate level diffusion of ICT technologies correlates with flexibility in product and labour markets (Cette and Lopez, 2008).

Also using sectoral data Bourlès et al. (2013) show that regulation matters for productivity, more so for countries close to the frontier (although Dabla-Norris, Ho, and Kyobe, 2013, find more mixed effects regarding the distance to the frontier).

When it comes to partial versus broad reforms, there is plenty of evidence that partial reforms are less successful than broad reforms (i.e. reforms that cut across several dimensions, such as both labour markets and product markets, tend to have stronger effects). For example, Aghion et al. (2008) found that the effects of reform on productivity can be higher when the labour market is more flexible. Similar results are found in Bassanini and Duval (2006), Estevão (2005) and Berger and Danninger (2006). There is similar evidence regarding the effectiveness of labour market reforms. Annett (2007) shows that successful labour market reformers combined their reforms with changes in product market regulations and overall reductions in government size. Bentolila et al. (2012) show that partial reforms in a dual labour market do not alter fundamental outcomes and can even generate negative impacts on productivity.

Finally, there is a question on when reforms are more successful. The experience of successful reformers shows that reforms are triggered by a sense of crisis (Annett, 2007). At the same time, structural reforms in crisis times can be counterproductive because of the potential negative effects on demand. In particular, in the case where monetary policy is constrained by the zero-lower bound, structural reforms can lead to lower growth (Eggertsson et al. 2014). This is confirmed by the recent study of International Monetary Fund (2015) showing that reforms are more productive during periods of expansion, and that they can have negative effects on productivity in the short-run.

The issue of timing of reforms and the business cycle is a key issue for Europe today given the cyclical performance of most countries over recent years. To get a perspective on this we can do a quick comparison between the cost of the recent crisis and the potential gains from reforms. Typically, gains from reforms are seen in a range of 5–20% of GDP. As an example, a recent review of reforms over the last ten years by the OECD estimates effects on productivity that range from 0 to 14%. And on labour utilization that can be as high as 7%. These are large magnitudes but they are not far from the estimates of changes in potential output as a result of the crisis. Using different vintages of the World Economic Outlook, the revisions to potential output as a consequence of the crisis that started in 2008 can be as high as 20% for Greece and in the range of 3–10% for some of the other periphery countries. This means that the potential benefits of reform are in a range that is similar to the permanent effects of the crisis.

## 1.7. Conclusion: An Agenda for Reforms in Europe

As a region, Europe's economic performance lags behind that of the USA, and has been seen for years as growing at rates that are below its potential. The degree of underperformance varies across countries as well as over time. Southern Europe has seen its convergence process slowed down or even reversed for the last decades. In Eastern Europe, while some countries have been on a path of convergence supported by continuous reform, others seem to be on a much slower path of both reforms and growth. The European core seems to be in better health but with signs that some countries cannot keep up with certain global trends or some of their future challenges (e.g. demographics).

The diagnosis of the causes of low performance is not uniform either. The distance to the frontier lies in a combination of gaps in productivity and employment that are very different across countries. There is no one recipe of reforms that applies to all countries.

This poor economic performance is certainly not new and some see it as the natural consequence of a different economic and social model. There are, however, increasing signs that the model is failing to cope with new economic circumstances. Countries that were keeping up with the technology frontier seem to have entered a downward trajectory, even when they have been pursuing reform efforts. And Europe has not managed well the recent large economic crises that have left permanent scars on both the economic and social model.

The good news, as discussed in Section 1.4, is that reforms are happening and they are happening faster in the countries in which they are most needed. European and OECD-wide initiatives seem to be having a positive effect on the process of designing and implementing reforms. However, the speed of reforms might not be fast enough and their positive effects are not as strong as desired. What would it take for reforms to happen faster? How can reforms be more effective?

There is very little disagreement on the direction in which reforms must go, although each country has to follow its own path. There is also general consensus on the ingredients that make reforms happen. From a recent review by the OECD on the last ten years of reforms (OECD, 2015), their successful implementation requires a combination of:

1. A sense of urgency through 'erosion of the status quo'
2. Effective communication backed by solid research and analysis.
3. Strong electoral mandate and government leadership and cohesion.
4. Persistence and patience to see the outcome of reforms.

There is no doubt that in many European countries there is a general sense of urgency and a desire to change, although it might not always translate into an agreed direction for the reforms. And this is partly because the understanding of what needs to be done is not always supported by 'effective communication backed by solid research and analysis'. What are the true priorities? Where are the bottlenecks? What are the preconditions required for certain reforms to work? There might be clarity on some of these questions when they are discussed at the technical level but this does not translate into clarity when they are part of the political debate. In that sense, the political process is not providing the leadership or vision to form a strong coalition that translates the urgency to change into a proper reform process.

The result is that reform becomes an 'always-on' process without clear deadlines and expected outcomes. Reforms take place in small steps, not always supported by complementary policies that ensure their success. The outcome tends to be one of political fatigue that is not conducive to the persistence needed to ensure the full implementation of reform plans.

And the business cycle generates the wrong incentives for reforms. In good years there is a sense of complacency that slows down the political urgency for reform. And during crisis, reforms are accelerated at the time when the effectiveness of reforms is likely to be the lowest and, in some cases, they could have counterproductive effects.

What is the role of Europe and European institutions in the reform process? Europe has served as a catalyst for reform in some of the least-advanced EU economies. Through the imposition of requirements to join certain European initiatives, it has fostered enough social consensus around the need for compromises. As an example, it worked well to transform and standardize the macroeconomic institutions of European countries, especially when it comes to monetary policy and inflation.

But these dynamics are not always productive. Reform is ultimately a domestic political business where trade offs are being made between economic efficiency, social goals and the way power and income are distributed in a society. Always giving Europe as the reason for reforms is likely to generate unhealthy dynamics. In addition, it is not always easy to link reforms to the benefits of European integration. As an example, current negotiations between Greece and its European partners have very strong support among the Greek population to stay in the Euro area but there is limited support to implement the reforms that 'Brussels' believe are necessary.

The only way to change these dynamics is through a much more contractual and ex-ante approach to reforms. This was partly the spirit of regulations of the Maastricht Treaty that established rules of behaviour to be a member of the Euro. But, as experience has shown, those were not enforceable rules. The rules only worked well as an entry condition, once the entry decisions were made the rules became very weak. Rules have been renegotiated, changed, and violated on numerous occasions. Why not make the entry conditions more binding? The reality is that if countries were asked to reform or adopt irreversible commitments before joining any process of European integration, there would be very few members of the EU or the Euro area left.

The second role that Europe could play is as a way to share best practices and to generate enough peer pressure (a process that also happens at the OECD level). This is partially working today but to make it more effective it requires clarity on the benefits ahead, a sense of the common good, and patience to see the results of those reform plans. For this to take place a much stronger shared sense of the political goals of the EU is needed.

As we look at a path for reforms ahead, there is one additional complication coming from the current state of many European economies. A long-lasting crisis and a weak recovery have created a very difficult environment to introduce reforms. While crises are wake-up calls for change, successful implementation of reforms requires consensus around policies and growth to ensure continued support. Consensus around policies has broken down because of what has been seen as a failure of European economic policies to handle the economic crisis. The crisis was handled through a package of economic policies that put together austerity and reform. These policies have resulted in a deep crisis and a slow recovery that has led to a fall in potential output by a magnitude that is, in some cases, comparable with the potential effects of reforms.

To get out of the current environment there is the need to come up with a combined growth and reform plan at the European level (see Enderlein and Pisani-Ferry, 2014; or PIIE, 2014). This plan needs to first address the lack of confidence and demand deficiencies that have impaired a proper economic recovery. It needs to generate sufficient investment, private and in some cases public, required to ensure continuing growth in the years ahead. It needs to reinforce key European-wide initiatives to reform sectors that are central to the generation of growth and new ideas (R.&D., financial sector). These initiatives will stress the European dimension of reforms and the benefits of the overall process. And the countries that are behind the traditional reforms (labour markets, product markets) need to use this opportunity to sell these policies and the resulting growth domestically to gain enough support for a strategy based on broad reforms.

Some will argue that providing a positive growth environment can slow down reforms because it buys time for governments that are not committed to change. This is possible but the alternative, to generate reforms out of forcing 'good behaviour' has already failed, at least in the current environment.

We need to be realistic as well and Europe needs to find a way to deal with countries and governments that do not want to go along with the reform process or that are unable to do so. Ultimately, the speed of reform remains the decision of individual countries. Its citizens are the ones that will suffer the consequences of no reforms and low growth. This is true for any country, advanced or emerging, and this is true for Europe.

The reason why the reform debate becomes more visible and relevant in the European context relative to other advanced economies that might struggle with similar issues of performance, is that the process of European integration might occasionally force countries to move together. When you share risk via the balance sheet of a central bank or when you design a programme of transfers from rich to poor regions, the reform agenda becomes a supranational issue, not simply a pure national debate. Perhaps Europe needs to find ways to separate the two? Either through a much more contractual approach to institutions that leaves no room for further negotiation, or by changing the design of those institutions so that the links between countries and the shared risks are minimized. This could be suboptimal as it might come at the cost of reducing the effectiveness of those institutions, but it might be the only way to make the process of European integration and economic reforms compatible.

## 1.8. References

Acemoglu, Daron, Simon Johnson, and James A. Robinson (2001), 'The Colonial Origins of Comparative Development: An Empirical Investigation', *The American Economic Review* 91, 1369–401.

Aghion, Philippe, Robin Burgess, Stephen J Redding, and Fabrizio Zilibotti (2008), 'The Unequal Effects of Liberalization: Evidence from Dismantling the License Raj in India', *The American Economic Review* 98, 1397–412.

Anderson, Derek, Bergljot Barkbu, Lusine Lusinyan, and Dirk Muir (2014), 'Assessing the Gains from Structural Reforms for Jobs and Growth', *Jobs and Growth: supporting the European recovery*, 151.

Andrea, Dall'Olio, Mariana Iootty, Naoto Kanehira, and Federica Saliola (2013), *Productivity growth in Europe*, The World Bank.

Annett, Anthony (2007), *Lessons from Successful Labor Market Reformers in Europe* (International Monetary Fund).

Ark, Bart van (2002), 'Understanding productivity and income gaps in the OECD area: are ICT and intangibles the missing links?'.

Barro, Robert J. (1996), 'Democracy and growth', *Journal of Economic Growth* 1, 1–27.

Barro, Robert J. (2012), *Convergence and modernization revisited*, National Bureau of Economic Research.

Barro, Robert J. and Xavier Sala-i-Martin (1992), 'Convergence', *Journal of Political Economy* 100, 223–51.

Barro, Robert J., Xavier Sala-i-Martin, Olivier Jean Blanchard, and Robert E. Hall (1991), 'Convergence across states and regions', *Brookings Papers on Economic Activity*, 107–82.

Bassanini, Andrea and Romain Duval (2006), 'The determinants of unemployment across OECD countries: Reassessing the role of policies and institutions', *OECD Economic Studies* 42, 7.

Bentolila, Samuel, Juan J. Dolado, and Juan F. Jimeno (2012), 'Reforming an insider-outsider labor market: the Spanish experience', *IZA Journal of European Labor Studies* 1, 1–29.

Berger, Helge and Stephan Danninger (2006), 'The employment effects of labor and product markets deregulation and their implications for structural reform'.

Boeri, Tito, (2011), 'Institutional reforms and dualism in European labor markets', *Handbook of Labor Economics* 4, 1173–236.

Bouis, Romain and Romain Duval (2011), *Raising Potential Growth After the Crisis: A Quantitative Assessment of the Potential Gains from Various Structural Reforms in the OECD Area and Beyond*, OECD Publishing.

Bourlès, Renaud, Gilbert Cette, Jimmy Lopez, Jacques Mairesse, and Giuseppe Nicoletti (2013), 'Do Product Market Regulations in Upstream Sectors Curb Productivity Growth? Panel Data Evidence for OECD Countries', *Review of Economics and Statistics* 95, 1750–68.

Cette, Gilbert and Jimmy Lopez (2008), 'What Explains the ICT Diffusion Gap Between the Major Industrialized Countries: An Empirical Analysis?', *International Productivity Monitor* 17, 28–39.

Dabla-Norris, Era, Giang Ho, and Annette Kyobe (2013), *Reforms and Distance to the Frontier*. IMF Technical Appendix.

De Bandt, Olivier and Olivier Vigna (2008), 'The macroeconomic impact of structural reforms', *Quarterly Selection of Articles*, 5.

De Michelis, Andrea, Marcello M. Estevão, and Beth Anne Wilson (2013), *'Productivity or Employment: Is It a Choice?'* 13–97 (International Monetary Fund).

Djankov, Simeon, Caralee McLiesh, and Rita Maria Ramalho (2006), 'Regulation and Growth', *Economics Letters* 92, 395–401.

Doppelhofer, Gernot, Ronald I. Miller, and Xavier Sala-i-Martin (2004), 'Determinants of Long-Term Growth: A Bayesian Averaging of Classical Estimates (BACE) Approach', *The American Economic Review* 94, 813–35.

Easterly, William and Ross Levine (2001), 'What have we learned from a decade of empirical research on growth? It's Not Factor Accumulation: Stylized Facts and Growth Models', *World Bank Economic Review* 15, 177–219.

Eggertsson, Gauti, Andrea Ferrero, and Andrea Raffo (2014), 'Can structural reforms help Europe?', *Journal of Monetary Economics* 61, 2–22.

Ek, Andreas (2015), 'Taking Culture Into Account(ing)', *Manuscript*.

Enderlein, Henrik and Jean Pisani-Ferry (2014), *Reforms, Investment and Growth: An Agenda for France, Germany and Europe*.

Estevão, Marcello (2007), 'Labor policies to raise employment', *IMF Staff Papers*, 113–38.

Estevão, Marcello M. (2005), *Product market regulation and the benefits of wage moderation*.

European Council (2000), *Lisbon Strategy Presidency Conclusions.*

Gillanders, Robert and Karl Whelan (2014), 'Open for business? Institutions, business environment and economic development', *Kyklos* 67, 535–58.

Glaeser, Edward L., Rafael La Porta, Florencio Lopez-de-Silanes, and Andrei Shleifer (2004), 'Do institutions cause growth?', *Journal of Economic Growth* 9, 271–303.

Hall, Robert E. and Charles I. Jones (1999), 'Why Do Some Countries Produce So Much More Output Per Worker Than Others?', *The Quarterly Journal of Economics* 114, 83–116.

International Monetary Fund (2015), 'Where Are We Headed? Perspectives on Potential Output', *World Economic Outlook* Chapter 3.

Kaufmann, Daniel, Aart Kraay, and Massimo Mastruzzi (2009), 'Governance matters VIII: aggregate and individual governance indicators', 1996–2008', *World bank policy research working paper.*

Mankiw, N. Gregory, David Romer, and David N. Weil (1992), 'A Contribution to the Empirics of Economic Growth', *The Quarterly Journal of Economics* 107, 407–37.

McQuinn, Kieran and Karl Whelan (2015), *Europe's Long-Term Growth Prospects: With and Without Structural Reforms.*

Nicoletti, Giuseppe, and Stefano Scarpetta (2003), 'Regulation, productivity and growth: OECD evidence', *Economic policy* 18, 9–72.

OECD (2005), *Economic Policy Reforms: Going for Growth* (Organization for Economic Cooperation and Development).

OECD (2013a), *OECD Employment Outlook* (Organization for Economic Cooperation and Development).

OECD (2013b), *The 2012 Labour Market Reform in Spain: A Preliminary Assessment,* Organization for Economic Cooperation and Development.

OECD (2015), *Economic Policy Reforms: Going for Growth* (Organization for Economic Cooperation and Development).

PIIE (2014), 'Rebuilding Europe's Common Future', *PIIE Briefing* 14.

Rodrik, Dani, Arvind Subramanian, and Francesco Trebbi (2004), 'Institutions rule: the primacy of institutions over geography and integration in economic development', *Journal of Economic Growth* 9, 131–65.

Romer, Paul M. (1986), 'Increasing returns and long-run growth', *Journal of Political Economy,* 1002–37.

Romer, Paul M. (1990), 'Endogenous Technological Change', *Journal of Political Economy* 98, S71–102.

Solow, Robert M. (1956), 'A contribution to the theory of economic growth', *Quarterly Journal of Economics,* 65–94.

Turrini, Alessandro, Gabor Koltay, Fabiana Pierini, Clarisse Goffard, and Áron Kiss (2014), *A Decade of Labour Market Reforms in the EU: Insights from the LABREF Database,* Institute for the Study of Labor (IZA).

Varga, Janos, Jan in 't Veld (2014), 'The potential growth impact of structural reforms in the EU. A benchmarking exercise', *European Economy Economics Papers.* European Economy.

## 1.9. Data Sources

- GDP PPP adjusted (2013): World Economic Outlook, October 2014 Database, IMF.
- Population, (2013): World Development Indicators, World Bank.
- Working-Age Population and Adult Population (2013): ILO.
- Number of hours worked (2013): Total Economy Database, Conference Board.
- Time series of GDP per capita, GDP per hour and hours per employment (1950–2013): Total Economy Database, Conference Board.
- Product and Market Regulations: Product and Market Regulations database, OECD.
- Employment Rates: Labour Database, OECD.
- Employment Protection: Employment Protection Database, OECD.
- Labour Tax Wedge, Social Security Charges (percentage of GDP): OECD Tax Database, OECD.
- Governance Indicators: Governance Indicators Database, World Bank.
- Doing Business Distance to Frontier: Doing Business Database, World Bank.

# 2

# Crisis Management and Economic Growth in the Eurozone

*Paul De Grauwe and Yuemei Ji*

## 2.1. Introduction

Since the financial crisis of 2007–8 most developed countries have been unable to return to their pre-crisis growth path. Nowhere in the developed world is this more visible than in the Eurozone. We show this in Figure 2.1, in which we compare the evolution of real Gross Domestic Product (GDP) in the Eurozone with real GDP in the USA and in the EU-countries not belonging to the Eurozone (EU10). The difference is striking. Prior to the financial crisis, the Eurozone real GDP was on a slower growth path than in the USA and in EU10. Since the financial crisis of 2008, the divergence has increased even further. Real GDP in the Eurozone stagnated and in 2014 was even lower than in 2008. In the USA and EU10 one observes (after the dip of 2009) a relatively strong recovery. Admittedly, this recovery is below the potential growth path of these countries (see Summers, 2014), but is much more pronounced than in the Eurozone where stagnation prevailed. Note also that there was a recovery in the Eurozone from 2009 to 2011, and that from 2012 to 2013 the Eurozone experienced a double-dip recession.

What is it that makes the Eurozone such a pronounced island of stagnation in the developed world? This is the question that we want to analyse in this chapter.

## 2.2. Eurozone Stagnation: Supply or Demand Problem?

The policy response to the sovereign debt crisis has very much been influenced by a supply side story of the origins of the low growth in the Eurozone.

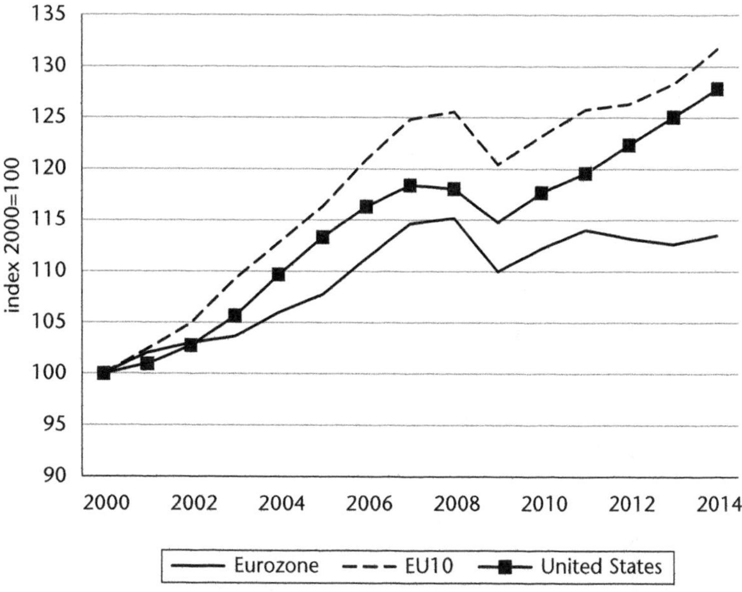


**Figure 2.1.** Real GDP (prices of 2010) in Eurozone, EU10, and USA.
*Source*: European Commission, Ameco database.

In this view, low growth is the result of structural rigidities, that is of a lack of flexibility in the way the supply side of the economy works. Labour markets are rigid, preventing demand and supply of labour from reaching equilibrium. As a result of these rigidities, production remains below its potential. Similarly, the goods markets are subject to price rigidities and other imperfections that also reduce potential output. Policies that eliminate these imperfections will increase potential output, so goes this story that has become the mainstream view among policymakers in Europe.

Implicit in this view is that the increase in potential output will automatically lead to an increase in realized output. Put differently, Say's Law, according to which supply creates its own demand, is implicitly assumed. Thus, policies that improve the supply side through structural reforms will automatically lead to more demand and thus to more production. The demand side of the economy adjusts automatically to the supply side.

From Brussels, Frankfurt, and Berlin we have been hearing incessantly that structural reforms are the key to economic recovery and higher growth rates. Making labour and output markets more flexible is the only way to boost economic growth in the Eurozone in a sustainable way, so we are told by European policymakers. This view has been very influential and has led countries into programmes of structural reforms of labour and product markets.

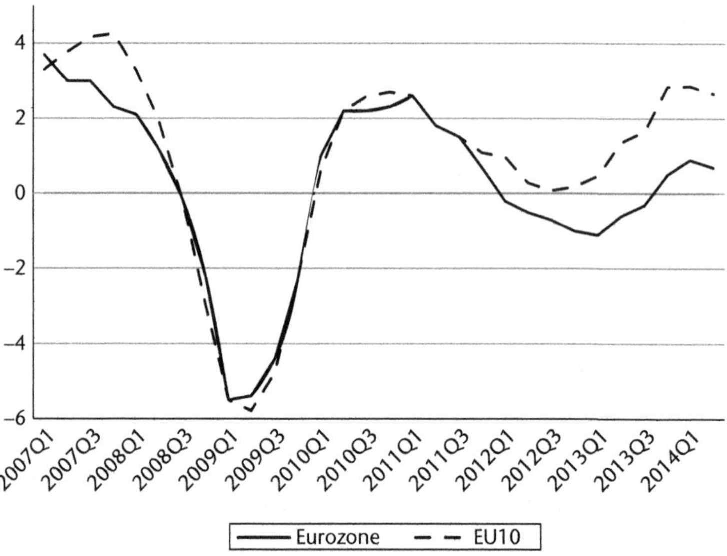


**Figure 2.2.** Growth GDP in Eurozone (EU18) and EU10 (per cent).
*Source*: Eurostat.

A quick look at Figure 2.2 makes us sceptical of this view. We observe that since 2010–11 the EU10 has experienced a strong recovery, whereas the Eurozone got caught in stagnation. Prior to those years, the Eurozone and the EU10 experienced similar movements of GDP growth. If stagnation in the Eurozone since the start of the sovereign debt crisis is the result of structural rigidities, it is difficult to understand why the same structural rigidities prevented the Eurozone from engineering an equally quick recovery from the Great Recession of 2008–9 as the EU10.

All this of course is only suggestive evidence. A more systematic empirical analysis is necessary to find out how important structural rigidities in the labour and product markets are for economic growth. To analyse this question we perform an econometric analysis of the factors that affect economic growth. We will rely on the theory and the econometrics of economic growth (see, e.g., Barro and Sala-i-Martin, 2003; Acemoglu, 2009).

## 2.3. Structural Rigidities and Growth: An Econometric Analysis

Since Robert Solow's seminal contribution, modern economic growth theory has identified a number of fundamental variables that drive the economic growth process. These variables are population growth, physical and human capital accumulation, and technological progress (the residual in Solow's growth model). Recent theoretical contributions have highlighted the importance of institutions as deep variables that influence the process of capital accumulation and technological progress (productivity growth). Influential contributions are Barro and Sala-i-Martin (2003) and Acemoglu and Robinson (2012).

There are many institutional features that can influence the economic growth process. The econometric literature has put a lot of emphasis on political institutions (nature of democracy, transparency of political system, rule of law, etc.) that affect the dynamics of physical and human capital accumulation and technological progress, and through this channel economic growth. The flexibility of labour and capital markets (or the lack thereof) is part of the institutional characteristics of countries that can affect economic growth. Surprisingly, relatively little importance has been given to these features in traditional econometric analyses of econometric growth.[1] In this section we present an econometric growth model using indicators of the degree of flexibility in labour and product markets as one of the institutions that can facilitate capital accumulation and productivity growth.

The study is limited in that it focuses on flexibility in labour and product markets and not the many other institutions that have been identified in the econometric growth literature (see Aghion and Howitt, 1998; Barro and Sala-i-Martin, 2003; Acemoglu, 2009). One institutional feature we introduce to the analysis is the quality of public governance. We use the World Bank's index of government effectiveness. We hope at a later stage to integrate more institutional variables into the analysis.

Our study is limited in another sense. We restrict our econometric analysis to Organization for Economic Co-operation and Development (OECD) countries. The main reason is that the indices of labour and output market flexibility in which we are interested have been constructed by the OECD for the OECD-member countries. We are not aware of similar indicators of labour and product market flexibility for other countries.

The econometric model is specified as follows:

$$\begin{aligned} y_{i,t} = a_i + \beta I_{i,t} + \mu H_{i,t} + \theta EPL_{i,t} + \lambda Age_{i,t} + \rho PM_{i,t} + \sigma GE_{i,t} \\ + \gamma R_{i,t} + \delta G_{i,t} + \varepsilon_{i,t} \end{aligned}$$

where $y_{i,t}$ = growth rate of per capita GDP in year t in country i. This way of defining the growth rate is equivalent to explaining the growth rate of GDP by population growth while assuming that the effect of population growth on GDP growth has a unitary elasticity; $I_{i,t}$ = the ratio of investment (private + public) to GDP in year t in country i. This measures the process

[1] There have been quite some empirical studies of the effect of structural reforms on economic growth. These have mainly been performed by official institutions such as the OECD, the European Commission and the European Central Bank (ECB). We review these in Section 2.4.

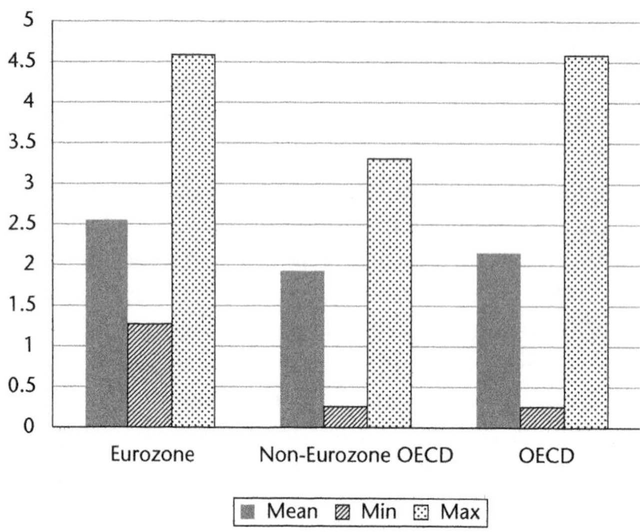


**Figure 2.3.** Employment Protection Legislation (EPL) Index (mean 1998–2013).
*Source*: OECD and authors' own calculation.

of capital accumulation on economic growth; $H_{i,t}$ = the proportion of the population with a tertiary education. This variable represents human capital accumulation. We expect it to have a positive effect on economic growth; $EPL_{i,t}$ = the employment protection legislation (EPL) index as measured by the OECD (in year t and country i). It is generally agreed that more intense employment protection legislation makes the labour market more rigid. Making firing more expensive also makes firms more reluctant to hire. As a result, employment growth will be curtailed and so will economic growth. Thus one expects a negative effect of EPL on economic growth. We show the mean EPL index in the OECD countries in Figure 2.3; $Age_{i,t}$ = this is the average effective retirement age in year t in country i. According to accepted wisdom a country that increases the retirement age of the working population should experience more economic growth; $PM_{i,t}$ = the product market regulation (PMR) index as computed by the OECD. According to conventional wisdom more product market rigidities have a negative effect on economic growth. We show the mean PMR index in the OECD countries in Figure 2.4; $GE_{i,t}$ = the government effectiveness index as computed by the World Bank. More effective government should boost economic growth.

We have added two other control variables that are often introduced in econometric growth equations, that is the real effective exchange rate,[2] $R_{i,t}$,

[2] This is measured by the effective exchange rate of country *i* in year *t* corrected for the ratio of consumer prices in country *i* versus the trading partners of country *i*.

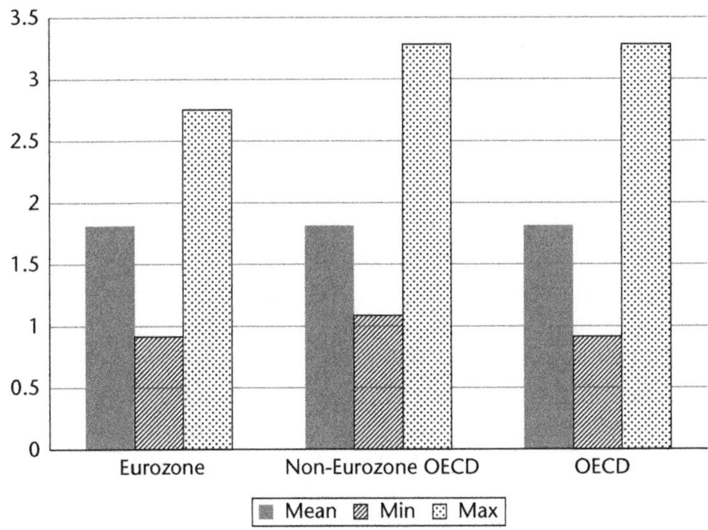


**Figure 2.4.** Product Market Regulation (PMR) Index (mean 1998–2013).
*Source*: OECD and authors' own calculation.

and government consumption as a per cent of GDP. The former should have a negative effect on economic growth, that is an overvalued currency should reduce economic growth; the latter is often assumed to have a negative effect on GDP growth. $a_i$ is the fixed country effect measuring time invariant idiosyncrasies of countries. An important one is the initial level of per capita income. Our empirical analysis relies on the fixed effect model.

The model was estimated for the OECD countries. One problem we encountered is that the sample of member-countries of the OECD has changed over time. Prior to 1993 the central European countries were not members. Therefore, we estimate the model first for the smaller group of OECD-countries (called advanced economies) that were members prior to 1993. This estimation is over the sample period 1985–2013. Then we estimate the model for the full sample of countries but over a shorter time period, that is 1998–2013. We also estimate one specification without a dummy for the financial crisis (starting in 2008) and one with such a dummy.

The results are presented in Table 2.1 (the sources of the data are presented in Appendix 2.1). These results lend themselves to the following interpretation.

First, the investment ratio has the expected positive sign and is significant for the OECD countries as a whole. Second, our index of human capital (the proportion of the population with tertiary education) has a strong and significantly positive effect on economic growth. Thus the traditional fundamental variables of economic growth, and physical and human capital accumulation are important in driving economic growth.

The most striking aspect of our results is the finding that the structural measures of the labour and product market rigidities do not seem to have any influence on the growth rate of GDP per capita. The OECD employment protection legislation index even appears to have a systematically positive effect on growth in the full sample of the advanced economies. This is not found in the shorter sample of all OECD-countries, where this effect is not significantly different from zero.

There is a possibility that labour market protection and product market regulations affect economic growth indirectly through their effect on investment. One should not exclude the possibility that rigidities in labour and product markets have a negative effect on investment, and through this channel reduce economic growth. To test for this hypothesis, we regressed investment (as a per cent of GDP) on our indices of labour and product market rigidities, together with a number of control variables. We show the results in Appendix 2.2. It appears that we can reject the hypothesis that labour market and product market rigidities are associated with lower investment. In fact, in the case of labour market protection we find a positive association, that is higher labour market protection is associated with higher investment.

Our conclusion is that employment protection is of no visible importance for economic growth. This may seem surprising. The Brussels–Frankfurt consensus has stressed that employment protection has a negative effect on hiring, and subsequently reduces prospects for growth. This may be true but there is another phenomenon that may more than compensate the positive effect of flexibility on economic growth. In economies in which employment protection is weak, the incentives for firms to invest in its labour force are weak. When turnover is high firms are unlikely to invest in personnel who are likely to quit early. In addition, employees that can be fired quickly have equally weak incentives to invest in firm-specific skills. As a result, labour productivity is negatively affected. More generally, the quality of human capital will be low.

One must also take into account that reverse causality may be at work, biasing the results. This reverse causality runs as follows. In countries with high growth, there is a high demand for labour protection. Workers and their representatives are strong and are pushing for legislation to provide strong employment protection. As a result, we will observe that high growth is correlated with employment protection.

To correct for this reverse causality, we used an instrumental variable method. We selected two instruments: the lagged EPL index and the ideological composition of the government along the scale right to left

**Table 2.1.** Estimation results (Ordinary Least Squares (OLS))

| | (1) Advanced economies 1985–2013 | (2) Advanced economies 1985–2013 | (3) OECD economies 1998–2013 | (4) OECD economies 1998–2013 |
|---|---|---|---|---|
| Investment/GDP | 0.131 | 0.083 | 0.337*** | 0.346*** |
| | (0.081) | (0.076) | (0.119) | (0.120) |
| Proportion of tertiary education | 1.739*** | 1.802*** | 1.400*** | 1.472*** |
| | (0.139) | (0.174) | (0.157) | (0.174) |
| Real effective exchange rate | −0.040*** | −0.034** | −0.044*** | −0.046*** |
| | (0.014) | (0.012) | (0.015) | (0.014) |
| Working population growth | −0.259 | −0.357 | −0.640** | −0.939*** |
| | (0.391) | (0.335) | (0.302) | (0.317) |
| Government consumption/GDP | −0.870*** | −0.633*** | −0.759*** | −0.500*** |
| | (0.134) | (0.130) | (0.155) | (0.156) |
| Effective retirement age | −0.135 | 0.107 | −0.122 | 0.103 |
| | (0.152) | (0.155) | (0.197) | (0.179) |
| Government effectiveness | 2.002** | 1.414 | 2.513** | 1.952** |
| | (0.911) | (0.984) | (0.962) | (0.878) |
| Crisis period | | −1.526*** | | −2.142*** |
| | | (0.272) | | (0.391) |
| Employment protection | 3.140*** | 2.383*** | −0.470 | −0.853 |
| | (0.779) | (0.748) | (2.932) | (2.884) |
| Product market protection | | | 0.484 | −0.989 |
| | | | (0.546) | (0.605) |
| Observations | 409 | 409 | 457 | 457 |
| R-squared | 0.396 | 0.430 | 0.297 | 0.344 |
| Number of countries | 24 | 24 | 32 | 32 |

Robust standard errors in parentheses.

*** $p<0.01$, ** $p<0.05$, * $p<0.1$.

Advanced economy: Australia, Austria, Belgium, Canada, Denmark, Finland, France, Germany, Greece, Ireland, Italy, Japan, South Korea, Luxemburg, Netherlands, New Zealand, Norway, Portugal, Spain, Sweden, Switzerland, UK, USA.

Regression: fixed effect module.

(for a description, see Appendix 2.1). This takes the view that employment protection is positively correlated with the ideological composition of governments, that is more leftist governments push for more employment protection. The results are presented in Table 2.2. We observe that the strongly positive effect of employment protection on growth disappears. We now find that employment protection has no significant effects on economic growth.

The same conclusion holds for product market regulations. The coefficients of this variable are never significant. Thus, product market regulations do not seem to matter in the process of economic growth. Again this goes against current mainstream thinking, which has been much influenced by, among others, Aghion et al. (2001), and which stresses that the model of perfect competition with free entry and price flexibility boosts economic growth innovation among firms that are close to the technological frontier. There is an older literature, however, going back to Joseph Schumpeter, stressing that innovation, investment, and growth are better promoted in an environment

**Table 2.2.** Estimation Results: Instrumental Variables

| | (1) Advanced economies 1985–2013 | (2) OECD economies 1998–2013 | (3) OECD economies 1998–2013 | (4) Advanced economies 1998–2013 | (5) Advanced economies 1998–2013 |
|---|---|---|---|---|---|
| Second stage: | | | | | |
| Investment GDP ratio | 0.111 | 0.270** | 0.339** | 0.192** | 0.257** |
| | (0.091) | (0.129) | (0.140) | (0.095) | (0.118) |
| Tertiary education/total population | 1.798*** | 1.492*** | 1.464*** | 1.456*** | 1.429*** |
| | (0.148) | (0.160) | (0.138) | (0.147) | (0.127) |
| Real effective exchange rate | −0.041*** | −0.039*** | −0.050*** | −0.040*** | −0.052*** |
| | (0.011) | (0.013) | (0.015) | (0.012) | (0.015) |
| Working population growth | −0.425 | −0.776*** | −0.901*** | −0.658** | −0.792*** |
| | (0.331) | (0.299) | (0.311) | (0.274) | (0.290) |
| Government consumption GDP ratio | −0.670*** | −0.597*** | −0.535*** | −0.733*** | −0.666*** |
| | (0.148) | (0.180) | (0.165) | (0.174) | (0.154) |
| Real retirement age | 0.170 | 0.080 | 0.085 | 0.192 | 0.189 |
| | (0.148) | (0.192) | (0.189) | (0.175) | (0.173) |
| Government effectiveness | 0.737 | 1.016 | 0.766 | 0.829 | 0.528 |
| | (1.019) | (0.961) | (0.932) | (0.991) | (0.946) |
| Crisis | −1.595*** | −1.771*** | −2.142*** | −1.415*** | −1.740*** |
| | (0.286) | (0.320) | (0.406) | (0.315) | (0.378) |
| Employment protection | 1.936* | −1.267 | −0.784 | 1.101 | 1.608 |
| | (1.069) | (2.484) | (2.509) | (1.066) | (1.138) |
| Product market protection | | | −0.775 | | −0.647 |
| | | | (0.590) | | (0.455) |
| First stage: | | | | | |
| Excluded instruments: | | | | | |
| Lagged employment protection | 0.877*** | 0.7893*** | 0.7728*** | 0.8660*** | 0.8365*** |
| | (0.085) | (0.0864) | (0.0872) | (0.0908) | (0.093) |
| Government (left) composition | 0.0004* | 0.0004** | 0.0004* | 0.0004* | 0.0003 |
| | (0.002) | (0.002) | (0.002) | (0.002) | (0.002) |
| Partial R-squared of excluded instruments | 0.6065 | 0.5387 | 0.5217 | 0.5720 | 0.5432 |
| Weak Identification F test | 0.0064 | 0.0068 | 0.0061 | 0.0064 | 0.0075 |
| Hansen J statistic | 0.7150 | 0.8469 | 0.8589 | 0.6875 | 0.7408 |
| Observations | 389 | 405 | 399 | 347 | 341 |
| R-squared | 0.464 | 0.387 | 0.404 | 0.452 | 0.473 |
| Number of countries | 23 | 28 | 28 | 23 | 23 |

Robust standard errors in parentheses, *** p<0.01, ** p<0.05, * p<0.1.

of market imperfections and market power. The empirical evidence suggests that both opposing views may be at work, thereby offsetting each other.

Among our control variables, first, the effect of investment and tertiary education are significant in most cases. Second, it appears that the real effective exchange rate matters. Countries with overvalued currencies experience below average growth rates of GDP per capita. Third, government consumption (excluding investment spending or spending on social transfers for instance) has a significant negative effect on growth. This is consistent with the findings in the literature: government consumption not including social

**Table 2.3.** Estimation Results (OLS): Five-year Averages and Cross-section

| | (1) Five-year average fixed effect model | (1) Cross-section model |
|---|---|---|
| Initial GDP per capita level | - | −0.0001** |
| | | (0.000) |
| Investment GDP ratio | 0.343** | 0.1471** |
| | (0.135) | (0.068) |
| Tertiary education/total population | 3.639*** | 0.2345 |
| | (0.882) | (0.908) |
| Real effective exchange rate | −0.035*** | 0.0210 |
| | (0.012) | (0.019) |
| Working population growth | −0.652 | 0.2870 |
| | (0.500) | (0.367) |
| Government consumption GDP ratio | −0.410* | −0.0770 |
| | (0.233) | (0.062) |
| Real retirement age | −0.040 | −0.1159** |
| | (0.268) | (0.045) |
| Government effectiveness | 1.663 | 0.1226 |
| | (1.062) | (0.560) |
| Employment protection | 0.941 | −0.1032 |
| | (1.634) | (0.251) |
| Product market protection | −0.602 | −0.6953 |
| | (0.570) | (0.714) |
| Crisis | −1.503*** | |
| | (0.424) | |
| Observations | 91 | 32 |
| Number of countries | 32 | 32 |
| R-squared | 0.754 | 0.427 |

Robust standard errors in parentheses.
*** $p<0.01$, ** $p<0.05$, * $p<0.1$.

security spending is considered to be unproductive and thus is negatively associated with real growth.

Finally, we also estimated the model using five-year averages (column (1) in Table 2.3) and a cross-section (column (2) in Table 2.3). The results in Table 2.3 confirm the previous results. Investments in physical and human capital are significant driving forces of economic growth in the medium and long run. In contrast, no significant effect can be detected of rigidities in labour and product markets on long-term economic growth.

## 2.4. Survey of the Literature

Many econometric studies have been performed measuring the impact of labour and output market rigidities on economic growth (and on productivity growth). In general, econometric studies involving developed countries (mainly OECD countries) find weak and often insignificant effects of measures of rigidity on economic growth. This is especially the case with measures of labour market regulation for which little evidence exists of any impact on economic growth in the OECD countries. This is confirmed by a recent study by the International Monetary Fund (IMF) (2015) that could not find a significant effect of employment protection on productivity growth in a sample of industrialized countries (see also Babecki and Campos, 2011). Older studies found mixed evidence. Nickell and Layard (1999) found a positive association between employment protection and productivity per capita, using cross-country variation only. Belot et al. (2007) used a richer data-set, including time-varying indicators of employment protection and legislation, and found that there is an inverse U-shaped relationship between employment protection and growth.

Whereas the previous studies looked at the macroeconomic effects of labour market regulation on economic growth (or productivity growth), Bassanini, Nunziata, and Venn (2009) used industry-level data to analyse the relationship between employment protection and productivity growth. These authors found that employment protection legislations have a depressing impact on productivity growth in industries where layoff restrictions are more likely to be binding. It is unclear, however, how large these sectoral effects are when we aggregate them to the economy as a whole.

The empirical evidence of the effect of product market regulation on economic growth confirms the theoretical uncertainty about this effect that we noted in the Section 2.3 (see Aghion et al., 2009). Some econometric evidence has been found that lower product market regulations increase economic growth (Nicoletti and Scarpetta, 2003; OECD, 2015). What is striking in these studies, however, is that these estimates are not very robust. Typically, researchers present a large number of different specifications and definitions and produce only a few significant results. In Nicoletti and Scarpetta (2003), out of seventeen estimated coefficients of product market regulation variables, only three are significant (see also IMF, 2015).

The previous studies were econometric analyses. The OECD has performed other empirical studies that simulate the effects of labour and product market deregulations on economic growth. Two approaches have been used: the first consists of taking some of the significant estimated coefficients of market regulation found in the literature and applying these to many countries (see, e.g., De Mello and Padoan, 2010; Barnes et al., 2011; Bouis and Duval, 2011). Sometimes it is not even estimated coefficients that are used, but 'calibrations by assumption' (Barnes et al., 2011). This typically produces complicated graphs showing how deregulation increases economic growth. It should be borne in mind that these simulations use only a small number of estimated coefficients that come from regression exercises in which most estimated coefficients of market regulation variables are insignificant.

A second approach also has been popular: this is to use a macroeconomic model of the Dynamic Stochastic General Equilibrium (DSGE) type and to simulate the effect of deregulation on output (European Central Bank, 2015; Eggertsson et al., 2014; Cacciatore et al., 2012). Invariably these simulations find that deregulation of labour and output markets lead to increases in output.[3] The problem with this approach is that the simulations just confirm *a priori* beliefs. To give an example, in most DSGE models unemployment is voluntary, that is results from a decision of individual agents to take more leisure time. Structural reforms are then interpreted as an intervention that changes the relative price of leisure versus labour, that is makes the former more expensive (e.g. by reducing unemployment benefits). As a result, agents will take less leisure time and decide to work longer. Lo and behold, output will increase.

In addition, most DSGE models used in the simulations are based on calibrations. They are not to be interpreted as empirical evidence. Unfortunately, quite often these simulations are interpreted as providing empirical evidence of how structural reform boosts economic growth.

A striking observation one can make is that econometric studies encompassing both developed and developing countries tend to find significant effects of labour and output market regulations on economic growth. A typical example is a study of the World Bank (Loayza et al., 2004). This study finds that a deregulation of output markets in the developing countries to the mean level achieved in the OECD countries would increase economic growth by up to 1.4% per year.

One may ask the question of why the econometric evidence involving both developing and developed countries tends to be stronger than the evidence about developed (OECD) countries alone? The main reason probably is that the developed countries have relatively low levels of regulation of product markets compared with developing countries. This is made clear in Figure 2.5, which shows a measure of product market regulation as computed by the World Bank. It can be seen that within the OECD countries the level and the variation of product market regulation is very low compared with that of developing countries.

This implies that once countries have reached the level of regulation achieved in OECD countries, few additional gains can be made in terms of increased productivity and growth. Put differently, moving from the very high levels of regulation observed in developing countries towards the low

[3] It should be noted that the Eggertson et al. study finds that this is the case in normal times, but not during recessions. Structural reforms during recessions make the recession worse. These authors conclude that during recessions and 'in the absence of the appropriate monetary stimulus, reforms fuel expectations of prolonged deflation, increase the real interest rate, and depress aggregate demand'.

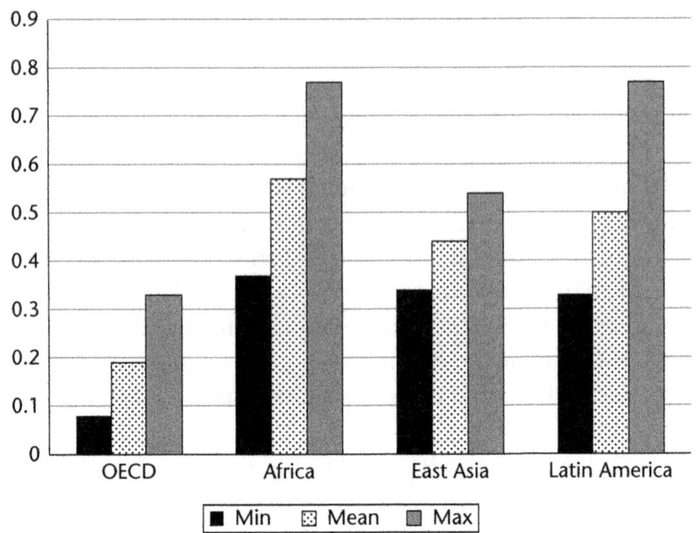


**Figure 2.5.** Product Market Regulation.
*Source*: Loayza et al. (2004).

levels reached in the OECD countries produces important and significant gains. These gains, however, tend to disappear when the levels of regulation have reached those observed in the OECD countries. There is then also very little point in trying to reduce these levels even further.

## 2.5. Growth and Macroeconomic Imbalances

In Sections 2.1–2.4 we argued that stagnation in the GDP of the Eurozone since 2008 has little to do with structural rigidities. In other words it is mostly unrelated to the supply side of the Eurozone countries. In this section we argue that stagnation of the Eurozone during 2008–14 is related to asymmetry in macroeconomic adjustment to external imbalances that has been pursued in the Eurozone since the start of the sovereign debt crisis.

Prior to the crisis, the Southern European countries (including Ireland) accumulated current account deficits, whereas the Northern Eurozone countries[4] built up current account surpluses. As a result, the Southern countries became the debtors and the Northern countries the creditors in the system (see Figure 2.6). This forced the Southern countries hit by sudden liquidity stops to beg the Northern ones for financial support. The latter

[4] We define Northern Eurozone countries to be Austria, Belgium, Finland, Germany, and the Netherlands.

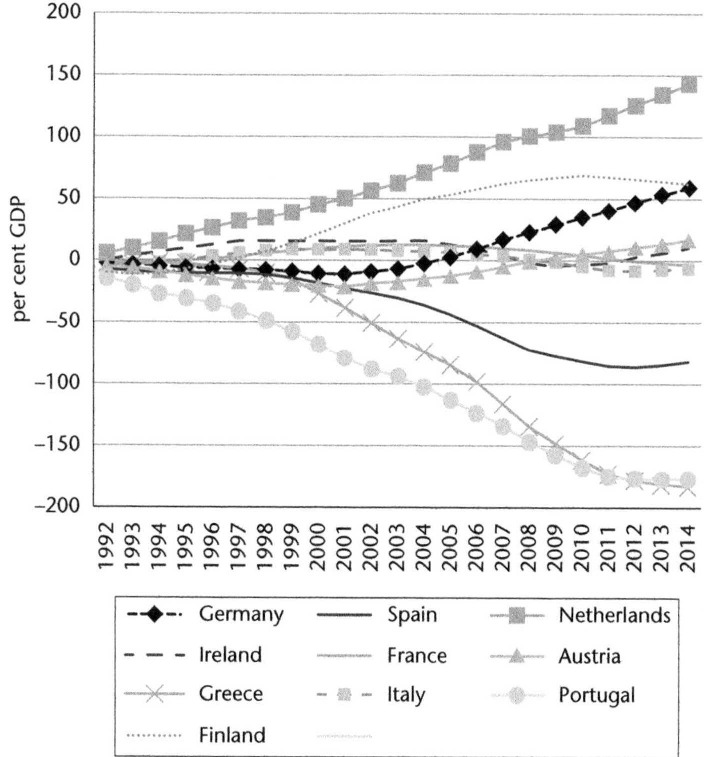


**Figure 2.6.** Cumulated Current Accounts.
*Source*: European Commission, Ameco.

reluctantly did do so, but only after imposing tough austerity programmes pushing these countries into quick and deep spending cuts and intense recessions.

As a result, the creditor nations in the Eurozone ruled and pushed austerity as the instrument to safeguard the interest of these nations. Another approach would have been possible and could have guided the conduct of macroeconomic policies in the Eurozone. This alternative approach is based on the view that the responsibilities for the current account imbalances are shared between the creditor and debtor nations. The debtor nations took on too much debt and are responsible for that. The creditor nations extended too much credit and are thus equally responsible for the imbalances. For every reckless debtor there must be a reckless creditor. This symmetric view, however, has not prevailed in relations between the creditor and debtor nations of the Eurozone. The former have been viewed as having followed virtuous policies and the latter as having followed foolish ones. As a result, the debtor nations have been forced to bear the full brunt of the adjustment.

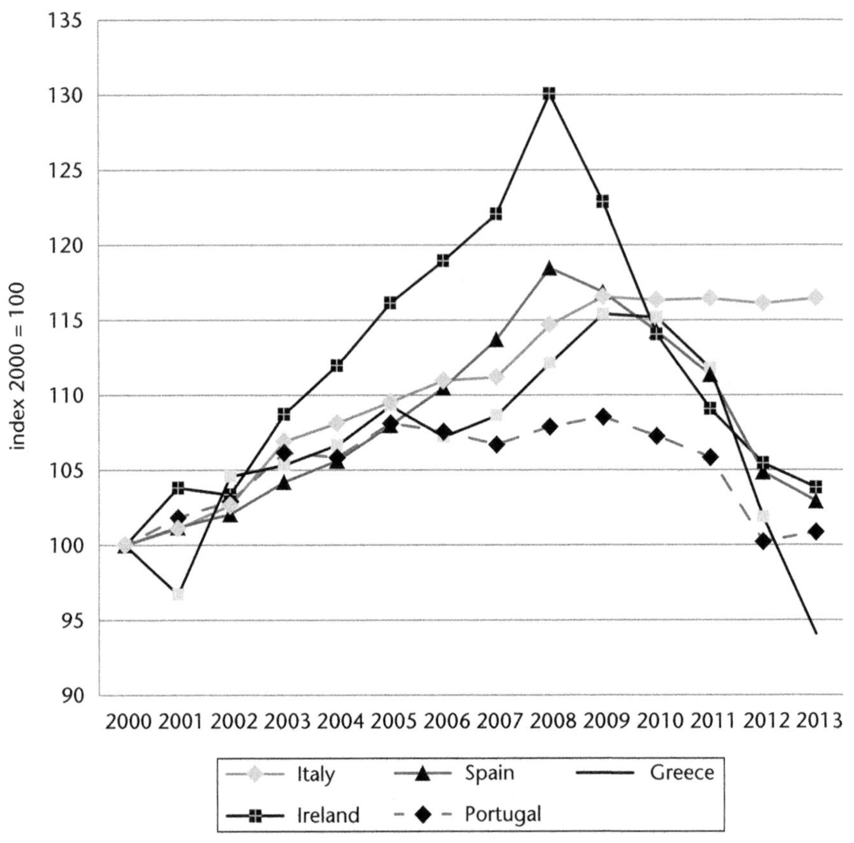


**Figure 2.7.** Relative Unit Labour Costs in Debtor Countries in the Eurozone.
*Source*: European Commission, Ameco.

This led to an asymmetric process where most of the adjustment has been done by the debtor nations. In the absence of the option to devalue, the debtor countries have been forced to reduce wages and prices relative to the creditor countries (an 'internal devaluation') without compensating wage and price increases in the creditor countries ('internal revaluations'). This has been achieved by intense austerity programmes in the South, whereas in the North no compensating stimulus has been imposed.

In Figure 2.7, we show some evidence about the nature of this asymmetry. The Figure shows the evolution of the relative unit labour costs[5] of the debtor countries (where we use the average over the 1970–2010 period as the base period). Two features stand out. First, from 1999 until 2008–9, one observes

[5] The relative unit labour cost of a country is defined as the ratio of the unit labour costs of that country and the average unit labour costs in the rest of the Eurozone. An increase in this ratio

a strong increase of these countries' relative unit labour costs. Second, since 2008–9 quite dramatic turnarounds of the relative unit labour costs have occurred (internal devaluations) in Ireland, Spain, and Greece, and to a lesser extent in Portugal and Italy.

These internal devaluations have come at a great cost in terms of lost output and employment in the debtor countries mainly because the expenditure-reducing effects of these internal devaluations were more intense than the expenditure switching (competitiveness) effects.

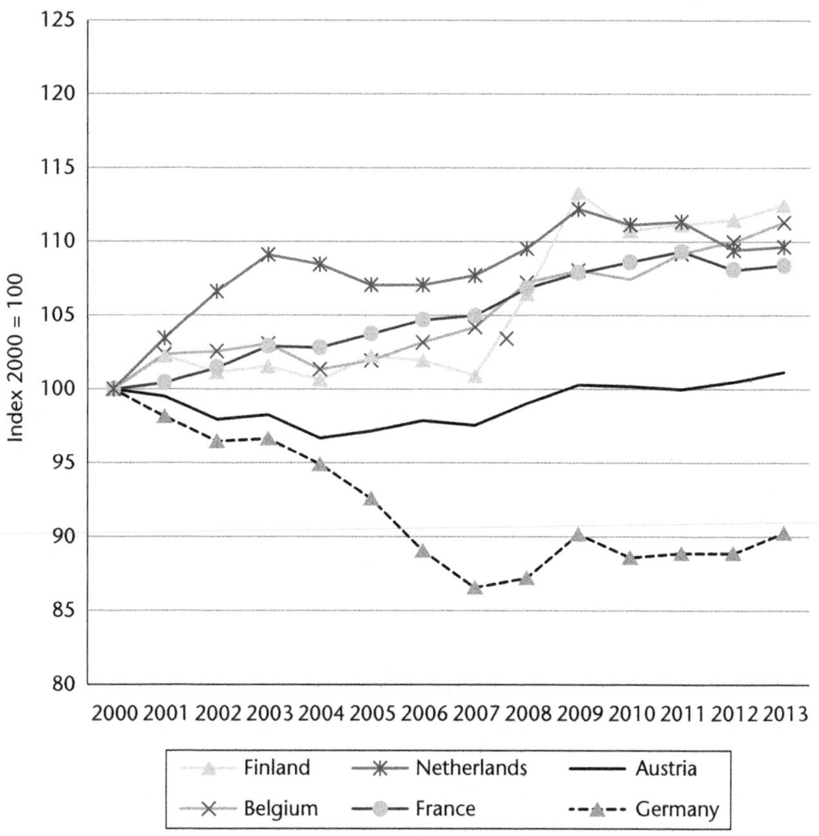


**Figure 2.8.** Relative Unit Labour Costs in Creditor Countries in the Eurozone.
*Source*: European Commission, Ameco databank.

indicates that the country in question has seen its unit labour costs increase faster than in the rest of the Eurozone, and vice versa. The relative unit labour costs are computed using the average of the other Eurozone countries. The weights to compute this average, however, are specific to each country as they depend on the shares of trade flows. For example, in the Dutch relative unit labour cost, Germany has a share that is larger than the share of Germany in the Spanish relative unit labour costs. Thus these indices do not have to be symmetrical.

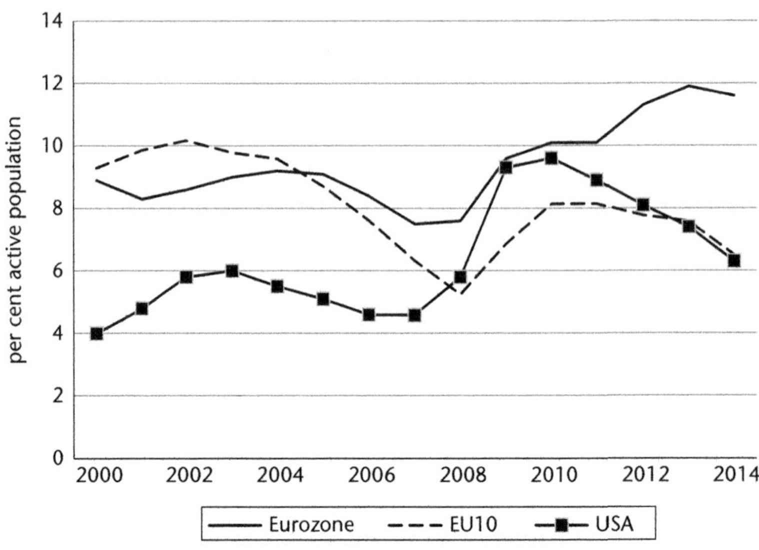


**Figure 2.9.** Unemployment Rate in the Eurozone, EU10, and USA.
*Source*: European Commission, Ameco databank.

Is there evidence that such a process of internal revaluations has been going on in the surplus countries? The answer is given in Figure 2.8, which presents an evolution of the relative unit labour costs in the creditor countries. One observes that since 2008–9 there has been very little movement in these relative unit labour costs in these countries.

Thus, one can conclude that at the insistence of the creditor nations, the burden of the adjustments to the imbalances in the Eurozone has been borne almost exclusively by the debtor countries in the periphery. This has created a deflationary bias that explains why the Eurozone has been pulled into a double-dip recession in 2012–13, and why real GDP has stagnated since 2008, in contrast with what has happened in the non-Euro EU countries and in the USA. It also helps to explain why the unemployment rate increased from 8% in 2008 to close to 12% in 2014, whereas in the EU10 and in the USA the unemployment rate started to decline significantly from 2010 (see Figure 2.9).

The deflationary forces to which the Eurozone was subjected as a result of the asymmetric adjustment policies led to two other effects. The first was to turn the current account deficit that existed in 2008 into a surplus of close to 3% of GDP in 2014 (Figure 2.10). As the debtor nations were forced into austerity, spending declined. The latter was not offset by increased spending in the creditor nations as these nations aimed at maintaining current account surpluses. Thus, the Eurozone adjustment process in all countries consisted of saving more, pushing the current account into a significant surplus.

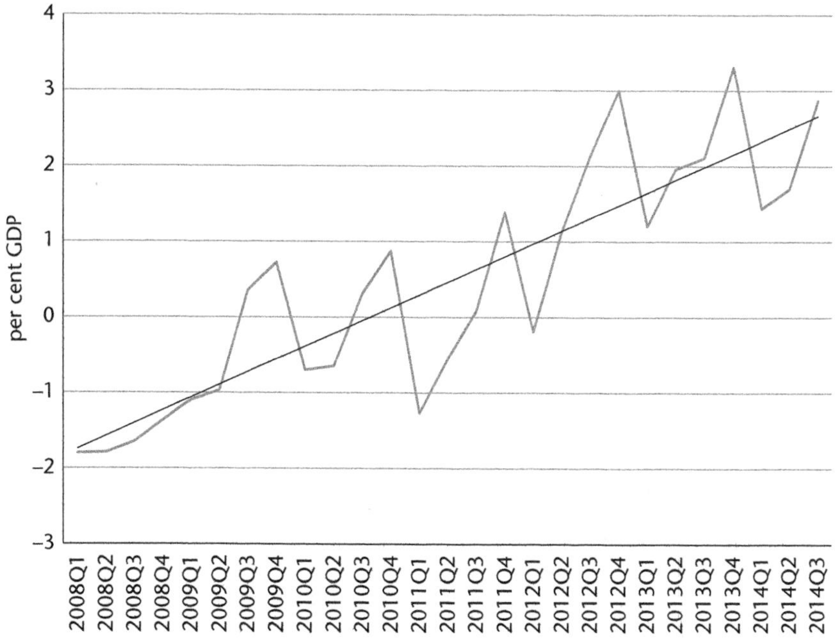


**Figure 2.10.** Current Account Euro Area.
*Source*: European Commission, Ameco databank.

The second effect of the deflationary dynamics produced by an asymmetric adjustment process was a sharp decline in inflation, which at the end of 2014 became negative in the Eurozone as a whole. We show this in Figure 2.11, in which we compare the rate of inflation in the Eurozone and the USA. It is striking to find that while the USA seems to have stabilized its inflation rate around a value of 1.5%, this is not the case in the Eurozone where we observe a continuous decline of inflation since 2011, until it became negative in December 2014.

From the preceding analysis one can conclude that all the phenomena associated with the secular stagnation hypothesis are present in the Eurozone in a significantly more intense manner than they are in the USA and the other EU countries. Increased attempts to save, triggered by external imbalances (and debt accumulation), and lack of an exchange rate instrument to rebalance the economies of the debtor nations, drove inflation into negative territory. This in turn prevented the real interest rate from declining further so as to equilibrate savings and investments. As a result, the Eurozone seems to be stuck in a low-growth. high-unemployment equilibrium.

It is interesting to make a historic parallel here. During the 1930s a number of European countries decided to stay on gold and to keep their exchange

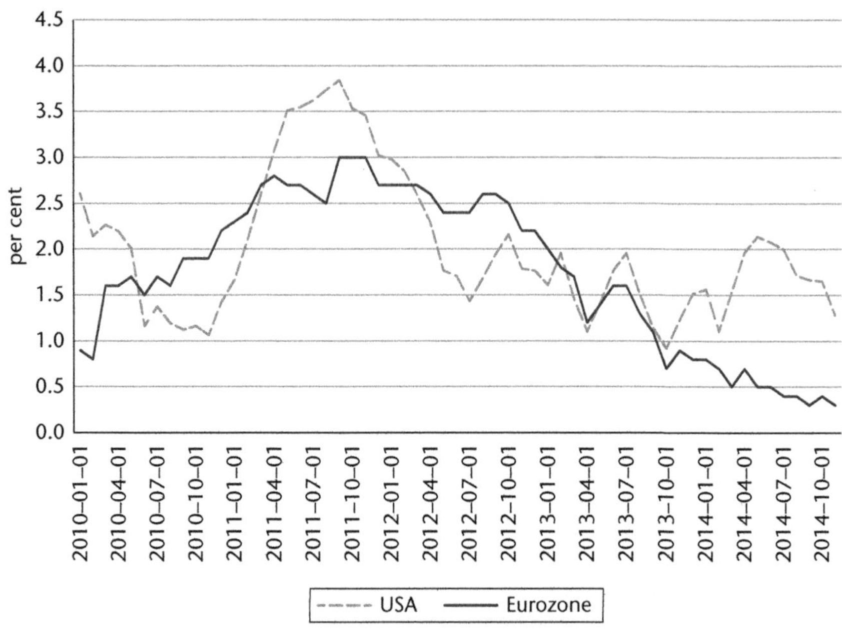


**Figure 2.11.** Inflation in the USA and the Eurozone.
*Source*: ECB.

rates fixed. This forced these countries into deflationary demand policies aimed at restoring balance of payments equilibrium. As a result, they failed to recover and performed significantly worse than the countries that went off gold and devalued their currencies (see Eichengreen, 1992). Something very similar has happened in the Eurozone since the Great Recession.[6]

The nature of macroeconomic policies in the Eurozone is illustrated in Figure 2.12, which shows the production possibility frontier. These policies focused on structural reform (supply side policies) aimed at shifting the production possibility frontier of the Eurozone outward. Our empirical analysis suggests that it is unclear whether these policies actually worked to generate such a positive shift. At the same time the austerity policies that were applied throughout the Eurozone reduced aggregate demand. As a result, effective production (shown by the dot inside the production possibility frontier) declined. The austerity policies had the effect of reducing public investment and spending for education. As a result, the two main drivers of economic growth, physical and human capital accumulation were affected negatively. Thus it is more likely that the macroeconomic policies pursued in the Eurozone had the effect of shifting the production possibilities frontier

[6] See also Eichengreen and O'Rourke (2009).

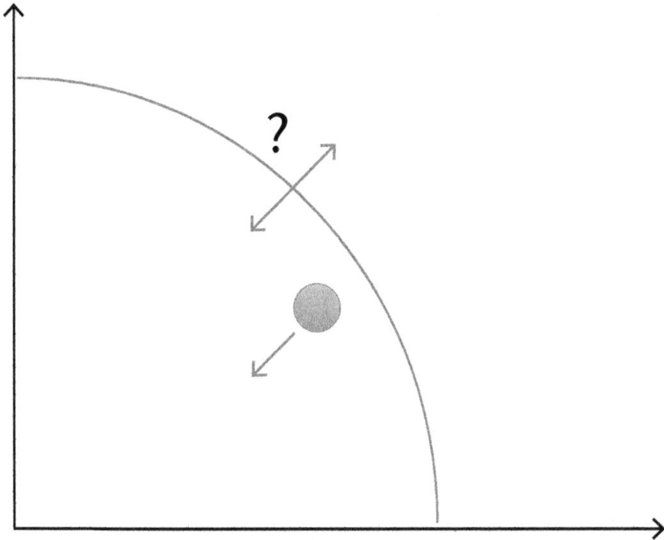


Figure 2.12. Production Possibility Frontier.

downwards, together with a decline in effective production (see Blanchard and Leigh, 2013).

## 2.6. What Should Be Done?

All this leads to the question of what to do today, in 2016? As stressed by many participants in the debate concerning secular stagnation (see Teulings and Baldwin, 2014; Summers, 2014), the policy mix to lift countries from the low growth and high unemployment equilibrium is a mix of monetary and fiscal expansion.

The European Central Bank (ECB) decided to do its part, albeit rather late, when it decided to start its QE programme in January 2015. Although this programme looks quite spectacular, it should not be forgotten that the ECB will be restoring the money base to its pre-crisis growth path. This is made clear in Figure 2.13, which contrasts the balance sheets of the ECB with those of the US Fed. The contrast since 2012 is spectacular. To stimulate the US economy, the Fed engaged in a dramatic increase of its balance sheet. During the same time, when the Eurozone turned back in a double-dip recession, the ECB allowed its balance sheet to contract by €1 trillion. Quite a surprising policy choice. The announced quantitative easing (QE) programme of €1 trillion will bring the money base back on track, not more than that.

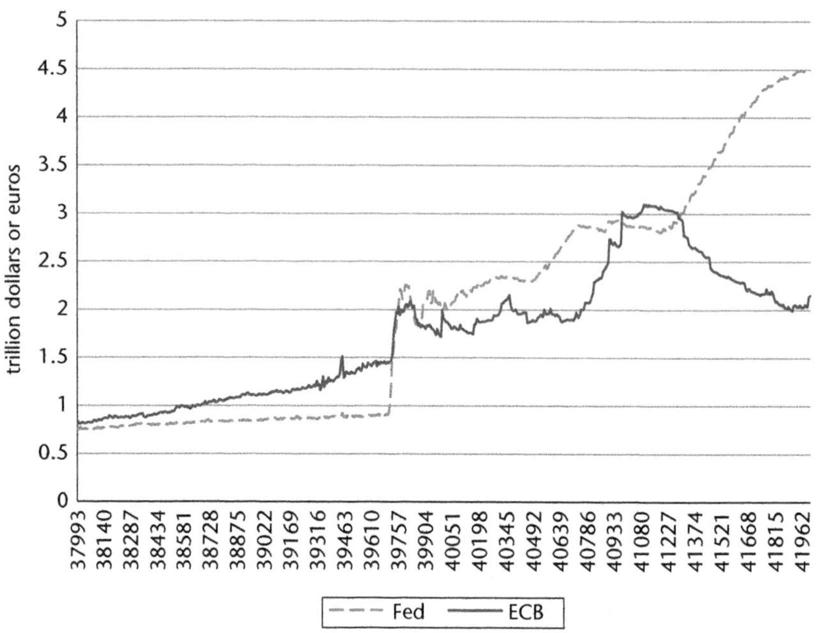


**Figure 2.13.** Balance Sheet Federal Reserve and ECB (2004–14).
*Source*: ECB and Federal Reserve.

It is now generally recognized that when the economy is in a liquidity trap, monetary policy is insufficient to stimulate aggregate demand, and that fiscal policies have to take the brunt of demand stimulus.

Governments of the Eurozone, in particular in the Northern member countries now face historically low long-term interest rates. The German government, for example, can borrow at less than 1% at a maturity of ten years. These historically low interest rates create a window of opportunities for these governments to start a major investment programme. Money can be borrowed almost for free, while in all these countries there are great needs to invest in the energy sector, the public transportation systems, and the environment.

This is therefore the time to reverse the ill-advised decisions made since 2010 to reduce public investments, as illustrated in Figure 2.14. This can be done at very little cost. The country that should lead this public investment programme is Germany. There are two reasons for this. First, as we argued earlier, the asymmetric nature of the macroeconomic adjustment programmes within the Eurozone unnecessarily magnified the cost of these programmes in the debtor nations, and is responsible for the stagnation of the Eurozone since 2008. Second, public investments as a per cent of GDP in Germany are among the lowest of all Eurozone countries. In 2013 public investment

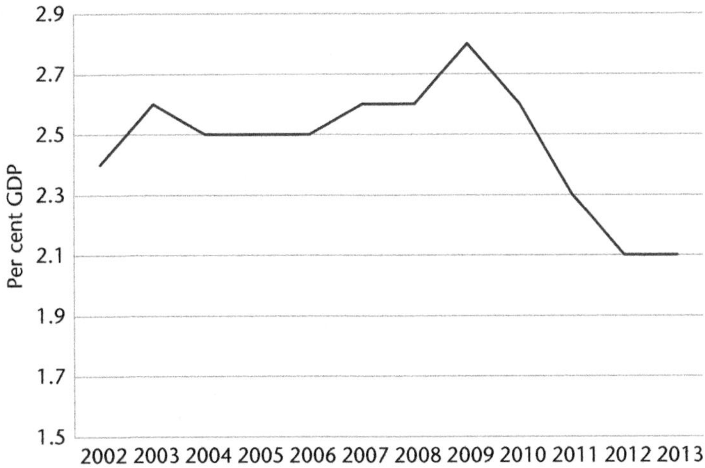


**Figure 2.14.** Public Investment in the Eurozone.
*Source*: Eurostat.

in German amounted to a bare 1.6% of GDP versus 2.3% in the rest of the Eurozone (see also Fratzscher, 2014, on this).

Such a public investment programme would do two things. First, it would stimulate aggregate demand in the short run and help to pull the Eurozone out of its stagnation. Second, in the long run it would help to lift the long-term growth potential in the Eurozone.

The prevailing view in many countries is that governments should not increase their debt levels lest they put a burden on future generations. The truth is that future generations inherit not only the liabilities but also the assets that have been created by the government. Future generations will not understand why these governments did not invest in productive assets that improve these generations' welfare, while present-day governments could do so at historically low financing costs.

There is a second factor that prevents European policymakers from using a large government investment programme to lift the Eurozone from its stagnation. These policymakers continue to believe that the stagnation since 2008 is a result of structural rigidities in the Eurozone. Thus the problem of stagnation is seen as originating exclusively from the supply side. In this view structural reforms (together with austerity) are the answer.

We have shown evidence that structural rigidities in the labour and product markets have insignificant effect on economic growth. As a result these rigidities cannot be seen as the primary cause of the Eurozone stagnation since 2008. It is time policymakers face this truth and start following policies that work. This will have to come mainly from fiscal programmes aimed at boosting investment.

## 2.7. Conclusion

Macroeconomic policies pursued since the financial crisis in the Eurozone have not been evidence-based. Supply side policies ('structural reforms') have been at the centre of policy-thinking in the Eurozone and member countries have been forced to implement such supply side policies. In this chapter, we have provided evidence against the view that supply side policies boost economic growth. In some cases the evidence even suggests that these policies might reduce economic growth. This is particularly the case with the forced breakdown of employment protection, which is likely to reduce investment in human capital.

Thus it appears that macroeconomic policies rather than being evidence-based have been ideology-based. This ideology claims that flexibility in labour and product markets should be pursued under all circumstances. The evidence that this will lead to more growth is extremely thin.

In contrast, the strong empirical evidence that investment in physical and human capital is key to economic growth has not been used. On the contrary, in the name of austerity and a phobia vis-à-vis government debt, a decline in public investment was set in motion endangering the long-term potential of the Eurozone. In addition, austerity had the effect of reducing spending for education, thereby reducing the potential for long-term economic growth.

The discussion in this chapter does not imply that no structural reforms are necessary. Some are, even if their implications for economic growth are uncertain. The main structural reform in the labour market consists of eliminating its dual nature. This has been a serious problem in countries like Italy and Spain, in which older workers are fully protected and the newcomers, the young, are not. As a result, the latter face extremely flexible labour contrasts with little protection. This duality in labour contracts has the effect of reducing human capital of the young as both the firms and the young have little incentives to invest in better skills. In addition, this duality leads to important negative social and political effects as a new generation feels it is not really integrated in society. Some steps have been taken in a number of countries (Italy, Spain) with new legislation that promises to do away with this duality. This is done by introducing a unified labour contract for young and old, whereby employment protection is gradually built up for the young that enter the labour market (see Boeri et al., 2013).

The crisis management that was set up in the Eurozone after the eruption of the government debt crisis can be said to be responsible for the economic stagnation experienced by the Eurozone. This crisis management was characterized by two features. One was the asymmetric adjustment to the current account imbalances that forced the deficit countries into intense austerity without a compensating policy of stimulus in the surplus countries. This led to a deflationary bias that created strong collateral damage on investment, both private and public.

The second feature of crisis management was its focus on supply policies. While the overriding macroeconomic problem was an insufficiency of demand, policymakers insisted on fixing the supply side of the economy in the hope that this would spur long-term economic growth. The evidence we have provided in this chapter is that these supply side policies have insignificant, and sometimes even negative effects on long-term economic growth. As a result, together with the negative effects of austerity on investment, it can be concluded that the crisis management in the Eurozone not only exacerbated a demand problem, but also harmed the long-term growth potential of the Eurozone.

## 2.8. Appendices

**Table A.2.1.** Description of the Variables

| Variable | Sources | Note |
|---|---|---|
| Real growth rate | OECD | |
| Investment/ GDP | World Bank WDI | |
| Real effective exchange rate | OECD | Measures the competitiveness-weighted relative consumer prices and unit labour costs for a country |
| Working population growth | OECD | |
| Government consumption/GDP | Oxford Economics | Value of government spending on goods and services expressed as a share of nominal GDP. This includes things like the public sector's payroll and procurement. It does not include investment spending or spending on social transfers for instance |
| Effective retirement age | OECD | |
| Government effectiveness | Worldwide governance indicator | |
| Proportion of tertiary education | World Bank education International Institute for Applied Systems Analysis (IIASA)/Vienna Institute of Demography (VID) Projection | Proportion of population by educational attainment, age 15–64, total, tertiary |
| Employment protection legislation (EPL) | OECD | Strictness of employment protection–individual and collective dismissals (regular contracts) |

(Continued)

**Table A.2.1.** (Continued)

| Variable | Sources | Note |
|---|---|---|
| Product market protection index | OECD | A comprehensive and internationally comparable set of indicators that measure the degree to which policies promote or inhibit competition in areas of the product market where competition is viable. They measure the economy-wide regulatory and market environments. The indicators cover formal regulations in the following areas: state control of business enterprises; legal and administrative barriers to entrepreneurship; barriers to international trade and investment |
| Government cabinet composition (left) % | Comparative political data | Government composition: cabinet posts of social democratic and other left parties as a percentage of total cabinet posts. Weighted by the number of days in office in a given year |

**Table A.2.2.** Investment GDP Ratio Regression (fixed effects model)

| | (1) Advanced economies 1985–2013 | (2) OECD economies 1998–2013 | (3) Advanced economies 1998–2013 | (4) Advanced economies 1998–2013 |
|---|---|---|---|---|
| Growth | 0.087 | 0.137*** | 0.107* | 0.106* |
| | (0.063) | (0.045) | (0.052) | (0.054) |
| Real effective exchange rate | 0.028 | 0.041*** | 0.032 | 0.047*** |
| | (0.021) | (0.013) | (0.019) | (0.016) |
| Working population growth | 2.330*** | 2.072*** | 2.405*** | 2.269*** |
| | (0.532) | (0.486) | (0.551) | (0.515) |
| Government consumption GDP ratio | −0.235 | −0.212* | −0.187 | −0.167 |
| | (0.175) | (0.123) | (0.168) | (0.162) |
| Real retirement age | 0.211 | 0.193 | 0.153 | 0.227 |
| | (0.178) | (0.193) | (0.175) | (0.168) |
| Government effectiveness | −0.152 | 0.417 | −0.178 | −0.039 |
| | (1.083) | (0.936) | (1.061) | (0.951) |
| Tertiary education/total population | −0.415* | −0.244* | −0.242 | −0.166 |
| | (0.206) | (0.129) | (0.162) | (0.144) |
| Employment protection | 5.707*** | 4.220*** | 5.952*** | 4.382*** |
| | (1.312) | (1.187) | (1.369) | (1.342) |
| Product market protection | | 0.734 | | 1.109 |
| | | (0.582) | | (0.719) |
| Observations | 409 | 457 | 365 | 359 |
| R-squared | 0.543 | 0.525 | 0.579 | 0.611 |
| Number of iid | 24 | 32 | 24 | 24 |

Robust standard errors in parentheses.

*** $p<0.01$, ** $p<0.05$, * $p<0.1$.

## 2.9. References


Acemoglu, D. (2009), 'Introduction to Modern Economic Growth', Princeton University Press.

Acemoglu, D. and J. Robinson (2012), 'Why Nations Fail: The Origins of Power, Prosperity, and Poverty', Crown Business.

Aghion, P. and P. Howitt (1998), 'Endogenous Growth Theory', Cambridge: Mass.: The MIT Press.

Aghion, P., C. Harris, P. Howitt, and J. Vickers (2001), 'Competition, Imitation and Growth with Step-by-Step Innovation', *Review of Economic Studies*, 2001, 68, 3, 467–92.

Aghion, P., R. Blundell, R. Griffith, P. Howitt, and S. Prantl (2009), 'The Effects of Entry on Incumbent Innovation and Productivity', *Review of Economics and Statistics*, 2009, 91, 1, 20–32.

Babecky, J. and N. Campos (2011), 'Does Reform Work? An econometric survey of the reform-growth puzzle', *Journal of Comparative Economics*, 39, 140–58.

Barnes, S., R. Bouis, Ph. Briard, S. Dougherty, and M. Eris (2011), 'The GDP Impact of Reform: A Simple Simulation Framework', Economics Department Working paper, no. 834, OECD.

Barro, R. and X. Sala-i-Martin (2003), 'Economic Growth', MIT Press.

Bassanini, A., L. Nunziata, and D. Venn (2009), 'Job protection legislation and productivity growth in OECD countries', *Economic Policy*, 24, 349–402.

Belot, M. V. K., J. Boone, and J. C. van Ours (2007), 'Welfare improving employment protection'. *Economica*, 74, 295, 381–96.

Blanchard, O. and D. Leigh (2013), 'Fiscal Consolidation: At What Speed?', VoxEU.org, 3 May.

Boeri, T., P. Garibaldi, and E. R. Moen (2013), 'The Economics of Severance Pay', IZA Discussion Papers 7455, Institute for the Study of Labor (IZA).

Bouis, R. and R. Duval (2011), 'Raising potential growth after the crisis: a quantitative assessment of the potential gains from various structural reforms in the OECD area and beyond', Economics Department Working Papers, no. 835, OECD.

Cacciatore, M., R. Duval, and G. Fiori (2012), 'Short-term gain or pain? A DSGE model-based analysis of the short-term effects of structural reforms in labour and product markets', Economics Department Working paper no. 948, OECD.

De Mello, and Padoan (2010), 'Promoting Potential Growth: The Role of Structural Reform', Economics Department Working paper, no. 793, OECD.

European Central Bank (ECB) (2015), 'Progress with structural reforms across the euro area and their possible impacts', *Economic Bulletin*, 2.

Eggertsson, G., A. Ferrero, and A. Raffo (2014), 'Can Structural reforms help Europe?', *Journal of Monetary Economics*, 612–22.

Eichengreen, B. (1992), 'Golden Fetters: The Gold Standard and the Great Depression', Oxford University Press, Oxford.

Eichengreen, B. and K. O'Rourke (2009), 'A tale of two depressions: What do the new data tell us?' February 2010 update, VoxEU.

Fratzscher, M. (2014), 'Die Deutschland-Illusion: Warum wir unsere Wirtschaft überschätzen und Europa brauchen', Hanser.

IMF World Economic Outlook (2015), Ch. 3, Box 3.5 on *The Effects of Structural Reforms on Total Factor Productivity*, 104–7.

Loayza, N., A. Oviedo, and L. Serven (2004), 'Regulation and Macroeconomic Performance', World Bank.

Nickell, S. J. and R. Layard (1999), 'Labour market institutions and economic performance'. In: O. Ashenfelter and D. Card (eds.), *Handbook of Labour Economics*. Amsterdam: North-Holland, 3029–84.

Nicoletti, G. and S. Scarpetta (2003), 'Regulation, Productivity and Growth'. OECD evidence, Policy Research Working Paper, The World Bank.

OECD (2015), 'Going for Growth', http://www.keepeek.com/Digital-Asset-Management/oecd/economics/economic-policy-reforms-2015_growth-2015-en#page11.

Summers, L. (2014), 'Reflections on the New "Secular Stagnation Hypothesis"', VoxEU, October, http://www.voxeu.org/article/larry-summers-secular-stagnation.

Teulings, C. and R. Baldwin (2014), 'Secular Stagnation. Facts, Causes and Cures'. A new vox ebook, October http://www.voxeu.org/article/secular-stagnation-facts-causes-and-cures-new-vox-ebook.

# 3

# Dealing with EMU Heterogeneity

## National Versus European Institutional Reforms

*André Sapir*

### 3.1. Introduction

In light of the recent financial and sovereign debt crisis, there is now a large consensus that something was fundamentally wrong with Europe's Economic and Monetary Union (EMU). There is less consensus, however, about what the deficiencies were and what the remedies should be. There are two broad schools of thought. One holds that the original Maastricht design—sometime referred to as 'EMU 1.0'—was basically fine but that the rules it embodies were not sufficiently well implemented. Those belonging to this school tend to emphasize fiscal rules, which were not respected by many Eurozone countries during the early years of the euro or even, in the case of Greece, already during the application process to euro membership. According to this view, fixing EMU requires first and foremost strengthening fiscal rules.

The other school of thought considers that the Maastricht blueprint was basically flawed and that a 'genuine EMU' cannot comprise only a monetary union but also requires an economic union, a banking (or financial) union, a fiscal union (including strengthened fiscal rules), and even a political union.[1]

My own view fits in with the second school and is based on an assessment that EMU 1.0 was deficient in three separate areas. First, it ignored that monetary integration has potential consequences for financial stability because of

[1] The expression 'genuine EMU' was first used in Van Rompuy (2012).

financial integration, and therefore that EMU needed mechanisms for supervision, resolution, and deposit insurance guarantee of banks. Second, EMU 1.0 disregarded that '[m]embers of a monetary union issue debt in a currency over which they have no control' (De Grauwe, 2011), and therefore that EMU needed mechanisms to prevent and resolve potential sovereign debt crises. Third, it underestimated the fundamental message of the optimum currency area (OCA) theory that countries in a monetary union can be subject to asymmetric shocks, and therefore that EMU needed mechanisms to adjust to such shocks.

Measures adopted since the crisis have attempted to correct some of these deficiencies. The new EMU 2.0 regime, which is now in place, contains important elements of a banking union, with a common supervision mechanism and a partially common resolution mechanism. It also contains elements of a fiscal union with stricter fiscal rules to reduce sovereign debt and a European Stability Mechanism (ESM) to mitigate sovereign debt crises.

Although a useful improvement on EMU 1.0, EMU 2.0 clearly falls short of what is needed to eliminate the three deficiencies listed above. A full common resolution mechanism and a common deposit insurance guarantee mechanism, both requiring a common fiscal backstop mechanism, would have to be put in place to create a genuine banking union capable of resolving financial crises in an appropriate fashion. A sovereign debt restructuring mechanism would need to be created to resolve sovereign debt crises in a timely manner, and the exposure of banks to sovereign debt would have to be reduced to avoid sovereign debt crises turning into financial crises. Finally, the issue of asymmetric shocks would need to be addressed by mechanisms in addition to those designed to deal with financial and sovereign debt crises, however useful they may be in and of themselves. All these mechanisms should be part of a future EMU 3.0 regime worthy of the label 'genuine EMU'.

This chapter concentrates solely on the problem of asymmetric shocks, an important feature in a Eurozone that continues to display serious economic heterogeneity among its member countries. It contains three main sections. Section 3.2 recalls the discussion of asymmetric shocks in the Optimum Currency Area (OCA) literature prior to the launch of the euro. Section 3.3 discusses the occurrence of asymmetric shocks during the early years of the euro, before the start of the financial and sovereign debt crisis, and proposes a combination of national and EMU mechanisms to reduce their occurrence in the future. Section 3.4 discusses the question of adjustment to asymmetric shocks, and proposes again a combination of national and EMU mechanisms to make adjustment smoother than it currently is. Finally, section 3.5 concludes.

## 3.2. Asymmetric Shocks: The Revenge of the Optimum Currency Area?

We all knew (or at least should have known) in the 1990s that the EU countries that were about to join the euro did not constitute an OCA. Two specific issues were raised at the time. First, there was a recognition that EU countries were heterogeneous in terms of their capacity to abandon the exchange rate instrument: some countries were deemed to be less exposed to idiosyncratic shocks and better equipped to deal with such shocks should they occur, whereas others were viewed as potentially more exposed to asymmetric shocks and less able to cope with them absent the exchange rate instrument because of their relatively rigid products and/or labour markets. The former, already labelled as 'core countries', were essentially those that belonged to the European Exchange Rate Mechanism (ERM) throughout the 1990s, including during the 1992–3 ERM crisis, namely Germany, France, and the Benelux countries; Austria, which only joined the EU in 1995, but had mimicked the other core countries in terms of exchange rate behaviour, was later added to the list of core countries. These six countries were often referred to as the D-Mark (DM) zone countries; the other EU countries were labelled as 'peripheral countries'.

The second issue was the absence of EMU mechanisms capable of substituting to or complementing national adjustment mechanisms (i.e. nominal exchange rate changes before EMU and labour market flexibility after the creation of the euro) in the event of idiosyncratic shocks. Two potential EMU mechanisms could have been labour mobility (as originally envisaged by Mundell, 1961) or fiscal transfers (as suggested first by Kenen, 1969) between EMU countries, but neither was promoted nor put in place in the Eurozone.

The heterogeneity of EMU countries, in particular structural differences between the former DM zone countries and the peripheral countries, combined with the absence of EMU mechanisms to handle idiosyncratic shocks should have alerted us to the potential fragility of the system in the case of such shocks. There were some warnings (even in official or semi-official publications like Buti and Sapir, 1998) on the eve of the creation of the euro that 'many aspects of product and labour markets in EU Member States are currently insufficiently flexible', but the hope was that 'adjustment in market structure and response [was] likely to emerge as an endogenous consequence of the Single Market and the new monetary regime' (as Frankel and Rose, 1997, had suggested), although it was acknowledged that 'these changes will emerge only gradually in the new regime'.[2]

[2] All quotations in this paragraph are from Buti and Sapir (1998).

In their assessment of EMU a few years later, Buti and Sapir (2002) found that 'heterogeneity and limited availability of adjustment instruments may have contributed to the heightening of economic divergence in the initial years of EMU', and wondered whether 'more symmetry in economic behaviour between current euro area members [was] going to occur during the next few years'. Their view was that 'a more homogenous economic behaviour can be expected provided [EU] policy surveillance is effective in fostering further adaptability and reducing exposure to asymmetric disturbances' but that such prospect was 'not yet in sight'.[3]

Buti and Sapir (2002) envisaged various scenarios for the Eurozone to become an OCA, all involving more symmetry between countries (and therefore less exposure to asymmetric shocks) and more flexibility in the labour markets (and therefore more ability to adjust to asymmetric shocks). The scenarios are depicted in Figure 3.1, which uses De Grauwe's OCA line (De Grauwe, 2012). Points on the OCA line define combinations of symmetry and labour market flexibility for which the costs of a monetary union (and in particular the giving up of exchange rate flexibility) exactly balance its benefits. The region above the OCA line is where the benefits of a monetary union outweigh the costs. Figure 3.1 shows that, at the start of the euro, the DM zone was above the OCA line, but the Eurozone was below. The implication was that peripheral countries needed either to become more like core countries or a lot more flexible than them. Unfortunately, neither happened.

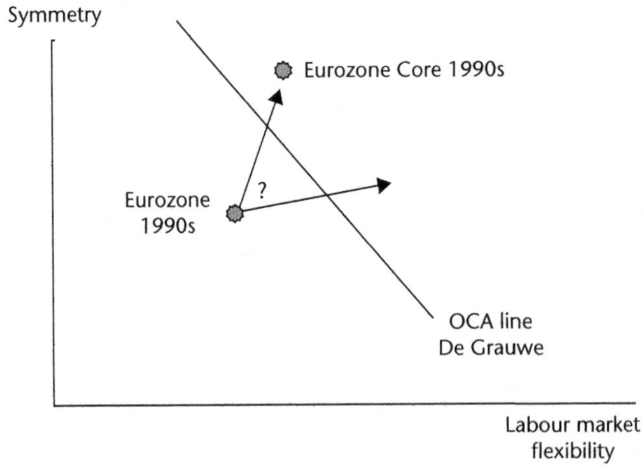


**Figure 3.1.** Symmetry and Labour Market Flexibility in the European Monetary Union.
*Source*: Adapted from Buti and Sapir (2002).

[3] All quotations in this paragraph are from Buti and Sapir (2002).

Heterogeneity among Eurozone countries continued or even increased and labour market flexibility remained insufficient.

The harsh reality therefore was that the Eurozone did not constitute an OCA at the time it was created, nor during its early years: economic heterogeneity between member countries was and remained a source of asymmetric shocks, and the absence of EMU mechanisms combined with national structural impediments rendered the adjustment to such shocks problematic. This situation has changed little since the crisis. The current state of affairs (EMU 2.0) still features a great deal of heterogeneity among Eurozone countries and risks of asymmetric shocks, and EMU mechanisms for adjusting to such shocks remain grossly insufficient. Hopefully EMU 3.0 will remedy the situation.

## 3.3. Exposure to Asymmetric Shocks

As already mentioned, prior to the creation of the euro the prevailing view in many European economic circles was that EMU would reduce the incidence of asymmetric shocks.[4] Policy-induced asymmetric shocks would be largely eliminated by the adoption of a single monetary policy and of fiscal rules that would impose sound national fiscal policies. Exogenous asymmetric shocks associated with structural differences between Eurozone countries were also considered less likely because EMU was supposed to produce structural convergence among these countries.

Unfortunately, '[w]hat happened instead was the mother of all asymmetric shocks—a shock that was, in a bitter irony, caused by the creation of the euro itself.' (Krugman, 2012). Buti and Sapir (2002) had correctly observed that the introduction of the euro had constituted an 'EMU shock' with asymmetric effects on three groups of countries: Germany, for whom the ECB monetary policy was too tight in the early years of the euro; the other core countries, for whom it was about right; and the peripheral countries, for whom the ECB policy was too lax, resulting in a demand boom. However, Buti and Sapir (2002) failed to draw the full consequences of the EMU-induced asymmetric shock.

Two of the early studies that fully grasped what was going on as a result of the EMU shock were both inspired by the Portuguese experience during the period starting before the launch of the euro in 1999 and ending before the financial crisis in 2007–8. Fagan and Gaspar (2007) characterized the EMU shock as a sharp decline in interest rates for the peripheral countries, where rates had been much higher than in the core countries prior to EMU. This

[4] See the discussion in Buti and Sapir (1998).

decline led to capital inflows, foreign debt, and a boom in domestic expenditure in peripheral countries, resulting in the sharp deterioration of their current account balance and a sizeable appreciation of their real exchange rate vis-à-vis the core countries.

Blanchard (2007) tells more or less the same story as Fagan and Gaspar (2007) but focusing entirely on Portugal and asking what happened after the boom turned into a slump. During the boom, wages grew consistently faster than productivity, causing unit labour costs (ULCs) to increase faster than in the rest of the Eurozone, implying a loss of competitiveness. Eventually the boom gave way to a slump, leaving the country in serious trouble, with low GDP growth, low productivity growth, high unemployment, and large fiscal and current account deficits. This was still before the financial crisis and already Portugal had no easy way out. Adjustment—in the form of 'competitive disinflation'—was viewed by Blanchard as likely to be long and painful, with sustained high unemployment and lower nominal wage growth until competitiveness improved, resulting in a current account surplus and the recovery of demand, output, and employment. Blanchard argued, however, that adjustment could be made shorter and less painful through structural reforms to boost productivity growth and fiscal policy measures linked to structural reforms and wage moderation.

What the previous discussion suggests is that the system of surveillance that operated in the Eurozone prior to the financial crisis was gravely deficient. Instead of continuing to monitor developments in real exchange rates (or competitiveness) as they did during the ERM days, when the nominal exchange rate instrument could be used to correct losses in competitiveness, national and European authorities seemed to have forgotten two elementary facts about a monetary union: first, that the loss of the nominal exchange rate instrument does not imply that real exchange rates cannot appreciate or depreciate, and, second, that competitiveness adjustment risks being long and painful given the loss of the nominal exchange rate instrument. As a result, real exchange rates in some Eurozone countries were allowed to become grossly over- or under-valued, creating difficult adjustment problems.

Figure 3.2 shows the evolution (in the non-agricultural business sector) of wage growth (measured on the vertical axis) and labour productivity growth (measured on the horizontal axis) in the Eurozone countries during the period 2001–7. Each point in the figure defines the combination of wage growth and labour productivity for a particular Eurozone country. Countries on the forty-five-degree line (shown by a solid line) are those where the growth in ULC (which is equal to the difference between the wage growth and the labour productivity growth) is zero, and therefore where the ULC-based real exchange rate (used here to measure of competitiveness) neither

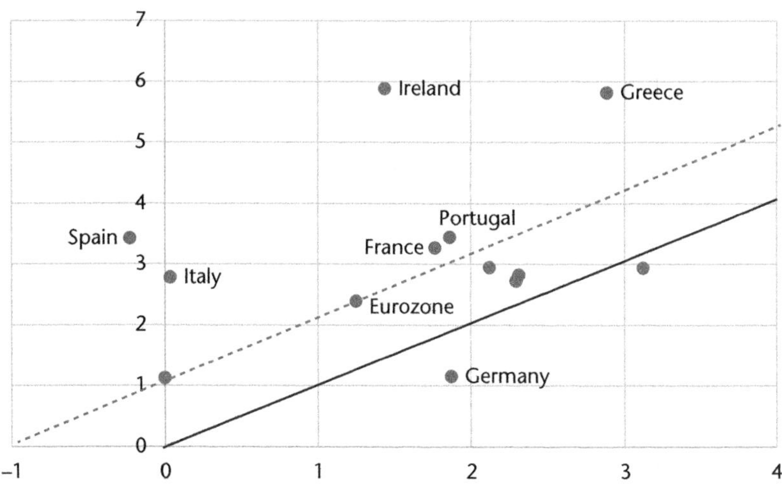


**Figure 3.2.** Wage Growth Versus Labour Productivity Growth in Eurozone Countries (Non-Agricultural Business Sector), 2001–7.
*Source*: Own calculations using OECD data.

appreciated nor depreciated during the period. Countries on the parallel above the forty-five-degree line (shown by a dashed line) are those where the growth in ULC is exactly equal to the growth in ULC for the Eurozone as a whole and therefore where the real exchange rate neither appreciated nor depreciated relative to the Eurozone during the period. The two parallel lines define three zones that correspond almost perfectly to the three groups of countries discussed earlier in the context of the EMU shock. The peripheral countries, which were subject to a positive EMU shock, are all in the zone above the highest line, reflecting the fact that they suffered a deterioration of competitiveness.[5] Germany, which was subject to a negative EMU shock, is in the zone below the lowest line, reflecting the fact that it not only improved its competitiveness vis-à-vis the Eurozone but even reduced its ULC in absolute terms as wages grew less rapidly than labour productivity growth.[6] In other words, the labour reforms undertaken by Germany in the early 2000s seemed to have more than compensated for the shock the country suffered after joining the euro, a situation akin to a 'competitive devaluation'. Finally, the other core countries (except Austria and France) are all in the zone between the two lines, reflecting the fact that they were subject to a relatively small EMU shock and witnessed little change of competitiveness.

[5] France also belongs to this zone but it lies much closer to the blue line than the peripheral countries.

[6] Austria also belongs to this zone but it lies much closer to the red line than Germany.

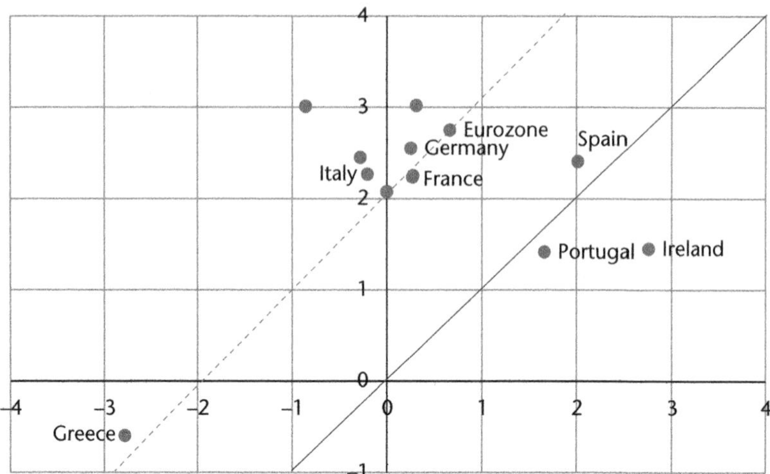


**Figure 3.3.** Wage Growth Versus Labour Productivity Growth in Eurozone Countries (Non-Agricultural Business Sector), 2007–13.
*Source*: Own calculations using OECD data.

Figure 3.3 repeats the same exercise for the period 2007–13. It shows that after the financial crisis, the peripheral countries split into two subcategories: those regaining competitiveness through wage moderation and productivity-enhancing reforms (Portugal, Spain, and especially Ireland); and those continuing to lose competitiveness (Greece and Italy).[7] By contrast, nearly all core countries lost competitiveness. This includes Germany, but excludes France, although in both cases only modestly so.

Misalignments of real exchange rates may not be the ultimate source of asymmetric shocks but they are typically their most visible and painful symptom. Whatever their fundamental cause, deviations of wage growth from labour productivity growth will tend to create adjustment problems in a monetary union and should therefore be closely monitored and corrected before they become protracted and painful to adjust.

As Carlin (2013) emphasizes, an important factor behind real exchange rate misalignment in the Eurozone, especially between the core and the periphery, has been the difference in national wage formation and bargaining systems among its members. There is no easy solution to this problem.

[7] The situation of Greece and Italy is somewhat different. Greece is the only Eurozone country where wages fell during the period 2007–13, but with labour productivity falling even more, its relative ULC continued to increase. Labour productivity growth was also negative in Italy during this period (after having been nil during the previous period as shown in Figure 3.2), but with wages continuing to increase at an annual rate of more than 2% (almost as rapidly as during the previous period), its relative ULC also continued to increase.

One solution would be to harmonize wage-setting systems, but this sounds hardly feasible given that national wage-setting systems have deep historical, political, and social roots. The alternative is to broadly maintain the existing systems but to constrain their functioning to ensure that they produce outcomes that are compatible with membership of a monetary union and the need to avoid persistent real exchange rate misalignment. This requires mechanisms to prevent and correct substantial misalignments of competitiveness between Eurozone countries.

The Macroeconomic Imbalance Procedure (MIP) established by the EU in 2011 in response to the economic and financial crisis has the potential to be an important tool to monitor and correct macroeconomic imbalances in all EU countries. This is especially the case for countries belonging to the Eurozone, for whom the MIP contains an enforcement mechanism, including the potential use of sanctions. The MIP's monitoring mechanism uses a set of indicators to assess 'macroeconomic imbalances and divergences in competitiveness'.[8] Currently, the MIP scoreboard covers 11 indicators, including the evolution of ULCs and of real exchange rates.

Sapir and Wolff (2015) proposed complementing the MIP by national procedures to monitor and, if needed, correct competitiveness problems and to increase ownership at the national level. These procedures would be required by EU legislation and their performance monitored by the European Commission.

All Eurozone countries would put in place a competitiveness-monitoring framework involving regular assessments and the definition of instruments to prevent problems. An interesting example is the Belgian legal framework, introduced in 1996 to preserve the country's competitiveness in EMU by keeping the evolution of wages in line with wage developments in the main trading partners. A national body regularly reports on the evolution of Belgian competitiveness relative to its three main trading partners (Germany, France, and the Netherlands). These reports are used by social partners to fix a wage norm for the next round of wage negotiations. Although the norm amounts only to a non-binding guideline, it has generally been respected by the private sector (to which the system applies). In case social partners fail to agree a wage norm compatible with the evolution of competitiveness, the government can step in and make the norm legally binding. The system has worked fairly well: it kept untouched the wage formation and bargaining system that existed prior to the euro, but made the behaviour of social partners compatible with membership of the euro. The result has been that ULCs in Belgium have evolved more-or-less in line with

[8] Regulation (EU) No 1176/2011 of the European Parliament and of the Council of 16 November 2011 on the Prevention and Correction of Macroeconomic Imbalances.

those in its main trading partners, thus avoiding significant competitiveness problems.

Apart from the fact that the Belgian system itself needs to be improved by targeting ULCs more directly than it does at the moment, it is clear that it cannot be exactly copied by other Eurozone countries as they feature different wage-setting systems. What is important is that all Eurozone countries put in place a mechanism to ensure that, although operating within their own system, the behaviour of social partners and the outcome of their wage negotiations is compatible with membership of the euro in terms of competitiveness and employment. These national mechanisms would be managed by national Competitiveness Councils.

Sapir and Wolff (2015) also proposed the creation of a Eurosystem Competitiveness Council (E.C.C.) consisting of both national Competitiveness Councils and the European Commission. The E.C.C.'s primary task would be to coordinate the actions of national Competitiveness Councils to ensure that no Eurozone country fixes a wage norm that implies significant competitiveness problems for itself and/or others. In case this fails, the Commission would have the power to require the relevant Competitiveness Councils to take appropriate corrective action using the Macroeconomic Imbalance Procedure.

These recommendations were endorsed by the Five Presidents' Report on Completing Europe's Economic and Monetary Union published in July 2015. The Report proposed the creation of national Competitiveness Authorities with a mandate to 'assess whether wages are evolving in line with productivity and compare with developments in other euro area countries and in the main comparable trading partners' (Juncker, 2015). It also proposed the creation of a Eurozone system of Competitiveness Authorities bringing together the national bodies and the Commission, 'which would coordinate the actions of national Competitiveness Authorities on an annual basis. The Commission should then take into account the outcome of this coordination... for decisions to be taken under the Macroeconomic Imbalance Procedure' (Juncker, 2015).

## 3.4. Adjustment to asymmetric shocks

The familiar downward-sloping OCA line popularized by De Grauwe (2012) and shown in Figure 3.1 conveys a simple but important message: the more a country joining a monetary union risks being subject to asymmetric shocks, the more it needs labour market flexibility to compensate for the absence of the exchange rate instrument and adjust to such shocks.

This view corresponds well with the Maastricht, or EMU 1.0, underlying philosophy: countries joining the euro can only count on EMU mechanism (the ECB with its monetary policy) in case of symmetric shocks that affect all EMU countries; adjustment to asymmetric shocks is the responsibility of national authorities who have to make sure that national labour markets are sufficiently flexible and (possibly) that national automatic fiscal stabilisers can sufficiently operate.

The Maastricht construction lacked one of the two adjustment mechanisms emphasized by the OCA theory, fiscal integration. The other mechanism, labour mobility, was theoretically possible by virtue of the EU treaties that guarantee the right of free movement of labour within the EU, but remained limited in practice.[9] In addition, as already discussed earlier, a number of Eurozone countries lacked sufficient labour market flexibility. The result is shown in Figure 3.4 which proposes a new OCA line, different from the one shown in Figure 3.1 used typically in the OCA literature. Points on the new OCA line define combinations of fiscal integration and labour market flexibility for which the costs of a monetary union (and in particular the giving up of exchange rate flexibility) exactly balance its benefits. The region above the OCA line is where the benefits of a monetary union outweigh the costs. Figure 3.4 shows that the USA is well above the new OCA line. By contrast, at the start of the euro, the Eurozone was well below the line: under EMU 1.0 it had virtually no fiscal union and some of its countries lacked sufficient labour market flexibility, a situation that prevailed until the start of the Eurozone's sovereign debt crisis in 2010.

The sovereign debt crisis came as a surprise. No one, leave alone the Maastricht treaty architects, had foreseen that a Eurozone government could face a liquidity or even a solvency problem. As a result, EMU 1.0 contained no mechanism to deal with such a problem when it occurred, first in Greece in 2010 and later in Ireland, Portugal, Spain, and Cyprus. All these countries found themselves suddenly unable to tap financial markets for their sovereign issuance and had to turn to supra-national public lenders. One source was the International Monetary Fund (IMF), but Eurozone countries needed their own rescue mechanism. In June 2010 they created the European Financial Stability Facility (EFSF), a temporary mechanism which provided financial assistance to Greece, Ireland, and Portugal during its three years of lending operation that ended in June 2013. In the meantime it was replaced by a permanent rescue mechanism, the ESM, established in February 2012,

[9] In addition, as Krugman (2012) rightly notes, 'lack of labour mobility has not played a major role in euro's difficulties... but lack of fiscal integration has had an enormous impact'. This, plus the reason given in the text, explains why Figure 3.4 and the remainder of the chapter focuses on fiscal integration and ignores the other OCA adjustment channel, labour mobility.

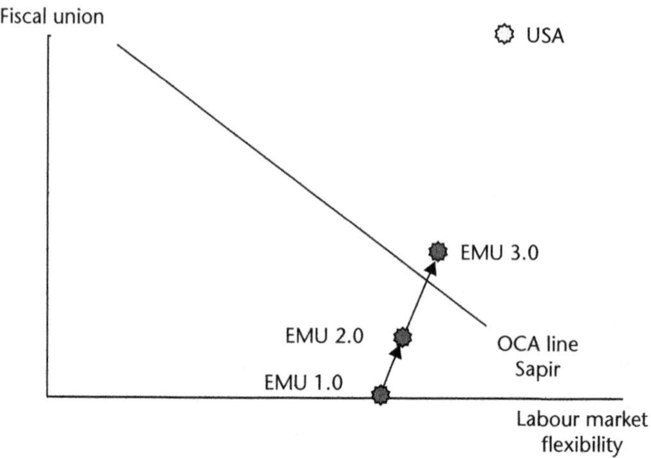


**Figure 3.4.** Fiscal Union and Labour Market Flexibility in Two Monetary Unions.

which so far has provided financial assistance to Spain, Cyprus, and Greece. EFSF/ESM loans come with conditionality that, so far, has always included making recipients' labour markets more flexible. Hence, the new EMU 2.0 regime set up in response to the financial and sovereign debt crisis includes an EMU risk-sharing mechanism in the form of fiscal assistance along with structural reforms in product and labour markets. This new regime is depicted by the dot EMU 2.0 in Figure 3.4, which is to the North and to the East of the EMU 1.0 dot. Note, however, that the EMU 2.0 dot is still below the OCA line. This reflects my judgement (and that of many others) that, although a clear improvement from EMU 1.0, EMU 2.0 still does not provide sufficient adjustment to qualify as a genuine and sustainable monetary union. As acknowledged by the Five Presidents' Report, a new regime—EMU 3.0 proposed here—is therefore needed.

What should EMU 3.0 contain in terms of adjustment mechanism? Many support the notion that what the Eurozone needs is not so much a fiscal union per se as an efficient risk-sharing mechanism that ensures both sufficient adjustment to asymmetric shocks and as little moral hazard as possible.

An international comparison of existing federations by the IMF shows that the Eurozone lacks the degree of risk sharing seen in other jurisdictions with respect to three dimensions.[10] First, contrary to federations such as the USA, Canada, or Germany that manage to smooth about 80% of local shocks, the Eurozone only manages to insulate half of that amount. Second, fiscal insurance does not account for the main share of total risk sharing in typical

[10] See IMF (2013).

federations, yet it compensates 25% of local shocks in Canada, 15% in the USA and 10% in Germany. In the Eurozone, fiscal insurance was virtually nil before the creation of the EFSF/ESM and remains very small. Third, most of the risk sharing in federations happens through private channels, mainly capital markets and banks. The Eurozone is no exception, but the absolute and relative (to banks) role of capital markets is much less than in other jurisdictions. But what is most peculiar to the Eurozone is the absence of a common fiscal backstop against financial risks, which explains why cross-border financial flows in the Eurozone were severely impaired during the financial and sovereign debt crisis. The establishment of a partial banking union (that comprises common supervision for Eurozone banks and partially common resolution, but so far no common deposit insurance) and the creation of an ESM direct bank recapitalization facility are important steps in the right direction, but what is still missing is a common fiscal backstop. As the IMF remarked, 'ultimately, a credit line from pooled fiscal resources would provide the best insurance against financial risks' (IMF, 2013).

The previous discussion suggests that the distinction between fiscal insurance and private insurance through financial markets, and the fact that the latter plays typically the dominant role in smoothing local shocks in federations, is not an argument against the need for a Eurozone fiscal union. On the contrary there is such a need but the fiscal union should not only aim to provide direct fiscal insurance. It should also provide a fiscal backstop against financial risks to allow private insurance to fully operate.[11]

Even if an efficient risk-sharing mechanism that provides appropriate adjustment to asymmetric shocks can be designed,[12] there is little chance that it will be implemented as long as the fear of moral hazard and of the related 'permanent fiscal transfers' is present in the Eurozone. In my view such fear partly or even largely reflects the heterogeneity that continues to prevail among Eurozone countries. The Five Presidents' Report was right to emphasize that 'there is significant divergence' across the Eurozone and that 'completion of a successful process of economic convergence... would pave the way for some degree of public risk sharing' (Juncker, 2015). What the Report has in mind is structural convergence predicated on structural reforms geared towards 'more efficient labour and product markets and stronger public institutions'.

Going back to Figure 3.4, the previous discussion suggests that the EMU 3.0 dot will need to lie to the North and to the East of the EMU 2.0 dot. In other words there will need to be progress along both the structural reform horizontal axis and the fiscal union vertical axis. Another way to interpret

[11] See Gros (2014).

[12] See Claeys, Darvas, and Wolff (2014) for a discussion about the benefits and costs of a much-discussed risk-sharing mechanism, European unemployment insurance.

the two axes is in terms of national and EMU institutional mechanisms, the former corresponding to structural reforms and the latter to fiscal union.[13]

## 3.5. Conclusion

The starting point of this chapter was the observation that the recent Eurozone crisis revealed major flaws in the original EMU design (EMU 1.0). It turns out that the architects of the Maastricht treaty had failed to foresee the risks of financial and sovereign debt crises and therefore to put in place institutional mechanisms to prevent and remedy them. They had also under-estimated the risks of asymmetric shocks and consequently had also not created sufficient mechanisms to prevent and adjust to them.

Even without the benefit of hindsight, the under-appreciation of the risks and consequences of asymmetric shocks by the euro's architects seems difficult to understand to someone versed in the economics literature on optimum currency areas. On the other hand, it is clear that prior to Maastricht, and even for quite a while afterwards, the economics profession was not sufficiently worried about the potential deficiencies of EMU with respect to financial crises and even less so to sovereign debt crises.[14] And certainly the vast OCA literature made no reference to either financial or sovereign debt crises.

This chapter has focused entirely on asymmetric shocks, but without ignoring financial and sovereign debt crises that have played such a central role in the Eurozone's recent predicament. The chapter has argued that, despite some important institutional innovations, EMU 2.0 is still insufficiently equipped to prevent and adjust to asymmetric shocks. It proposed a series of new institutional mechanisms that should form part of EMU 3.0, a new and sustainable design broadly along the lines envisaged by the Five Presidents' Report. The proposals are a combination of market-based and fiscal mechanisms. They also contain a mix of national and EMU mechanisms for I strongly feel that EMU 3.0 should not consider asymmetric shocks as a matter that simply requires Eurozone countries to put their individual national houses in order and implement national structural reforms. It must also

[13] A more in-depth discussion of structural reforms and of fiscal union may suggest however that, although mainly national, structural reforms would benefit from a coordinated Eurozone mechanism (see Draghi, 2015), and likewise that, although mainly supranational, fiscal union also should have an important national component (see Sapir and Wolff, 2015). Such discussion is however beyond the scope of this chapter.

[14] To my knowledge, the first paper warning that the EMU was institutionally ill-prepared to deal with financial crises is Prati and Schinasi (1999).

consider asymmetric shocks as a matter that requires putting the common EMU house in order by creating appropriate EMU institutions.

## 3.6. References


Blanchard, O. (2007), 'Adjustment within the euro. The difficult case of Portugal', *Portuguese Economic Journal*, 6(1) 1–21.

Buti, M. and A. Sapir (eds.) (1998), *Economic policy in EMU*, Oxford University Press, Oxford.

Buti, M. and A. Sapir (2002), 'EMU in the early years: differences and credibility', in M. Buti and A. Sapir (eds.), *EMU and economic policy in Europe: the challenge of the early years*, Edward Elgar, Cheltenham.

Carlin, W. (2013), 'Real exchange rate adjustment, wage-setting institutions, and fiscal stabilization policy: lessons of the Eurozone's first decade', *CESifo Economic Studies*, 59(3), 489–519.

Claeys, G., Z. Darvas, and G. Wolff (2014), 'The benefits and drawbacks of European unemployment insurance', *Bruegel Policy Brief*, no. 2014/06, Bruegel, Brussels.

De Grauwe, P. (2011), 'The governance of a fragile Eurozone', *CEPS Working Document*, no. 346, Centre for European Policy Studies, Brussels.

De Grauwe, P. (2012), *Economics of monetary union*, 9th edn. Oxford University Press, Oxford.

Draghi, M. (2015), 'Structural reforms, inflation and monetary policy', introductory speech by the president of the ECB, ECB Forum on Central Banking, Sintra, 22 May.

Fagan, G. and V. Gaspar (2007), 'Adjusting to the euro', *ECB Working Paper Series*, no. 716, European Central Bank, Frankfurt.

Frankel, J. A. and A. Rose (1997), 'The endogeneity of the optimum currency area criteria', *The Economic Journal*, 108(449), 1009–25.

Gros, D. (2014), 'A fiscal shock absorber for the Eurozone? Lessons from the economics of insurance', VoxEU.org, 19 March.

IMF (2013), 'Toward a fiscal union for the euro area', *IMF Staff Discussion Note*, no. SDN/13/09, prepared by C. Allard, P. Koeva Brooks, J. C. Bluedorn, F. Bornhorst, K. Christopherson, F. Ohnsorge, T. Poghosyan, and an IMF staff team, International Monetary Fund, Washington, DC.

Juncker, J. C. (in close cooperation with D. Tusk, J. Dijsselbloem, M. Draghi, and M. Schulz) (2015), *Completing Europe's economic and monetary union*, European Commission, Brussels.

Kenen, P. (1969), 'The theory of optimum currency areas: an eclectic view', in R. Mundell and A. Swoboda (eds.), *Monetary problems of the international economy*, University of Chicago Press, Chicago.

Krugman, P. (2012), 'Revenge of the optimum currency area', The conscience of a liberal (blog), The New York Times, 24 June, http://krugman.blogs.nytimes.com/2012/06/24/revenge-of-the-optimum-currency-area/.

Mundell, R. (1961), 'A theory of optimum currency areas', *American Economic Review* 51(4), 657–65.

Prati, A. and G. G. Schinasi (1999), 'Financial stability in European economic and monetary union', *Princeton Studies in International Finance*, 86, August.

Sapir, A. and G. Wolff (2015), 'Euro-area governance: what to reform and how to do it', *Bruegel Policy Brief*, no. 2015/01, Bruegel, Brussels.

Van Rompuy, H. (2012), *Towards a genuine economic and monetary union*, report issued by the president of the European Council on 25 June, European Council, Brussels.

# 4

# Macro-Financial Stability Under EMU

*Philip R. Lane*

## 4.1. Introduction

The aim of this chapter is to address whether monetary union affects the growth process for member countries. While it is typically assumed that real variables (such as the level of output) should be unaffected by monetary factors in the long run, it is possible that short-term and medium-term output might be affected by the nature of the monetary regime through a number of mechanisms. Moreover, if hysteresis mechanisms are operative, such temporary output losses may have permanent costs (Fatas, 2000; De Long and Summers, 2012).

At the level of an individual member country, there are two types of misallocation that may harm growth performance. First, there may be a chronic/persistent misallocation by which an economy may have an inappropriate sectoral composition of output (tradables versus non-tradables; investment in construction versus investment in machinery and equipment). Second, there may be acute/sharp intertemporal misallocations (spending levels too high relative to income levels) that result in a crisis, with an attendant post-crisis adverse impact on medium-term output (Reinhart and Rogoff, 2009; Romer and Romer, 2015).

The nature of a monetary union may foster both types of misallocation. There is considerable evidence that European Monetary Union (EMU) increased the degree of cross-border financial integration among euro area member countries, especially in relation to external debt positions (Lane, 2006; Lane, 2013a). In turn, financial integration facilitated an increase in the size and persistence of current account imbalances (Blanchard and Giavazzi, 2002; Lane and Pels, 2012). Large-scale and persistent current account imbalances raise the likelihood of both the chronic and acute misallocation risks outlined above. In relation to chronic risks, surplus countries may see excessive growth in export-orientated sectors and insufficient growth in domestically orientated sectors, with the opposite pattern prevailing in deficit countries. In relation to acute risks, external debt liabilities are a robust predictor of external crises (Catao and Milesi-Ferretti, 2014). While crises primarily affect debtors, crises also adversely affect creditor economies through wealth losses on external asset positions and trade channels.

In the other direction, international financial integration may also have positive effects on output growth. First, cross-border net financial flows may accelerate convergence, if capital is reallocated from capital-abundant economies to capital-scarce economies. Second, international risk sharing (through trade in equity-type instruments) may facilitate the selection of higher-return, higher-risk projects that generate faster (if more volatile) output growth (Obstfeld, 1994). Moreover, for a given level of output volatility, international risk sharing reduces the welfare costs of volatility by insulating wealth and consumption from domestic production shocks.

However, monetary union has had relatively little impact on cross-border equity positions relative to cross-border debt positions. Also, the scale and composition of current account imbalances in the mid-2000s are consistent with 'inefficient' imbalances that reflected excessive risk-taking by under-regulated national banking systems in some countries, over-investment in property assets (residential and non-residential), and delayed adjustment to adverse external shocks (Lane, 2013b). Following Forbes and Warnock (2012) and Bruno and Shin (2015), such domestic factors interacted with low global interest rates and 'easy' financial conditions (as captured by the VIX and global liquidity indicators).

In addition to the direct impact of international financial integration, monetary union also alters the behaviour of important adjustment mechanisms. In particular, the absence of national currencies may make it more difficult to accomplish stabilizing shifts in the real exchange rate. In turn, lack of adjustment in the real exchange rate may increase the persistence of external imbalances and sectoral misallocations (for both surplus and deficit economies). Going further, demand-type shocks may generate destabilizing movements in the real exchange rate (and the real interest rate, as price level movements are typically persistent), with current account deficits associated with real exchange rate appreciation and a decline in the real interest rate through a positive and persistent inflation differential.

However, in the other direction, it is also true that a monetary union offers insulation against non-fundamental national-level exchange rate shocks. There is a sizeable literature emphasizing the possible allocative inefficiencies associated with floating exchange rates, given the scope for speculative/noise shocks to shift currency values away from current fundamentals (see, amongst others, Berka et al., 2012). A concrete recent example is provided by Iceland: the sharp appreciation of the Icelandic krona in the mid-2000s was an aggravating factor during its boom phase. Accordingly, it is not clear ex ante whether monetary union would increase or decrease the efficiency of the exchange rate adjustment mechanism. In similar vein, the limited scope for independent monetary policies in mitigating international financial shocks is emphasized by Rey (2013).[1]

Along another dimension, conditional on a crisis occurring, membership of a monetary union provides a buffer through the operation of system-wide central bank liquidity mechanisms.[2] Through such cross-border liquidity flows (as captured by Target 2 balances in the eurosystem), the immediate output consequences of a sudden stop in private capital flows are mitigated. However, the existence of this buffer mechanism in turn may reduce private-sector incentives to maintain liquidity buffers and increase risk-taking incentives by banks (Fagan and McNelis, 2014). Given these mixed effects, whether monetary union increases or decreases the costs associated with external crises cannot be firmly established on an ex ante basis.

Of course, at a broader level, the crisis exposed the inadequacy of crisis management tools in many countries. In particular, insufficiently capitalized banks and the absence of effective bank resolution regimes raised the costs of crisis management. The high degree of cross-border financial linkages within the euro area meant that national-level banking policies had large area-wide spillover effects, which interacted with spillovers between the euro area and the financial systems of other advanced regions. In related fashion, the emergence of a diabolic loop between domestic banking systems and domestic sovereigns made management of the emerging sovereign debt crisis yet more problematic. In overall terms, the crisis highlighted the inefficiency of national banking policies in a common currency area, which also necessitated a clarification of the role of the eurosystem in underpinning area-wide financial stability. We return to the policy reform agenda in relation to financial integration and financial union in section 4.3.

In terms of the contribution of this chapter, we first examine the empirical evidence on whether membership of the euro area was associated with a shift in the cyclical behaviour of key macro-financial variables. If the euro has amplified pro-cyclical patterns in these variables, it reinforces the importance of designing and implementing offsetting stabilization policies and ensuring that balance sheets are sufficiently resilient to absorb the impact of higher volatility. Our empirical strategy is to examine these issues in the context of the 'initial phase' of EMU (1999–2007) and also the 'crisis' phase

[1] However, the degree of effective monetary autonomy is certainly non-zero, as shown by Klein and Shambaugh (2013).

[2] In relation to cross-border portfolio holdings, Galstyan and Lane (2013) also show that bond investors from outside the euro area were more likely to run for the exit during the crisis than were bond investors from fellow member countries.

(2008–12/2014). Second, we turn to the policy reform agenda in relation to improving macro-financial stability for the aggregate euro area and the individual member countries.

The structure of the rest of the chapter is as follows. We report our empirical work in Section 4.2. The policy agenda is discussed in Section 4.3. Finally, Section 4.4 concludes.

## 4.2. Empirical Analysis

In this section, we conduct three empirical exercises. First, we examine whether membership of the euro area has been associated with different cyclical behaviour of selected macro-financial variables relative to the experience of a large set of OECD countries over a long time span.[3] Second, for the set of member countries, we investigate whether deviations in macro-financial variables from euro area aggregate values are associated with cyclical output deviations from the euro area aggregate. Third, we examine whether external adjustment since 2008 has been different for members of the euro area.

This empirical approach is broader than the method of calculating country-specific hypothetical Taylor-type interest rates rules for each member country and inferring the costs of monetary union from the deviations of these estimated shadow policy rates from the European Central Bank (ECB) policy rate (Honohan and Lane, 2013; Ahrend et al., 2008; Taylor, 2008). Moreover, it is not clear that simulated Taylor rules provide a sufficient guide to the costs of monetary union during this period. First, while divergence in inflation rates and output gaps were significant in the initial years of EMU (1999–2002), inflation dispersion was relatively narrow by the mid-2000s and real-time estimates of output gaps were relatively small.[4] Second, interest rate policies would have been a costly way to tackle the financial imbalances emerging during the mid-2000s, in view of the limited impact of minor interest rate hikes on speculative behaviour during an asset price boom (Assenmacher-Wesche and Gerlach, 2010). Third, interest rate hikes can have perverse effects for small open economies with poorly regulated financial systems during periods of high global liquidity, as the associated currency appreciation may induce domestic speculators to increase foreign-currency leverage (Bruno and Shin, 2015). Fourth, the evidence indicates that small open economies tend to deviate from Taylor-indicated interest

[3] Estrada et al. (2013) present related evidence but focus on different variables, a different comparator set of countries and different empirical methods. See also Giannone et al. (2010) for related work on the characteristics of business cycles for members of the euro area.

[4] Of course, output gap estimates for the pre-crisis period have been heavily revised on the basis of ex-post information.

rates to limit differentials with the policy rates of the major central banks (Taylor, 2013).

Accordingly, we take a more indirect approach by investigating whether monetary union has been associated with a shift in the cyclical behaviour of key macro-financial variables. We first report some empirical results in relation to whether the cyclical behaviour of macro-financial variables has been different under EMU. To have a basis for comparison, we examine the member countries in the context of a wider group of thirty-four Organization for Economic Co-operation and Development (OECD) countries for the both the pre-EMU and post-EMU periods.[5]

Over 1984–2013, we examine the following specification

$$\Delta X_{it} = \alpha_i + \phi_t + \beta GROW_{it} + \sigma GROW_{it} * euro_{it} + \gamma GROW_{it} * noneuro_{it} \\ + \delta euro_{it} + \theta noneuro_{it} + \rho \Delta X_{it-1} + \varepsilon_{it} \tag{4.1}$$

where $X_{it}$ is a macro-financial variable (inflation, the real exchange, the current account balance and the fiscal balance) or an international financial flow variable (net debt flows, net portfolio flows, net other investment flows, and net FDI flows), $\alpha_i$ is a country fixed effect, $\phi_t$ is a time fixed effect, $GROW_{it}$ is the output growth rate, $euro_{it}$ is a dummy for membership of the euro area (taking the value 1 from 1999–2013), and $noneuro_{it}$ is a dummy for non-membership of the euro area (taking the value 1 for 1999–2013).[6]

The parameter $\beta$ captures the cyclicality coefficient between output growth and $\Delta X_{it}$, while $\sigma$ and $\theta$ capture any shifts in cyclicality from 1999 onwards for members of the euro area and non-members of the euro area, respectively. It is necessary to allow the cyclicality coefficient to change for even non-members of the euro area, as global factors may have altered the cyclical patterns in $\Delta X_{it}$ even in the absence of monetary union.

In terms of priors, we may expect $\sigma$ to be positive for inflation and the real exchange rate to the extent that fluctuations in output are driven by demand-type shocks. Such shocks mean that surges in growth are associated with upward pressure on wages and prices. In the absence of countervailing policy measures, this will result in positive comovement patterns between output growth and inflation and the real exchange rate. Similarly, demand-driven output fluctuations should be associated with a negative value for $\sigma$ in relation to the current account balance, with increases in domestic demand boosting imports. The prediction for the fiscal balance is

[5] The country list is: Australia, Austria, Belgium, Canada, Chile, Czech Republic, Denmark, Estonia, Finland, France, Germany, Greece, Hungary, Iceland, Ireland, Israel, Italy, Japan, Korea, Luxembourg, Mexico, Netherlands, New Zealand, Norway, Poland, Portugal, Slovak Republic, Slovenia, Spain, Sweden, Switzerland, Turkey, the UK, and the USA.

[6] We also examined an alternative sample interval 1984–2007. These results are available upon request.

Table 4.1. Macro-Financial Cyclical Elasticities I, 1984–2013

| | $\pi$ | $\Delta RER$ | $\Delta CAB$ | $\Delta FB$ |
|---|---|---|---|---|
| GROW | −1.7*** | 0.5** | −0.3*** | 0.3*** |
| | (0.4) | (0.2) | (0.04) | (0.1) |
| GROW*euro | 1.3* | −0.4 | −0.0 | −0.2** |
| | (0.7) | (0.4) | (0.1) | (0.1) |
| GROW*neuro | 0.8 | 0.5 | −0.2*** | −0.1** |
| | (0.6) | (0.4) | (0.1) | (0.1) |
| euro | −23.3*** | 0.8 | −1.1* | −4.0*** |
| | (6.2) | (3.2) | (0.7) | (0.7) |
| neuro | −27.7*** | 0.1 | −0.4 | −3.7*** |
| | (6.1) | (3.1) | (0.6) | (0.7) |
| LDV | 0.5*** | 0.1** | −0.1*** | −0.1** |
| | (0.03) | (0.03) | (0.03) | (0.03) |
| $R^2$ (within) | 0.37 | 0.05 | 0.17 | 0.32 |
| $R^2$ (between) | 0.83 | 0.03 | 0.0004 | 0.0002 |
| $R^2$ (overall) | 0.42 | 0.05 | 0.15 | 0.31 |
| N | 975 | 878 | 962 | 850 |
| Country FE | Yes | Yes | Yes | Yes |
| Year FE | Yes | Yes | Yes | Yes |

Standard errors in parentheses. ***,***,* denote significance at 1, 5, and 10 per cent levels, respectively. $\pi$ is the inflation rate; $\Delta$ Real Exchange Rates (*RER*) is the log change of the real effective exchange rate; $\Delta CAB$ is the first difference of the current account balance scaled by GDP. $\Delta FB$ is the first difference of the fiscal balance scaled by GDP; GROW is the percentage change of GDP at constant prices; euro is a dummy that equals one if a country is member of the euro area and zero otherwise; neuro is a dummy that equals one if a country is not member of the euro area during its existence and zero otherwise; LDV is the lagged dependent variable.

ambiguous: if membership of the euro area induces more fiscal prudence, we may expect a positive value for $\sigma$; whereas, if it induces less-disciplined fiscal policies (i.e. caused by the breaking of the link between national fiscal balances and countervailing actions by the monetary authority), we would observe a negative value for $\sigma$. In relation to the international financial flow variables, a procyclical pattern in net debt inflows may be viewed as a risk-enhancing pattern, whereas a procyclical pattern in net equity-type inflows might be a risk-mitigating pattern.

Table 4.1 shows the results for inflation, the real exchange rate, the current account balance and the fiscal balance, while Table 4.2 shows the results for various categories of international financial flows. It turns out that membership of the euro area (compared with the pre-EMU period and the comparator group of non-member countries) is associated with a significantly different cyclical pattern for only two variables: inflation and net international portfolio flows.

In relation to the former, inflation has been relatively more procyclical for the member countries. This is consistent with a pattern of demand-type shocks that induce both faster growth and local inflation pressures. In relation to the latter, the negative estimated value of $\sigma$ indicates that faster

**Table 4.2.** Macro-Financial Cyclical Elasticities II, 1984–2013

| | FDI | PORT | DEBT$^B$ | DEBT$^T$ |
|---|---|---|---|---|
| GROW | 0.1 | −0.1 | −0.1 | 0.5 |
| | (0.2) | (0.3) | (0.6) | (0.7) |
| GROW∗euro | −0.2 | −1.8*** | 1.6 | 0.9 |
| | (0.4) | (0.6) | (1.1) | (1.3) |
| GROW∗neuro | −0.1 | 0.005 | −0.4 | −0.9 |
| | (0.3) | (0.5) | (0.9) | (1.1) |
| euro | −1.4 | 3.9 | −1.2 | 8.0 |
| | (3.4) | (5.4) | (9.3) | (10.8) |
| neuro | −0.2 | 1.2 | 0.7 | 10.7 |
| | (3.3) | (5.2) | (9.0) | (10.5) |
| LDV | −0.2*** | −0.3*** | −0.4*** | −0.2*** |
| | (0.03) | (0.03) | (0.03) | (0.03) |
| $R^2$ (within) | 0.20 | 0.14 | 0.16 | 0.09 |
| $R^2$ (between) | 0.02 | 0.33 | 0.82 | 0.004 |
| $R^2$ (overall) | 0.20 | 0.13 | 0.15 | 0.09 |
| N | 946 | 921 | 961 | 953 |
| Country FE | Yes | Yes | Yes | Yes |
| Year FE | Yes | Yes | Yes | Yes |

Standard errors in parentheses. ***,***,* denote significance at 1, 5, and 10 per cent levels, respectively. FDI is the first difference of net FDI outflows scaled by GDP; PORT is the first difference of net portfolio outflows scaled by GDP; DEBT$^B$ is the first difference of net other investment outflows scaled by GDP; DEBT$^T$ is the first difference of net debt outflows scaled by GDP.

output growth for member countries was associated with greater net portfolio inflows, which is a destabilizing pattern. Otherwise, we do not observe in the data any euro-specific shift in the relation between output growth and this set of macro-financial variables. In this limited sense, it seems that the euro did not amplify cyclical risks along most dimensions.

Next we perform an intra-group comparison by asking whether deviations in output growth among the member countries were associated with procyclical behaviour in a range of macro-financial variables. Procyclical patterns in these variables might be interpreted as contributing to an amplification of national business and financial cycles within the euro area.

We run specifications of the following format

$$\Delta Z_{it} = \alpha_i + \theta_t + \beta * GROW_{it} + \varepsilon_{it} \tag{4.2}$$

where the inclusion of time dummies means that $\beta$ captures the covariation between the growth deviation for country $i$ in year $t$ and the deviation in variable $Z$ for country $i$ in year $t$, relative to the area-wide common patterns in growth and variable $Z$. The sample period is 1999–2013.[7]

[7] We also examined an alternative sample interval 1984–2007. These results are available upon request.

We consider a wide range of macro-financial variables: (i) the growth rate of private consumption; (ii) the growth rate of private investment; (iii) the growth rate of government absorption (consumption plus investment); (iv) the fiscal balance; (v) the current account balance; (vi) the log change in the real effective exchange rate; (vii) the C.P.I. inflation rate; (viii) the GDP deflator inflation rate; (ix) the change in the ratio of domestic credit to GDP; (x) net international debt flows; (xi) net international equity flows; and (xii) net FDI flows.

Tables 4.3–4.6 show the results. All specifications include time dummies but we consider both pooled and fixed effects estimates. The former specification takes into account the information in cross-country variation in the data, whereas the latter specification focuses on within-country variation. In

**Table 4.3.** Macro-Financial Deviations I, 1999–2013

| | (1) C | (2) I | (3) G | (4) CAB | (5) C | (6) I | (7) G | (8) CAB |
|---|---|---|---|---|---|---|---|---|
| GROW | −2.1*** | 0.4*** | −0.3*** | 0.7*** | −0.1 | 0.5*** | −0.01 | 0.1 |
| | (0.4) | (0.1) | (0.1) | (0.2) | (0.1) | (0.1) | (0.1) | (0.1) |
| $R^2$ (within) | | | | | 0.04 | 0.30 | 0.05 | 0.07 |
| $R^2$ (between) | | | | | 0.72 | 0.01 | 0.23 | 0.26 |
| $R^2$ (overall) | 0.04 | 0.30 | 0.05 | 0.07 | 0.10 | 0.11 | 0.01 | 0.02 |
| N | 180 | 180 | 180 | 180 | 180 | 180 | 180 | 180 |
| Country FE | No | No | No | No | Yes | Yes | Yes | Yes |
| Year FE | Yes | Yes | Yes | Yes | Yes | Yes | Yes | Yes |

Standard errors in parentheses. ***,**,* denote significance at 1, 5, and 10 per cent levels, respectively. GROW is the percentage change of GDP at constant prices; C is the deviation of private consumption from the euro area aggregate; I is the deviation of private investment from the euro area aggregate; G is the deviation of government spending from the euro area aggregate; CAB is the deviation of the current account balance from the euro area aggregate. All variables are scaled by GDP.

**Table 4.4.** Macro-Financial Deviations II, 1999–2013

| | (1) $\Delta$ *RER* | (2) $\pi$ | (3) $\pi^Y$ | (4) $\Delta$ *RER* | (5) $\pi$ | (6) $\pi^Y$ |
|---|---|---|---|---|---|---|
| GROW | 0.1 | 0.1*** | 0.3*** | 0.1 | 0.1*** | 0.3*** |
| | (0.1) | (0.04) | (0.1) | (0.1) | (0.04) | (−0.1) |
| $R^2$ (within) | | | | 0.82 | 0.15 | 0.18 |
| $R^2$ (between) | | | | 0.03 | 0.001 | 0.06 |
| $R^2$ (overall) | 0.82 | 0.15 | 0.18 | 0.80 | 0.11 | 0.17 |
| N | 168 | 180 | 168 | 168 | 180 | 168 |
| Country FE | No | No | No | Yes | Yes | Yes |
| Year FE | Yes | Yes | Yes | Yes | Yes | Yes |

Standard errors in parentheses. ***,**,* denote significance at 1, 5, and 10 per cent levels respectively. GROW is the percentage change of GDP at constant prices; $\Delta RER$ is the deviation of the log change of the real exchange rate from the euro area aggregate; $\pi$ is the deviation of the consumer price index from the euro area aggregate; $\pi^Y$ is the deviation of the log change of the GDP deflator from the euro area aggregate.

Table 4.3, the pooled estimates indicate that countries that grow more quickly in a given year typically experience faster investment growth but slower growth in private consumption and government absorption, while running a more positive current account balance. The only systematic within-country pattern is that an increase in a country's growth rate is associated with faster investment growth.

Table 4.4 shows that domestic inflation (both consumption and GDP deflator indices) is significantly positively associated with output growth in both the pooled and within-country estimates. This is a destabilizing pattern in that, holding fixed the area-wide policy interest rate, an increase in the expected inflation rate implies a decline in the real interest rate, which further boosts demand.[8] However, it turns out that the real effective exchange rate

**Table 4.5.** Macro-Financial Deviations III, 1999–2013

| | FB | DC | FB | DC |
|---|---|---|---|---|
| GROW | 0.7*** | 1.7*** | 0.5*** | 1.6*** |
| | (0.1) | (0.3) | (0.1) | (0.3) |
| $R^2$ (within) | | | 0.19 | 0.23 |
| $R^2$ (between) | | | 0.22 | 0.23 |
| $R^2$ (overall) | 0.18 | 0.23 | 0.17 | 0.23 |
| N | 180 | 176 | 180 | 176 |
| Country FE | No | No | Yes | Yes |
| Year FE | Yes | Yes | Yes | Yes |

Standard errors in parentheses. ***,**,* denote significance at 1, 5, and 10 per cent levels, respectively. GROW is the percentage change of GDP at constant prices. FB is the deviation of the the fiscal balance from the euro area aggregate; DC is the log change in domestic credit.

**Table 4.6.** Macro-Financial Deviations IV, 1999–2013

| | $PORT^N$ | $FDI^N$ | $PORT^N$ | $FDI^N$ |
|---|---|---|---|---|
| GROW | −1.8*** | 0.1 | −2.0*** | 0.01 |
| | (0.3) | (0.2) | (0.4) | (0.2) |
| $R^2$ (within) | | | 0.27 | 0.11 |
| $R^2$ (between) | | | 0.00 | 0.02 |
| $R^2$ (overall) | 0.24 | 0.09 | 0.24 | 0.09 |
| N | 150 | 148 | 150 | 148.00 |
| Country FE | No | No | Yes | Yes |
| Year FE | Yes | Yes | Yes | Yes |

Standard errors in parentheses. ***,**,* denote significance at 1, 5, and 10 per cent levels, respectively. GROW is the percentage change of GDP at constant prices. $PORT^N$ is the deviation of net portfolio outflows from the euro area aggregate; $FDI^N$ is the deviation of net FDI outflows from the euro area aggregate. All dependent variables are scaled by GDP.

[8] Inflation differentials tend to be persistent so an increase in inflation in one period is associated with an increase in expected inflation.

is orthogonal to the growth rate, which can be explained by the dominant role of the external value of the euro in driving the real effective exchange rates of member countries.

We turn to the evolution of the fiscal balance and domestic credit growth in Table 4.5. The fiscal balance shows a stabilizing pattern: faster output growth is associated with a larger fiscal surplus.[9] Domestic credit growth is significantly procyclical, which underlines the importance of macroprudential policies in ensuring macro-financial stability. We examine net international financial flows in Table 4.6.[10] While net FDI flows are orthogonal to output deviations, positive output deviations are associated with significantly larger net portfolio inflows. Again, this is a destabilizing pattern to the extent that these portfolio inflows contribute to domestic asset price dynamics and domestic credit growth.[11]

Finally, we examine whether the nature of external adjustment in the aftermath of the crisis has been different for members of the euro area. In one direction, the inability to adjust nominal exchange rates at a national level may have constrained the external adjustment process; in the other direction, access to cross-border eurosystem liquidity flows (as captured by Target 2 imbalances) may have cushioned the required scale of adjustment.

For this exercise, the sample consists of sixty-four advanced and emerging economies. Lane and Milesi-Ferretti (2012, 2015) examined cross-country variation in external adjustment since 2008 conditioning on the scale of pre-crisis current account imbalances. In particular, a standard empirical model of current account imbalances was estimated on four-year averaged data over 1969–2008 and the level of pre-crisis 'excessive' imbalances was calculated as the gap between the actual current account balance over 2005–8 relative to the model-fitted value for the current account balance.[12] That is, $CAGAP_{0508} = CAB_{0508} - CAB^{FIT}_{0508}$. A country running an excessive pre-crisis surplus is marked by a positive *CAGAP* value and a country running an excessive pre-crisis deficit is marked by a negative *CAGAP* value. Table 4.7 shows the largest *CAGAP* values for the advanced economies in the sample. It is clear that excessive imbalances were not confined to members of the euro area.

[9] If output growth is driven by the financial cycle, the scale of surpluses required to ensure a stabilizing pattern may be larger, given the procyclical nature of revenue streams generated by asset price booms and high construction investment.

[10] We exclude Ireland and Luxembourg, as the financial flow data for these countries are plagued by interpretation problems in relation to the mutual fund sector.

[11] See also Lane and McQuade (2014) and Carvalho (2014).

[12] The empirical model includes widely employed covariates such as demographic variables, the level of development, the fiscal balance, and correction factors for financial crises.

**Table 4.7.** Current Account Gap 2005–8: Large Excess Values

| Country | Negative | Country | Positive |
|---|---|---|---|
| Croatia | −2.1 | Sweden | 10.1 |
| Slovakia | −2.4 | Germany | 7.3 |
| Australia | −3.1 | Austria | 4.3 |
| Slovenia | −3.2 | Japan | 4.1 |
| Greece | −3.6 | Finland | 3.8 |
| Ireland | −3.7 | Netherlands | 3.5 |
| Portugal | −3.8 | Norway | 2.6 |
| United States | −4.0 | | |
| New Zealand | −4.7 | | |
| Spain | −4.9 | | |
| Estonia | −5.0 | | |
| Lithuania | −5.4 | | |
| Serbia | −7.2 | | |
| Romania | −7.3 | | |
| Latvia | −9.9 | | |
| Bulgaria | −16.3 | | |
| Iceland | −17.7 | | |

Advanced economies with current account gap values (2005–8) in excess of 2 per cent of GDP in absolute value.

To assess whether membership of the euro area affected the external adjustment process in the wake of the crisis, we run specifications of the following format

$$\Delta Z_{it} = \alpha + \beta * CAGAP_{i0508} + \delta * euro_i + \sigma * euro_i * CAGAP_{i0508} + \varepsilon_{it} \qquad (4.3)$$

where $Z_{it}$ is a macro-financial variable that is typically associated with external adjustment, $CAGAP_{0508}$ is the measure of 'excessive' pre-crisis current account imbalances and $euro_i$ is a dummy for membership of the euro area.[13] We examine adjustment in: (i) the current account balance; (ii) the real exchange rate; (iii) domestic demand; (iv) output; (v) inflation; (vi) the fiscal balance; (vii) the stock-flow adjustment term in the net international investment position (a proxy for international valuation effect); (viii) export volumes; (ix) import volumes; and (x) domestic credit growth.

Tables 4.8 and 4.9 show the results. Up to 2012, external adjustment has typically involved a closing of excessive current account imbalances, with those countries with negative current account gaps entering the crisis

[13] Lane and Milesi-Ferretti (2012) estimated a model of medium-term current account balances over 1969–2008 and calculated *CAGAP* as the deviation of the average current account balance in 2005–8 from the model-predicted current account balance. The empirical model associates current account imbalances with demographic patterns, fiscal positions, the terms of trade, the rate of output growth, the level of development, and historical exposure to financial crises. A positive value of *CAGAP* means an 'excessive' surplus and a negative value of *CAGAP* means an 'excessive' deficit.

**Table 4.8.** External Adjustment I

| | (1) CAB | (2) DD | (3) Y | (4) $\Delta DC$ | (5) FB |
|---|---|---|---|---|---|
| *CAGAP* | −0.74*** | 1.51*** | 0.90*** | 1.30 | −0.002 |
| | [−6.96] | [6.34] | [4.57] | [1.02] | [−0.05] |
| *CAGAP*euro* | −0.28 | 0.41 | −0.14 | −1.54 | −0.16 |
| | [−1.29] | [1.21] | [−0.53] | [−0.89] | [−0.73] |
| *euro* | 0.03*** | −0.17*** | −0.13*** | 0.06 | 0.01 |
| | [2.98] | [−7.21] | [−6.76] | [1.10] | [1.50] |
| $\alpha$ | −0.0008 | 0.10*** | 0.10*** | 0.12*** | −0.02*** |
| | [−0.14] | [5.69] | [7.43] | [3.20] | [−4.22] |
| *N* | 64 | 64 | 64 | 59 | 62 |
| $R^2$ | 0.66 | 0.58 | 0.45 | 0.11 | 0.07 |

CAB is current account adjustment between 2005–8 and 2012; DD is the change in domestic demand between 2007–8 (average) and 2012; Y refers to the change in real GDP between 2007–8 (average) and 2012; $\Delta DC$ is the change in ratio of domestic credit to GDP; FB refers to the change in general government structural balance as per cent of potential GDP between 2005–8 (average) and 2012. OLS estimation. ***,**,* denote significance at 1, 5, and 10 per cent levels, respectively.

**Table 4.9.** External Adjustment II

| | (1) $\pi$ | (2) RER | (3) EXP | (4) IMP | (5) SFA |
|---|---|---|---|---|---|
| *CAGAP* | 0.07 | 0.67 | −0.08 | 0.52*** | 2.82 |
| | [1.46] | [1.58] | [−1.05] | [3.68] | [0.86] |
| *CAGAP*euro* | 0.26** | −1.45*** | −0.36 | 0.06 | −1.78 |
| | [2.06] | [−3.24] | [−1.27] | [0.22] | [−0.49] |
| *euro* | 0.004 | −0.04* | −0.02 | −0.06*** | 0.17 |
| | [0.82] | [−1.86] | [−1.39] | [−3.51] | [1.54] |
| $\alpha$ | −0.01*** | 0.02 | 0.05*** | 0.05*** | −0.12 |
| | [−4.39] | [1.22] | [7.09] | [5.70] | [−1.39] |
| *N* | 64 | 64 | 64 | 64 | 64 |
| $R^2$ | 0.14 | 0.13 | 0.06 | 0.33 | 0.12 |

$\pi$ is change in inflation between 2005–8 and 2009–12; RER refers to the log change in real effective exchange rate between 2005–8 and 2012; EXP and IMP are volume growth in exports and imports, respectively, between 2007–8 and 2012; SFA is the cumulative stock flow adjustment term in the net international investment position over 2009–12. OLS estimation. ***,**,* denote significance at 1, 5, and 10 per cent levels respectively.

experiencing greater declines in domestic demand, output and import volumes. As highlighted by Lane and Milesi-Ferretti (2012, 2015), there was no cross-country correlation between current account adjustment and the real exchange rate up to 2012, so that the overall pattern for excessive-deficit countries is that of adjustment through 'expenditure reduction' rather than 'expenditure switching.'

In relation to the differential experience of the euro area, the interaction term between *CAGAP* and the *euro* dummy is not significant except for the real exchange rate and inflation regressions. In relation to the latter, the evidence does support some role for intra-area adjustment: inflation has declined by more over 2009–12 (relative to 2005–8) for those member countries with the most negative *CAGAP* values. However, in the other direction, these countries experienced the smallest real exchange rate depreciations. This configuration can be reconciled by differences in trade patterns across the member countries. Still, the broad message from Tables 4.8 and 4.9 is that membership of the euro area has not substantially altered the external adjustment pattern relative to a broader sample of advanced and emerging economies.[14]

Next, we consider an extended specification

$$\begin{aligned} \Delta Z_i = \alpha + \beta * CAGAP_{i0508} + \delta * euro_i + \sigma * euro_i * CAGAP_{i0508} \\ \theta * BELL_i + \gamma * BELL_i * CAGAP_{i0508} + \varepsilon_i \end{aligned} \tag{4.4}$$

where $BELL_i$ is a dummy that takes the value 1 for the group of new member states that pegged to the euro (Bulgaria, Estonia, Latvia, and Lithuania). This is a relevant comparison group, as these countries were bound by the peg to the euro but did not have access to eurosystem liquidity facilities.[15]

Tables 4.10 and 4.11 show the results. Relative to the *BELL* group, high-deficit members of the euro area experienced a less severe adjustment in the current account balance and a smaller compression in trade volumes. In this limited sense, it seems as if the cross-border liquidity support provided by the eurosystem facilitated a gentler form of adjustment.

In summary, the pattern in Table 4.1–4.6 is that the covariation between the output cycle and the financial cycle (as captured by domestic credit growth, net portfolio inflows, and variation in national-level real interest rates) grew more intense under EMU. As shown in Tables 4.7–4.11 in relation to external adjustment, this proved costly as the macro-financial costs of closing excessive current account imbalances in the wake of the crisis have been severe.[16] These cyclical patterns and the crisis experience have generated a wide-ranging policy debate about macro-financial stabilization under EMU. We turn to this debate in the Section 4.3.

[14] Lane and Milesi-Ferretti (2015) do show that countries with floating exchange rates were able to cut policy interest rates during the crisis. The common policy rate for the euro area has meant that interest rate differentials have not contributed to minimizing the cost of external rebalancing within the euro area.

[15] See also Gross and Alcidi (2013). Of course, there are also other important differences between this group and members of the euro area (level of GDP per capita, country size, importance of foreign-owned banks).

[16] Tables 4.8–4.11 also show that the adjustment experience has not been markedly different for euro area member countries relative to a broad comparator group and has been somewhat gentler than the sudden stop experienced by the BELL group.

**Table 4.10.** External Adjustment III

| | (1) CAB | (2) DD | (3) Y | (4) $\Delta DC$ | (5) FB |
|---|---|---|---|---|---|
| *CAGAP* | −0.65*** | 1.55*** | 0.94*** | 1.52 | 0.02 |
| | [−6.78] | [5.48] | [4.13] | [1.03] | [0.46] |
| *CAGAP*euro* | −0.20 | 0.54 | 0.07 | −3.03* | −0.02 |
| | [−0.87] | [1.19] | [0.18] | [−1.79] | [−0.09] |
| *CAGAP*BELL* | −0.52** | −0.03 | 0.09 | −5.02* | 0.08 |
| | [−2.58] | [−0.05] | [0.21] | [−1.80] | [0.32] |
| *euro* | 0.03*** | −0.17*** | −0.14*** | 0.10* | 0.01 |
| | [2.94] | [−6.45] | [−6.16] | [1.95] | [1.02] |
| *BELL* | −0.01 | 0.03 | 0.05 | −0.62*** | 0.04 |
| | [−0.42] | [0.40] | [1.01] | [−3.19] | [0.96] |
| $\alpha$ | −0.003 | 0.10*** | 0.10*** | 0.11*** | −0.02*** |
| | [−0.52] | [5.44] | [7.21] | [2.69] | [−4.10] |
| *N* | 64 | 64 | 64 | 59 | 62 |
| $R^2$ | 0.69 | 0.58 | 0.46 | 0.19 | 0.11 |

BELL is dummy for group consisting of Bulgaria, Estonia, Latvia, and Lithuania. CAB is current account adjustment between 2005–8 and 2012; DD is the change in domestic demand between 2007–8 (average) and 2012; Y refers to the change in real GDP between 2007–8 (average) and 2012; $\Delta$DC is the change in ratio of domestic credit to GDP; FB refers to the change in général government structural balance as per cent of potential GDP between 2005–08 (average) and 2012. OLS estimation. ***,**,* denote significance at 1, 5, and 10 per cent levels, respectively.

**Table 4.11.** External Adjustment IV

| | (1) $\pi$ | (2) RER | (3) EXP | (4) IMP | (5) SFA |
|---|---|---|---|---|---|
| *CAGAP* | 0.03 | 0.89** | −0.08 | 0.54*** | 3.63 |
| | [0.70] | [2.13] | [−0.82] | [3.15] | [0.96] |
| *CAGAP*euro* | 0.19** | −1.21*** | 0.07 | 0.58* | −1.72 |
| | [2.17] | [−2.76] | [0.24] | [1.83] | [−0.46] |
| *CAGAP*BELL* | 0.27** | −1.33* | 0.90*** | 0.99*** | −6.69 |
| | [2.35] | [−1.91] | [3.79] | [3.00] | [−1.14] |
| *euro* | 0.004 | −0.04* | −0.03** | −0.07*** | 0.19 |
| | [1.03] | [−1.83] | [−2.22] | [−4.01] | [1.50] |
| *BELL* | −0.0002 | −0.02 | 0.15*** | 0.18*** | −0.35 |
| | [−0.02] | [−0.29] | [4.14] | [3.73] | [−0.91] |
| $\alpha$ | −0.01*** | 0.02 | 0.05*** | 0.05*** | −0.14 |
| | [−3.99] | [0.91] | [6.79] | [5.46] | [−1.43] |
| *N* | 64 | 64 | 64 | 64 | 64 |
| $R^2$ | 0.21 | 0.18 | 0.17 | 0.40 | 0.17 |

BELL is dummy for group consisting of Bulgaria, Estonia, Latvia and Lithuania. $\pi$ is change in inflation between 2005–8 and 2009–12; RER refers to the log change in real effective exchange rate between 2005–8 and 2012; EXP and IMP are volume growth in exports and imports, respectively, between 2007–8 and 2012; SFA is the cumulative stock flow adjustment term in the net international investment position over 2009–12. OLS estimation. ***,**,* denote significance at 1, 5, and 10 per cent levels, respectively.

## 4.3. Policy Reforms

The high costs associated with resolving excessive external imbalances and recovering from financial crises have underlined the importance for all economies of maintaining macro-financial stability and improving the resilience of the real economy and the financial system to large-scale shocks. The absence of national currencies makes these issues even more acute for members of the euro area.

At a national level, there are three main challenges. First, macroprudential regulation of the financial system has the potential to mitigate financial risks. However, this is no easy task and is made more difficult by the rise of shadow banking and shifts in financial activity towards non-regulated sectors. In addition, the scope for cross-border spillovers and leakages in relation to macroprudential policies means that appropriate coordination through the European Systemic Risk Board (ESRB) is essential.

Second, fiscal policy should at the same time both maintain long-term sustainability while also contributing to macroeconomic stability by moving counter-cyclically against both the output cycle and financial cycle (Calmfors, 2003; Benetrix and Lane, 2013). To this end, it is necessary that the European fiscal framework be intelligently interpreted to enable the attainment of these twin goals.

Third, national legal and financial systems and domestic labour markets should be designed to tolerate inter-sectoral reallocations. For smooth adjustment, the capital ratios and credit policies of banks should be sufficiently resilient to absorb losses in declining sectors while funding new lending in expanding sectors; bankruptcy and debt restructuring should be efficiently processed by the legal system; and labour market institutions should be capable of facilitating separations between workers and firms in contracting sectors and new matches in expanding sectors.

At the European level, there has been considerable progress in setting up bank recovery and resolution plans and important elements of banking union, including the establishment of the Single Supervisory Mechanism (SSM) and the initiation of a Single Resolution Fund. Still, a full-scale banking union requires further progress in developing a robust harmonized area-wide deposit insurance scheme and ensuring a joint fiscal backstop (Marzinotto et al., 2011).

The stability of the European banking system would be further assured by reforms that limit excessive holdings of domestic sovereign bonds by banks (see also European Systemic Risk Board, 2015). Brunnermeier et al. (2011) and Corsetti et al. (2015) highlight the benefits of a multi-country diversification requirement in the sovereign bond portfolios held by banks. Furthermore, a pooled bundle of sovereign bonds could be divided into senior and junior tranches, with the senior tranche constituting an area-wide safe asset. As argued by Corsetti et al. (2015), these senior tranche bonds could become the main instrument for eurosystem liquidity operations and quantitative easing programmes. The eurosystem could help develop the market for this security by stipulating that only these types of securities can achieve the highest rating in relation to risk weighting of assets and the calculaton of liquidity coverage ratios. In turn, if the links between banks and national government are weakened, the growth of pan-European banks will be encouraged. Through geographical diversification, such banks are more likely to be robust in the event of regional shocks.

In addition, the dilution of bank exposures to any individual sovereign also mean that it will be more feasible in the future to allow for sovereign debt restructuring if a national government loses market access (Corsetti et al. 2015). International Monetary Fund (2014) provides a useful guide to the criteria that could be used to determine the role of sovereign debt restructuring (as a precursor to any official funding) in a given situation. The lending framework of the ESM should be aligned with these criteria.

The scope for international risk sharing can also be improved by the types of reforms envisaged under the Capital Markets Union (C.M.U.) initiative. Deeper and more integrated corporate bond and asset-backed securities markets can provide extra cushioning relative to a bank-dominated credit system, while the integration of equity markets and the market for corporate control (by fostering higher FDI flows) can improve the equity-debt mix in cross-border flows. At the same time, it is important to design policy frameworks so that growth in non-bank debt markets does not damage the capacity of macroprudential regulation to tackle excessive credit growth.

The crisis has also posed challenges for the conduct of monetary policy by the ECB. Working out the appropriate roles of eurosystem liquidity policies and national-level Emergency Liquidity Assistance (ELA) in stabilizing distressed national banking systems (especially in the context of simultaneously distressed sovereigns) has been an ongoing challenge for the eurosystem. In a similar vein, the effectiveness of interest rate policies was compromised by the fragmentation of the interbank markets during the crisis and compromised state of bank balance sheets in many member countries. Most severely, speculation about redenomination risk induced elevated spikes in sovereign bond yields for a number of member countries.

Through the 2012 announcement of the Outright Monetary Transactions (OMT) programme and 2014–15 adoption of large-scale asset purchase programmes, the ECB has addressed uncertainty about the degree of its commitment to meeting its inflation target and supporting financial stability in Europe. Given the limitations of conventional and unconventional monetary policies at the 'near zero' lower bound, the desirability of revising upwards the inflation target warrants debate. While this debate is also relevant for other major central banks, it has special relevance for the euro area in view of the desirability of facilitating adjustment of real exchange rates within the euro area.

In relation to fiscal policy, national fiscal policies should be embedded in an area-wide aggregate fiscal position that is appropriate for the broad macroeconomic environment.[17] To this end, further reform of the European fiscal process may be necessary. In particular, the first stage of the European Semester could be devoted to determining the appropriate aggregate fiscal position for the euro area, with national fiscal plans subsequently framed to ensure that the aggregate position is achieved while also ensuring that national fiscal positions are sustainable. To support this two-step process, the establishment of an independent, non-political European Fiscal Council could be helpful in formulating the appropriate area-wide aggregate fiscal position.

In principle, European-level surveillance of macro-financial risks may also be helpful to avoid national-level group think problems and reconcile the aggregate implications of diverse trends across the member economies.[18] While the European Union's Macroeconomic Imbalances Procedure (MIP) spans a wide range of relevant national-level macro-financial risk factors, country-level risk analysis should be embedded in a broader framework that is capable of providing a coherent account of area-wide risk. While an EU framework has been established to monitor financial stability risks through the ESRB, there is no similar institutional arrangement to monitor broader macroeconomic risks.

Finally, high legacy debt levels in a number of member countries make it more difficult to implement the range of reforms outlined in this section, even if debt servicing problems are certainly less acute at current low interest rates. Corsetti et al. (2015) outline a range of options to alleviate the burden of high debt levels, to support the transition to a safer, more stable euro area.

## 4.4. Conclusions

This chapter has examined whether monetary union has been associated with a shift in the cyclical behaviour of an array of national-level macro-financial variables. In common with other advanced economies, the euro area experienced a major financial boom-bust cycle during 2003–10. Along several important dimensions, this cycle was more severe within the euro area.

[17] In this chapter, I do not explore the scope for a larger-scale fiscal union that would involve cross-border net fiscal transfers in response to asymmetric shocks. The degree of political integration required for a large-scale fiscal union does not seem imminent. In any event, if the reforms discussed in this chapter are implememted, the scope for large-scale asymmetric shocks (which have primarily emerged from the financial system) should be sharply curtailed.

[18] Lunn (2013) provides an insightful account of decision-making biases during the Irish credit boom.

The failure to implement sufficiently countercyclical macroprudential and fiscal policies during the boom phase was costly, as was the absence of effective area-wide crisis management institutions once the crisis emerged. While there has been considerable progress in remedying these policy and institutional failures, much remains to be done, with the recent Five Presidents's Report outlining the range of reforms required to ensure a more robust monetary union. Whether Europe has the political appetite to implement these reforms is a major question for the coming years.

*Acknowledgements*

I thank Rogelio Mercado and Yannick Timmer for excellent research assistance. I also gratefully acknowledge research support from the Irish Research Council.

## 4.5. References

Ahrend, Rudiger, Boris Cournede, and Robert Price (2008), 'Monetary Policy, Market Excesses and Financial Turmoil', *OECD Economics Department Working Paper No. 597.*

Assenmacher-Wesche, Katrin and Stefan Gerlach (2010), 'Monetary Policy and Financial Imbalances: Facts and Fiction', *Economic Policy* 25, 437–82.

Benetrix, Agustin S. and Philip R. Lane (2013), 'Fiscal Cyclicality and EMU', *Journal of International Money and Finance* 24, 164–73.

Berka, Martin, Michael B. Devereux, and Charles Engel (2012), 'Real Exchange Rate Adjustment in and out of the Eurozone', *American Economic Review (Papers and Proceedings)* 102, 179–85.

Blanchard, Olivier and Francesco Giavazzi (2002), www.ideas.repec.org/a/bin/bpeajo/v33y2002i2002-2p147-210.html, 'Current Account Deficits in the Euro Area: The End of the Feldstein Horioka Puzzle?', www.ideas.repec.org/s/bin/bpeajo.htm, Brookings Papers on Economic Activity, 33(2), 147–210.

Brunnermeier, Markus K., Luis Garicano, Philip R. Lane, Marco Pagano, Ricardo Reis, Tano Santos, Stijn Van Nieuwerburgh, and Dimitri Vayanos (2011), 'European Safe Bonds: ESBies', *mimeo*, Euro-nomics.com.

Bruno, Valentina and Hyun Song Shin (2015), 'Cross-Border Banking and Global Liquidity', *Review of Economic Studies* 82(2), 535–64.

Corsetti, Giancarlo, Lars P. Feld, Philip R. Lane, Lucrezia Reichlin, Helene Rey, Dimitri Vayanos, and Beatrice Weder di Mauro (2015), 'A New Start for the Eurozone: Dealing with Debt', *Monitoring the Eurozone Report*, Centre for Economic Policy Research.

Calmfors, Lars (2003), 'Fiscal policy to stabilise the domestic economy in the EMU: What can we learn from monetary policy?', *CESifo Economic Studies* 49(3), 3–19.

Carvalho, Daniel (2014), 'Financial Integration and the Great Leveraging', *Banco de Portugal Working Paper No. 2014–07.*

Catao, Luis and Gian Maria Milesi-Ferretti (2014), 'External Liabilities and Crises', *Journal of International Economics* 94(1), 18–32.

DeLong, J. Bradford and Lawrence H. Summers (2012), 'Fiscal Policy in a Depressed Economy', *Brookings Papers on Economic Activity* 44(1), 233–97.

Estrada, Angel, Jordi Gali, and David Lopez-Salido (2013), 'Patterns of Convergence and Divergence in the Euro Area', *IMF Economic Review* 61(4), 601–30.

European Systemic Risk Board (2015), *Report on the Regulatory Treatment of Sovereign Exposures*.

Fagan, Gabriel and Paul McNelis (2014), 'TARGET Balances and Macroeconomic Adjustment to Sudden Stops in the Euro Area', *IIIS Discussion Paper No. 465*.

Fatas, Antonio (2000), 'Do Business Cycles Cast Long Shadows? Short-Run Persistence and Economic Growth', *Journal of Economic Growth* 5(2), 147–62.

Forbes, Kristin and Francis E. Warnock (2012), 'Capital Flow Waves: Surges, Stops, Flight and Retrenchment', *Journal of International Economics* 88(2), 235–51.

Galstyan, Vahagn and Philip R. Lane (2013), 'Bilateral Portfolio Dynamics During the Global Crisis', *European Economic Review* 57(1), 63–74.

Giannone, Domenico, Michele Lenza, and Lucrezia Reichlin (2010), 'Business Cycles in the Euro Area', in *Europe and the Euro* (Alberto Alesina and Francesco Giavazzi, editors), University of Chicago Press.

Gross, Daniel and Cinzia Alcidi (2013), 'Country Adjustment to a 'Sudden Stop': Does the euro Make a Difference?', *European Economy Economic Paper No. 492*.

Honohan, Patrick and Philip R. Lane (2013), 'Divergent Inflation Rates under EMU', *Economic Policy* 37, 358–94.

International Monetary Fund (2014), *The Fund's Lending Framework and Sovereign Debt-Preliminary Considerations*.

Klein, Michael and Jay C. Shambaugh (2013), 'Rounding the Corners of the Policy Trilemma: Sources of Monetary Policy Autonomy', *NBER Working Paper No. 19461*.

Lane, Philip R. (2006), 'The Real Effects of European Monetary Union', *Journal of Economic Perspectives* 20, 47–66, Fall 2006.

Lane, Philip R. and Gian Maria Milesi-Ferretti (2012), 'External Adjustment and the Global Crisis', *Journal of International Economics* 88(2), 252–65.

Lane, Philip R. and Gian Maria Milesi-Ferretti (2015), 'Global Imbalances and External Adjustment After the Crisis', in *Global Liquidity, Spillovers to Emerging Markets and Policy Responses* (edited by Claudio Raddatz, Diego Saravia, and Jaume Ventura), Central Bank of Chile, 105–39.

Lane, Philip R. and Barbara Pels (2012), 'Current Account Imbalances in the Europe', *Moneda y Credito* 234, 225–61.

Lane, Philip R. and Peter McQuade (2014), 'Domestic Credit Growth and International Capital Flows', *Scandinavian Journal of Economics* 116(1), 218–52.

Lunn, Pete (2013), 'The Role of Decision-Making Biases in Ireland's Banking Crisis', *Irish Political Studies* 28(4), 563–90.

Marzinotto, Benedicta, Andre Sapir, and Guntram B. Wolf (2011), 'What Kind of Fiscal Union?', *Bruegel Policy Brief No. 2011/06*.

Obstfeld, Maurice (1994), 'Risk-Taking, Global Diversification, and Growth', *American Economic Review* 84(5), 1310–29.

Reinhart, Carmen M. and Kenneth S. Rogoff (2009), *This Time is Different: Eight Centuries of Financial Folly*, Princeton University Press.

Rey, Helene (2013), 'Dilemma not Trilemma: The Global Financial Cycle and Monetary Policy Independence', in *Global Dimensions of Unconventional Monetary Policy*, Proceedings of the 2013 Federal Reserve Bank of Kansas City Economic Policy Symposium, 285–333.

Romer, Christina and David Romer (2015), 'New Evidence on the Impact of Financial Crises in Advanced Countries', *mimeo*, UC Berkeley.

Taylor, John B. (2008), 'The Financial Crisis and the Policy Responses: An Empirical Analysis of What Went Wrong', *Critical Review* 21 (2–3), 341–64.

Taylor, John B. (2013), 'International Monetary Coordination and the Great Deviation', *Journal of Policy Modeling* 35(3), 463–72.

# 5

# Demographics and the Secular Stagnation Hypothesis in Europe

*Carlo A. Favero and Vincenzo Galasso*

## 5.1. Introduction

Do demographic trends support the secular stagnation hypothesis for the euro area? The issue of secular stagnation was first raised in 1938 by Alvin Hansen (Hansen, 1939) in his presidential address 'Economic Progress and Declining Population Growth', delivered nine years after the onset of the Great Depression, when he worried that low population growth would produce a situation of persistently inadequate output growth. The wording has been recently revamped by Larry Summers (see Teulings and Baldwin, 2014), who argued that negative real interest rates are currently needed to equate saving and investment with full employment. With low inflation and zero lower bound on policy interest rates, it may be impossible for an economy to achieve full employment, satisfactory growth, and financial stability (as low real rates increase the probability of bubbles). The rate of growth of population has traditionally been the main concern of economists, and Alvin Hansen made no exception. Demographers (see, e.g., Bloom et al. 2003) take a different view and insist on the importance of the age structure of the population (i.e. the way in which the population is distributed across different age groups) for growth and real rates.

In this chapter, we assess the importance of the age structure of population for the secular stagnation hypothesis by deriving a mortality trend from a standard model of mortality, the Lee–Carter model, and combining it with the projected age structure of population to generate long-term projections for the trend in output per capita and real interest rates for euro area economies. Our evidence shows that demographic-based projections deliver for the next twenty years a lower long-run potential growth rate but a reversion of real interest rates to their historical mean. The increase in life expectancy with lower fertility increases the supply of loanable funds savings, but ageing and a higher share of old age population more than compensate this effect to deliver projected higher real rates. Evidence on real rates is that they moved from 5% in the 1980s to 2% in the 1990s to an average of −1% after the Lehman collapse; the demographics based projected rates are back in the positive range for the next ten years with a between country variability that reflects the heterogeneity in the age structure of population.

On the basis of this evidence, we proceed to assess the role of age structure on productivity and labour markets, to understand to what extent the evidence on the empirical relationship between age structure and long-term growth could be related to the impact of age structure on reforms in labour and product market. First, we exploit the Organization for Economic Co-operation and Developent (OECD) labour and product market indicators to show that a large share of middle aged and elderly individuals in the population is associated with a lower reform effort. Second, using Eurobarometer data, we show that middle aged and elderly individuals have a more negative view of reforms, competitiveness, and globalization than young. We conclude by evaluating the importance of our results for the debate on the best strategy to promote growth in the current macroeconomic conditions. In particular we discuss the importance of our evidence for the two different views that are currently debated: the structural reforms view versus the macroeconomic adjustment view. The first one underlines the relevance of structural policies to promote growth in potential output after the crisis while the macro adjustment view suggests that structural reforms may prove detrimental if more flexibility in the labour market cannot be accommodated by the central bank with expansionary policy that cannot in any case deliver the negative real rates necessary to restore equilibrium. Our results suggest that the real interest rates projected by taking into account the age structure of the population will be positive and moderately raising over the next decade. However, the implementation of product and labour market reforms will not be facilitated by the same age structure of population.

## 5.2. The Demographic Scenario for Europe

Demographic dynamics is seldom empirically modelled in economics, we shall make an exception here and base our analysis of the demographic scenario on an explicit dynamic model of mortality. We consider the Lee–Carter (1992) mortality model to derive a mortality trend that we will combine with the age structure of population in Europe[1] to generate demographic-driven

[1] We thererefore model the demographic dynamics only partially as we do not explicitly combine our mortality model with a migration model and a natality model.

trends for real output and real interest rates. We analyse fifteen European countries (Austria, Belgium, Denmark, Spain, Finland, France, Great Britain, Germany, Ireland, Italy, The Netherlands, Norway, Portugal, Switzerland, and Sweden) to generate a sample of 10 euro area countries and 5 non euro area countries. Data on mortality for the sample 1956–2009 are taken from the Berkeley Human Mortality Database website.[2] The data are annual observations of central mortality rates. $m_{x,t}$ denotes the mortality for individuals of age x in year t, where mortality is the probability that a person aged x and alive at the beginning of the year dies by the end of the year. $s(x,t)$ is instead the survivor probability for individuals of age x in year t, which is the probability that an individual will be alive at age $x$ given that he has survived up to age $x-1$. Given mortality rates, survivor probabilities are derived recursively for individuals aged T and over: If $x = T$ then $s(x,t) = 1 - m_{x,t}$, if $x > T$ then $s(x,t) = s(x-1,t)[1 - m_{x,t}]$. Frequencies of death for individuals of age $x$ at time $t$ are determined as first differences of survival probabilities: $fod(x,t) = s(x,t) - s(x+1,t)$. Finally, life expectancy at age $x$ in period t is defined as follows $E_{x,t} = \sum_{j=1}^{\infty} s(x+j, t+j)$.

The Lee–Carter (1992) model consists of a system of equations for logarithms of mortality rates for age cohort $x$ at time $t$, $\ln[m_{x,t}]$, and a time-series equation for an unobservable time-varying mortality index $k_t$:

$$\begin{aligned} \ln\left(m_{x,t}\right) &= a_x + b_x k_t + \epsilon_{x,t} \\ k_t &= c_0 + c_1 k_{t-1} + e_t \\ \epsilon_{x,t} &\sim NID\left(0, \sigma_\epsilon^2\right) \\ e_t &\sim \text{MeanZero} - \text{Stationary Process} \end{aligned} \tag{5.1}$$

where $a_x$ and $b_x$ are age-specific constants. The error term $\epsilon_{x,t}$ captures cross-sectional errors in the model based prediction for mortality of different cohorts, while the error term $e_t$ captures random fluctuations in the time series of the common factor $k_t$ driving mortality at all ages. This common factor, usually known as the unobservable mortality index, evolves over time as an autoregressive process and the favourite Lee–Carter specification makes it a unit-root process by setting $c_1 = 1$. The model allows to identify the unobservable stochastic mortality trend, common to all cohorts, and to construct empirical counterparts for survivor probabilities, frequencies of death, and life expectancy at every age.[3]

[2] www.mortality.org.

[3] Identification and estimation of the Lee–Carter model are discussed in Appendix 5.2.

The model fits well the data for all countries considered in our sample and the results from estimation and model projection are very helpful in describing the demographic scenario for Europe. Figure 5.1 reports historical data and projections (with associated 95% confidence intervals) for expected residual lifetime at sixty-five years. The typical scenario of an increase of expected lifetime of 'six hours a day' is confirmed for all countries and also projected to continue in the future with a considerable longevity risk surrounding the point estimates. Figure 5.2 reports the frequency of death from sixty-five onwards in 1980 and 2009, which shows how the increasing concentration of death around the mode of the curve of deaths ('compression of morbidity', see, e.g., Robine et al., 2008) has made the profile of frequencies of death for ages above the mode closer and closer to a straight vertical line on the left of the range.

Figure 5.3 complements the picture by reporting the observed and projected age distribution of population based on the databases of the U.N. Population Division and of the US Census Bureau; we consider four age groups: zero to nineteen, twenty to thirty-nine, forty to fifty-nine, and over sixty. The trend of share of total population in each group shows a clear upward movement in the over sixty group, a downward movement in the zero to nineteen group, and hump-shaped patterns in the twenty to thirty-nine and forty to fifty-nine groups, who have already both peaked, respectively, at the beginning of the eighties and at the beginning of the new millenium. Ageing and the increased expected lifetime are the two major demographic forces at work. These two major forces might have heterogenous economic consequences. Consider, for example, the impact on savings and real interest rates: on the one hand the increase in expected lifetime at middle age has an expansionary effect on the supply of savings and pushes downward the equilibrium real rates, on the other hand the increase in longevity and the higher share of population in retirement age decreases the supply of saving and pushes the equilibrium real rates upward. Quantifying these effects is crucial to understanding the impact of demographic trends on equilibrium real rates. Similar arguments apply to the output effect of demographic trends. On the one hand, the increased expected lifetime might reflect technological progress that generates higher output per capita but, on the other hand, productivity decreases with age and the equilibrium output might be lowered by an ageing population.

In Section 5.3 we shall try to quantify the effect of demographic forces on output and real rates by specifying demographically driven models for these variables.

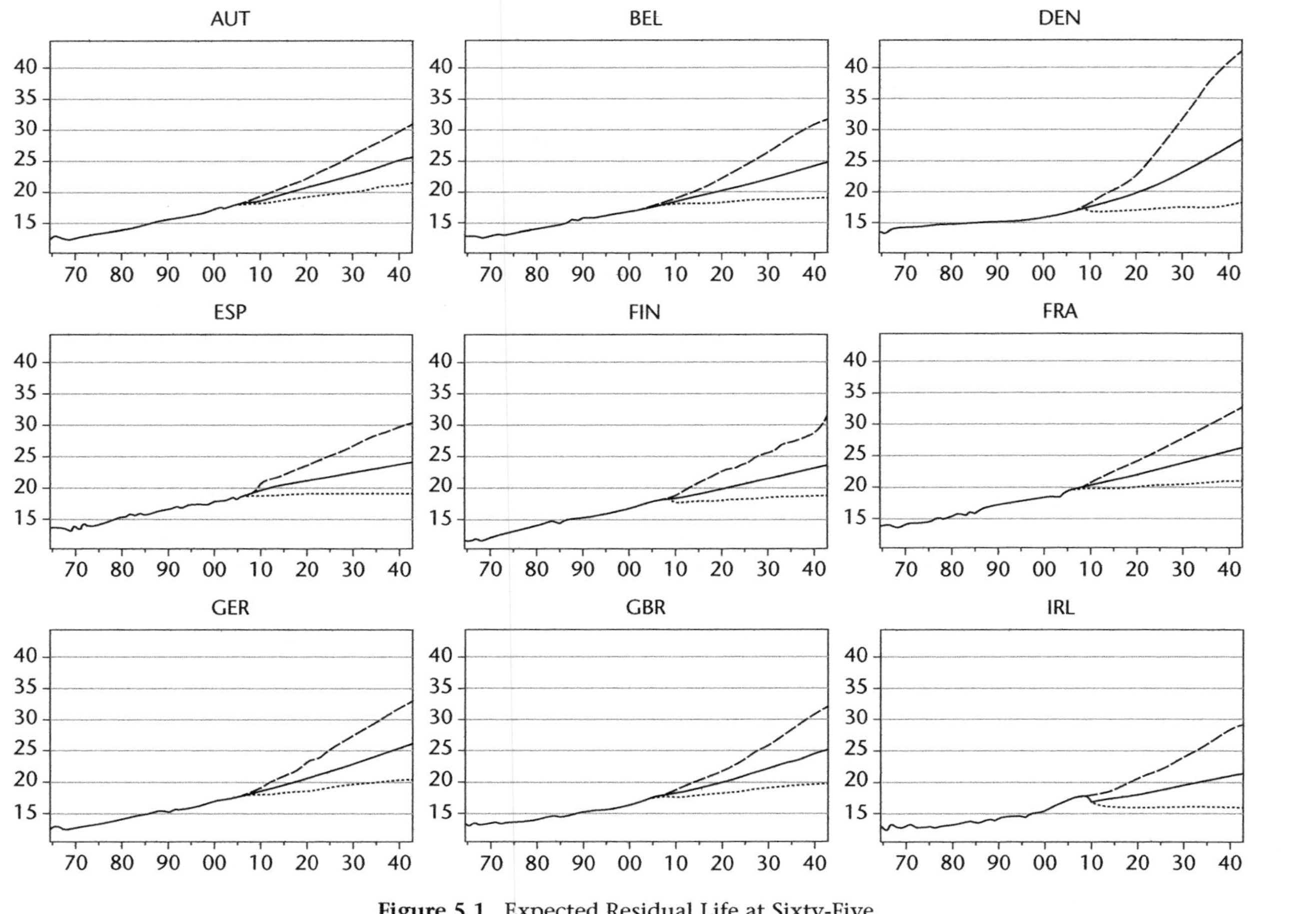


**Figure 5.1.** Expected Residual Life at Sixty-Five.

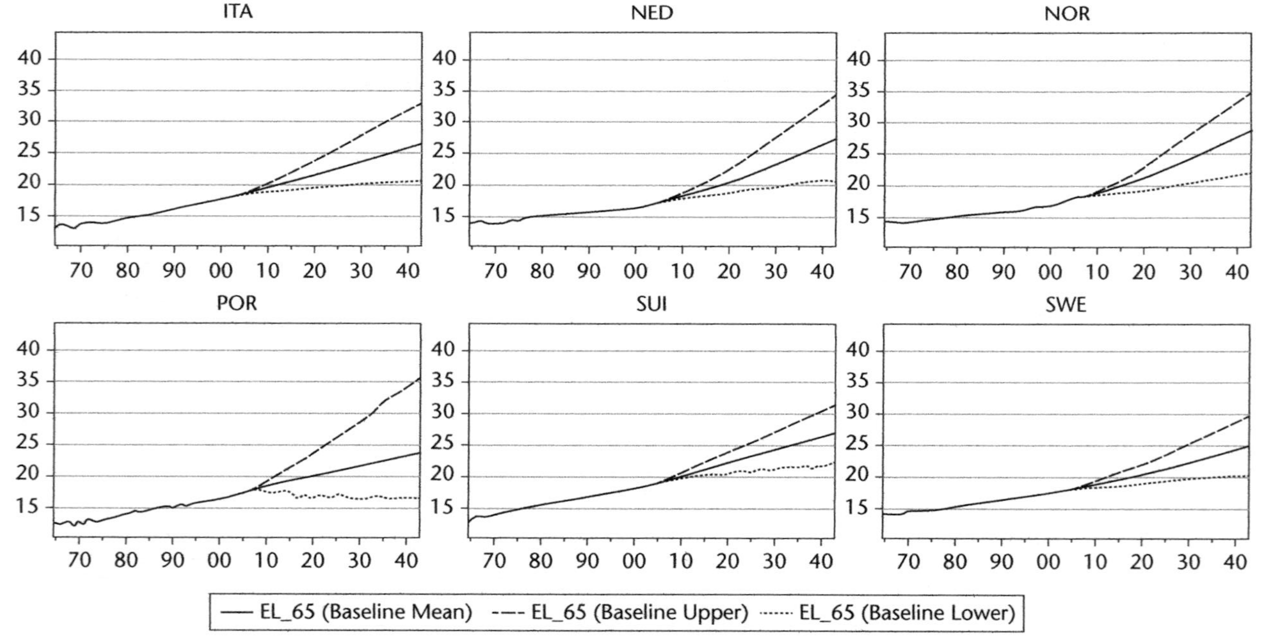


**Figure 5.1.** Continued

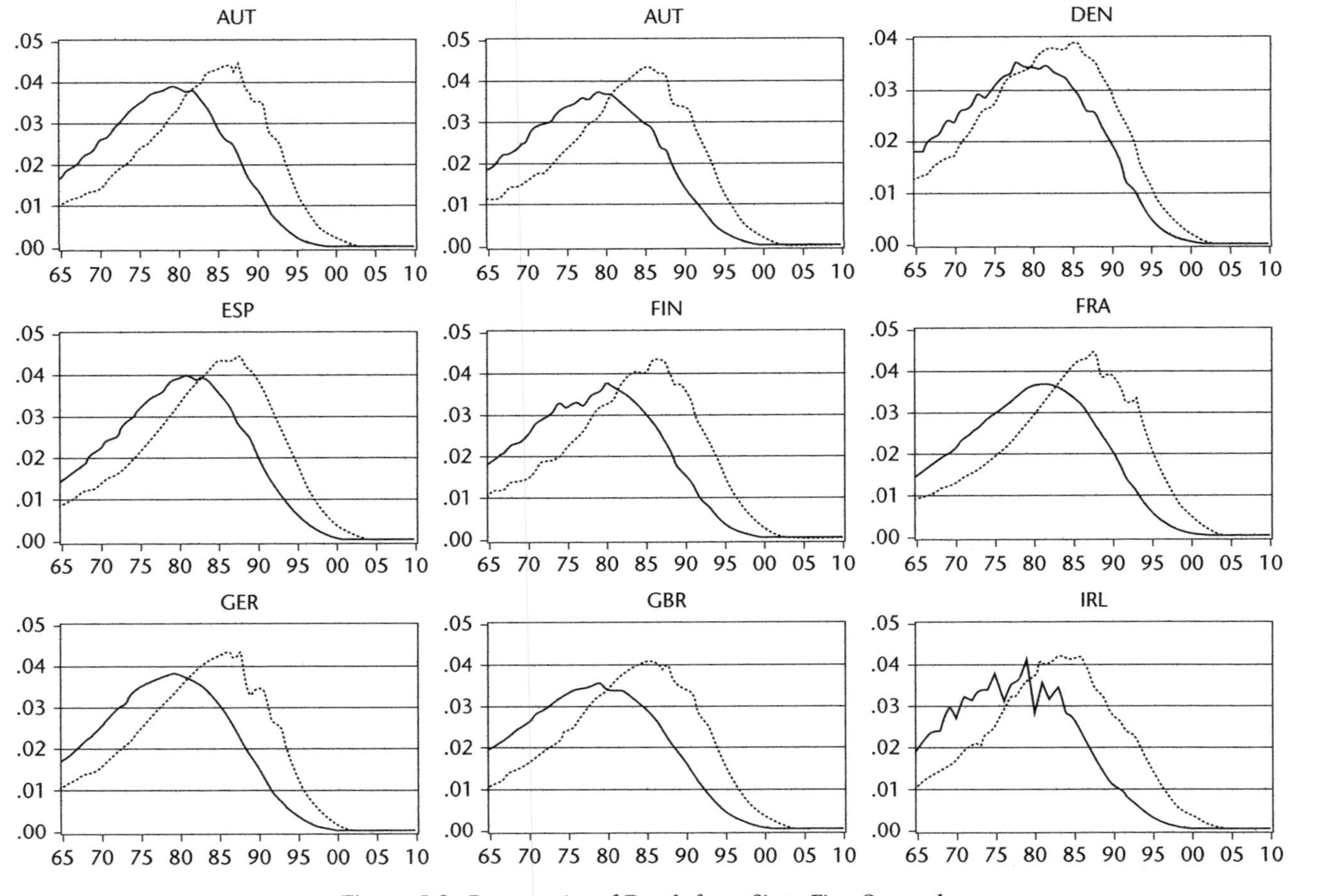


**Figure 5.2.** Frequencies of Death from Sixty-Five Onwards.

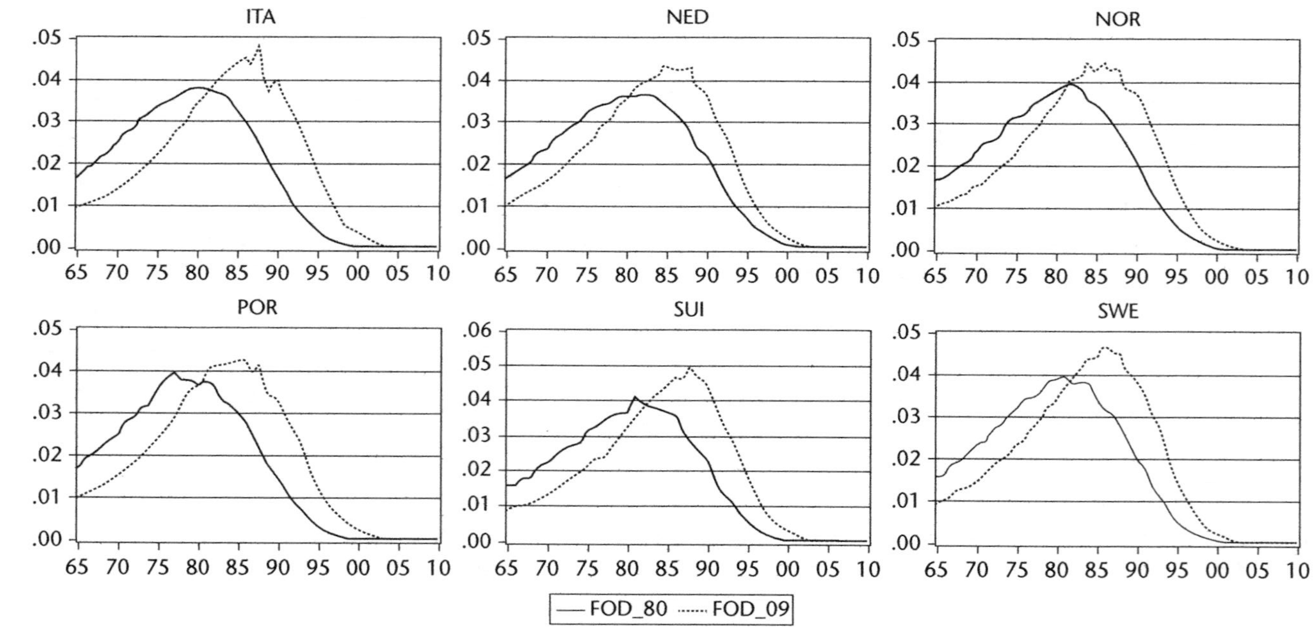


**Figure 5.2.** Continued

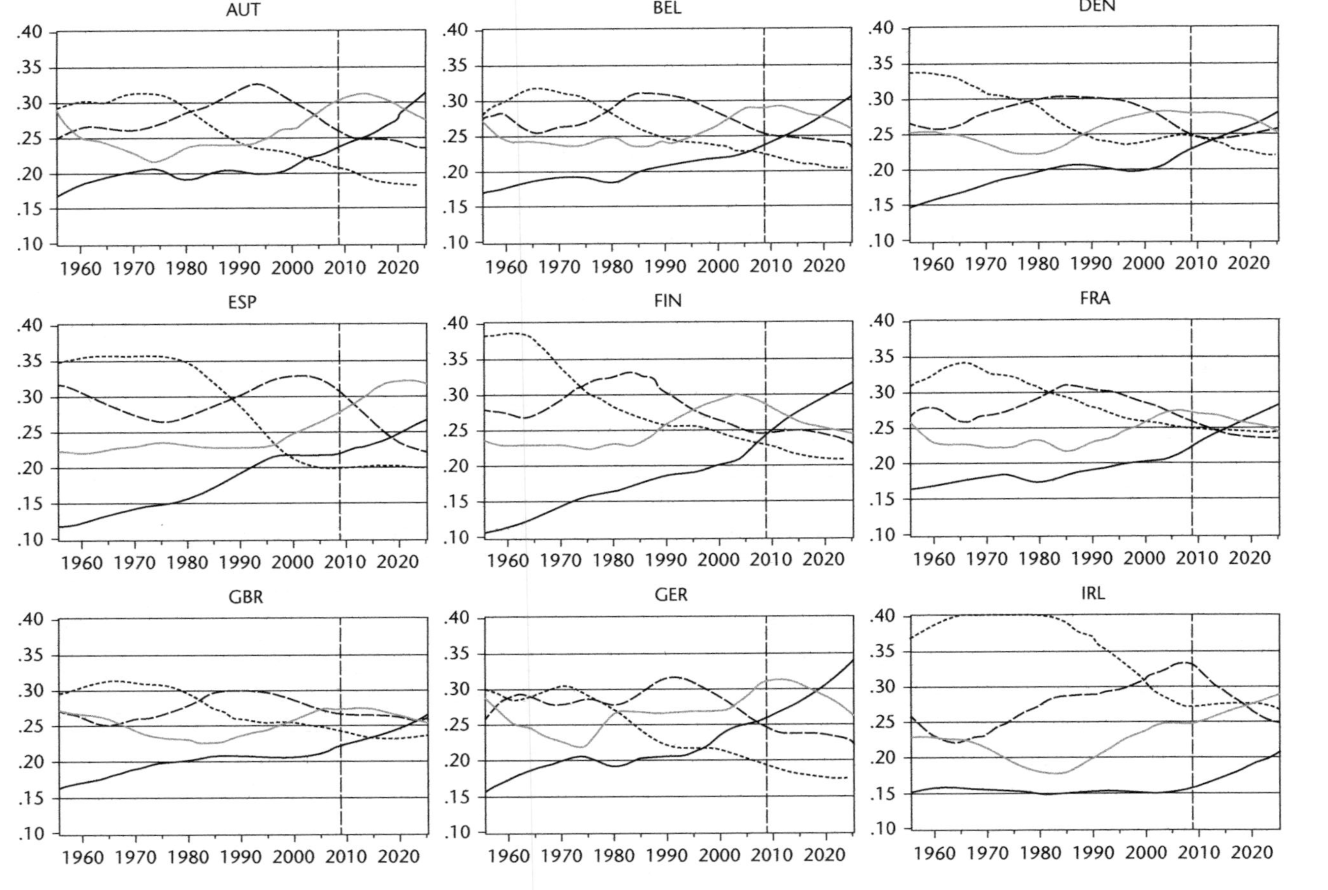


**Figure 5.3.** Shares of Total Population for Age Group.

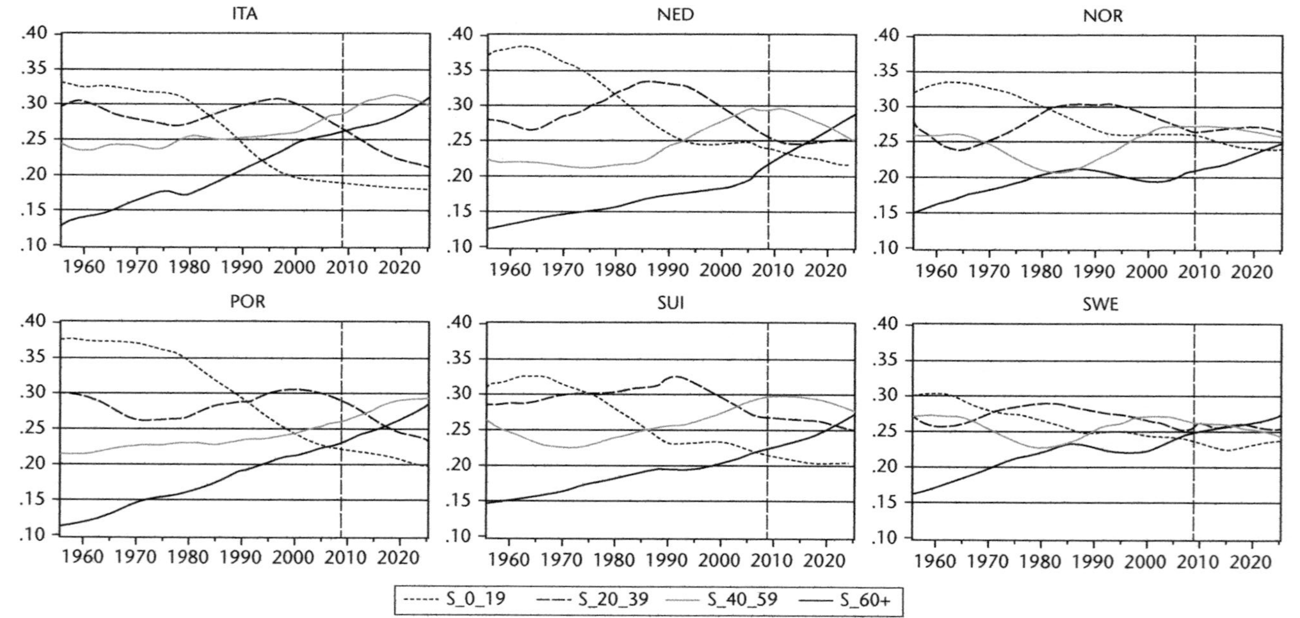


**Figure 5.3.** Continued

## 5.3. Demographic-Based Projections for Output and Real Interest Rates

To derive demographically based trends for output and real interest rates we take annual data from the Penn World Table 8 database for Expenditure-side Real GDP at Chained PPP (Millions of 2005 US$) and Total Population (Millions) and data for Long-Term Nominal Interest Rates, and GDP deflator (OECD base year i.e. 2005) from the OECD statistics.

We consider log of real per capita output at chained PPP, and we derive real long-term rates using dynamic forecasts for inflation from a country-specific recursively estimated first order autoregressive model.

We then adopt a model for a panel regression in levels of the logarithm of per capita GDP at PPP US dollars, $y_{i,t}$, and the real long-term interest rate, $rr_{i,t}$, on the logarithms of age shares, $a_{j,i,t}$, and the Lee–Carter country-specific mortality trend $k_{i,t}$:

$$\begin{aligned} z_{i,t} &= \beta_1 k_{i,t} + \sum_{j=0-19}^{60+} \beta_j a_{j,i,t} + \lambda_i + \chi_t + u_{i,t} \\ k_{i,t} &= c_{0,i} + c_{1,i} k_{i,t-1} + e_{i,t} \end{aligned} \tag{5.2}$$

where $j = 0-19, 20-39, 40-59, 60+$, $z_{i,t} = y_{i,t}, rr_{i,t}$. The specification also includes a country fixed effect and time-dummies; the model is estimated by Seemingly Unrelated Regression Estimation (SURE) to deal with cross-country correlations of residuals $u_{i,t}$. We use the model to project within-sample and out-of-sample the variables of our interest, by taking the age shares as exogenous and using the US Census Bureau projections. The results from estimation (over the sample 1956–2009 for $y_{i,t}$ and over the sample 1971–2014 for $rr_{i,t}$) are reported in Table 5.1.

The estimation results show a positive impact of the longevity trend both on output and interest rates, the coefficients on age-shares show that the replacement of population aged forty to fifty-nine with population aged sixty and over has a negative impact on output and a positive impact on real rates. Impact on output trend is linearly related to the age structure with a uniformly decreasing impact of the coefficient of age-shares on the trend for individuals aged twenty and over, while the effect on real rates is U-shaped with a trough at the forty to fifty-nine age share, that is the phase in life in which most savings should be cumulated. To provide further model evaluation and further insight on the implications of the empirical estimates, we perform within-sample and out-of-sample dynamic simulations for the two variables of our interest. Out-of-sample projections are based on the predicted shares of population made available by the US Census Bureau

Table 5.1. Demographic-Based Projections for Output and Real Interest Rates

| Log(GDP/capita), Seemingly Unrelated Regression (SURE), 1956–2009 | | | | |
|---|---|---|---|---|
| | Coefficient | Std. Error | t-Statistic | Prob. |
| $a_{0-19}$ | 1.238014 | 0.049163 | 25.18180 | 0.0000 |
| $a_{20-39}$ | 2.139490 | 0.047767 | 44.79056 | 0.0000 |
| $a_{40-59}$ | 1.540705 | 0.040224 | 38.30345 | 0.0000 |
| $a_{60+}$ | 0.931189 | 0.030463 | 30.56808 | 0.0000 |
| $k_t$ | −0.003238 | 0.000218 | −14.84704 | 0.0000 |
| **Real Interest Rate, Seemingly Unrelated Regression (SURE), 1971–2014** | | | | |
| | Coefficient | Std. Error | t-Statistic | Prob. |
| $a_{0-19}$ | 19.05117 | 1.873710 | 10.16762 | 0.0000 |
| $a_{20-39}$ | 24.50064 | 1.975536 | 12.40202 | 0.0000 |
| $a_{40-59}$ | 17.96599 | 2.017357 | 8.905707 | 0.0000 |
| $a_{60+}$ | 21.73423 | 1.525143 | 14.25062 | 0.0000 |
| $k_t$ | −0.139914 | 0.007949 | −17.60123 | 0.0000 |

and the out-of-sample predicted common stochastic trend generated by our estimated Lee–Carter model. The results are reported in Figures 5.4 and 5.5.

Figure 5.4 shows that the estimated model is capable of fitting well the observed trend in output within the estimation sample and that it predicts a clear break in this trend for the out-of-sample simulation: the trend output consistent with the age structure of population has a clear different and flatter slope in the out-of-sample simulations. This flatter slope is driven by the progressive increased importance of the sixty plus share over time in the out-of-sample period and by the significantly smaller coefficient of this age share in the estimated equation for output. The tipping point in the output trend is naturally related to baby boomers reaching retirement age, with the subsequent increase in the share of the population in retirement age and the decrease in the share of population in working age. This evidence is consistent with the results in Aksoy et al. (2015), who investigate the relation between demographic structure and macroeconomic trends in a Panel VAR framework that features a richer dynamic specification for the macroeconomic variables but a more parsimoniuos one for the demographic structure, limited to the inclusion of the age share with no mortality trend. Similar within-sample evidence is observed for real rates but the implications for the out-of sample simulations are cleary in constrast with the 'secular stagnation' hypothesis. The impact of the overall ageing population on real rates dominates that of longer expected lifetime of the savers. As a consequence real rates are predicted to increase out-of-sample. The overall demographic 'new normal' is one with slower trend growth (if any) and higher real interest rates.

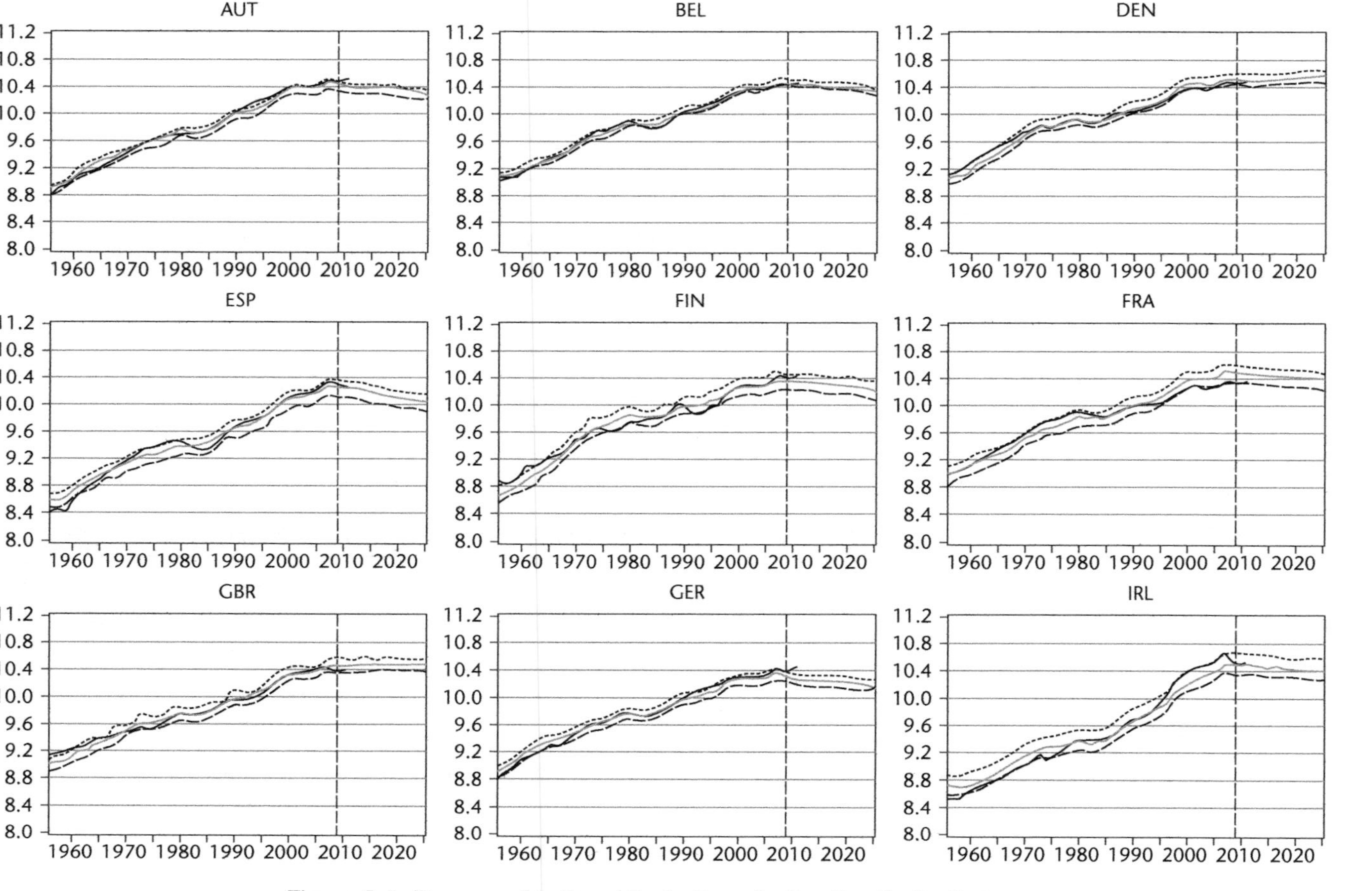


**Figure 5.4.** Demographic-Based Projections for Log Per Capita Output.

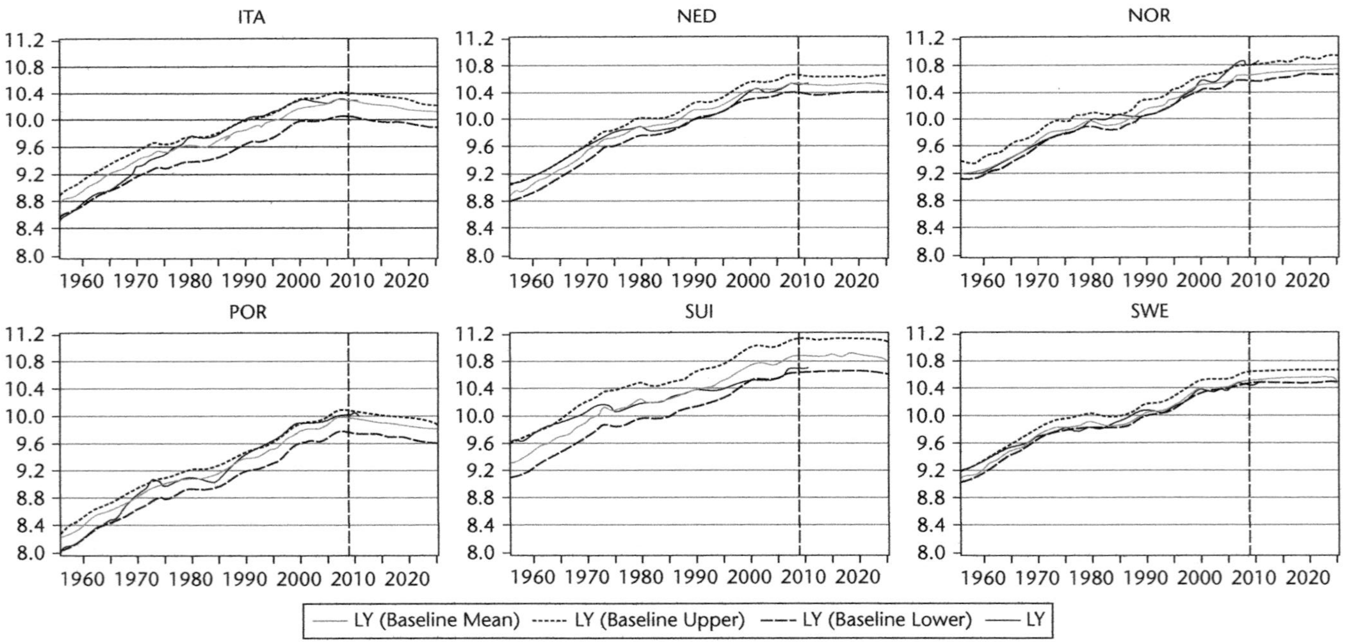


**Figure 5.4.** Continued

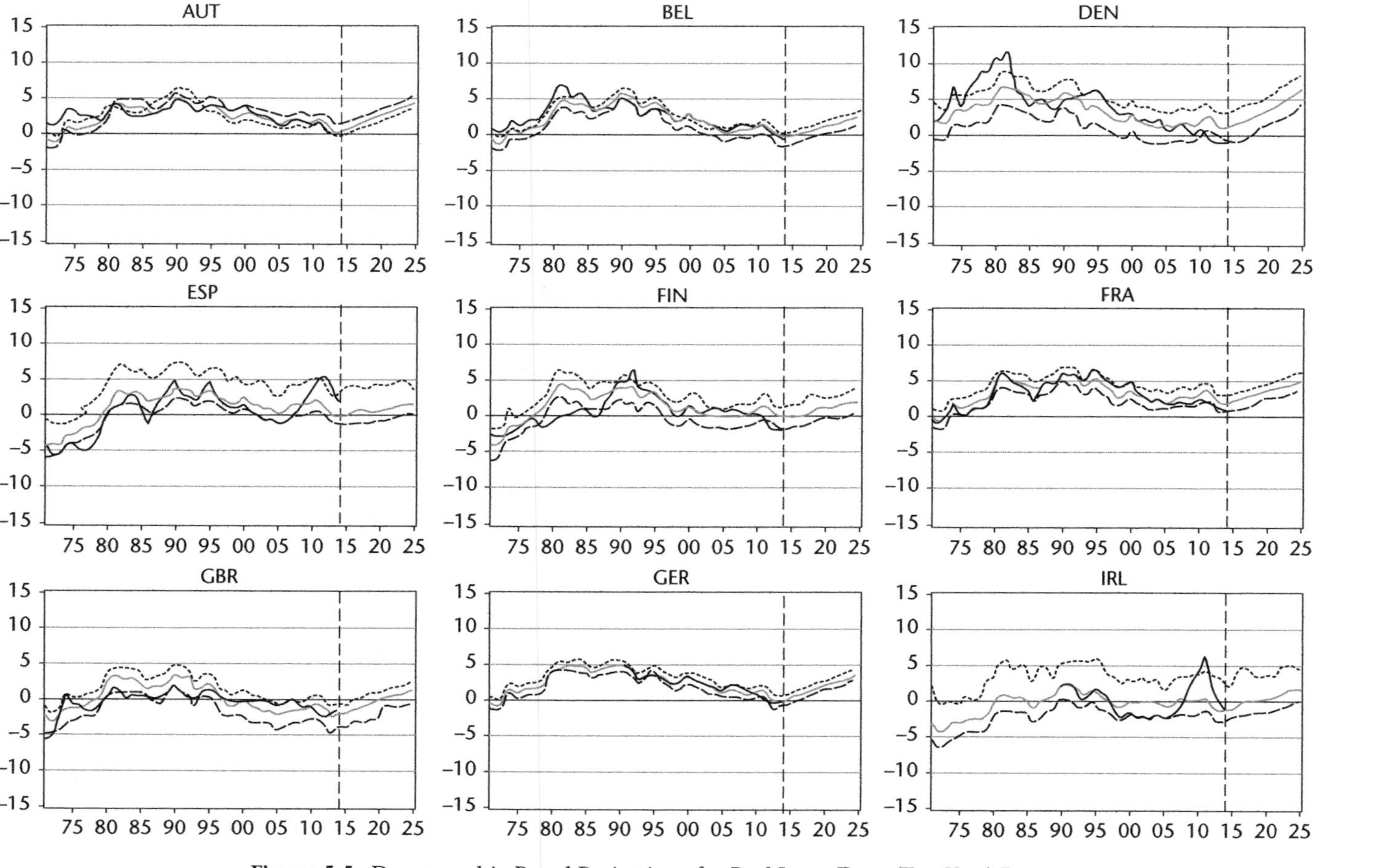


**Figure 5.5.** Demographic-Based Projections for Real Long-Term (Ten-Year) Rates.

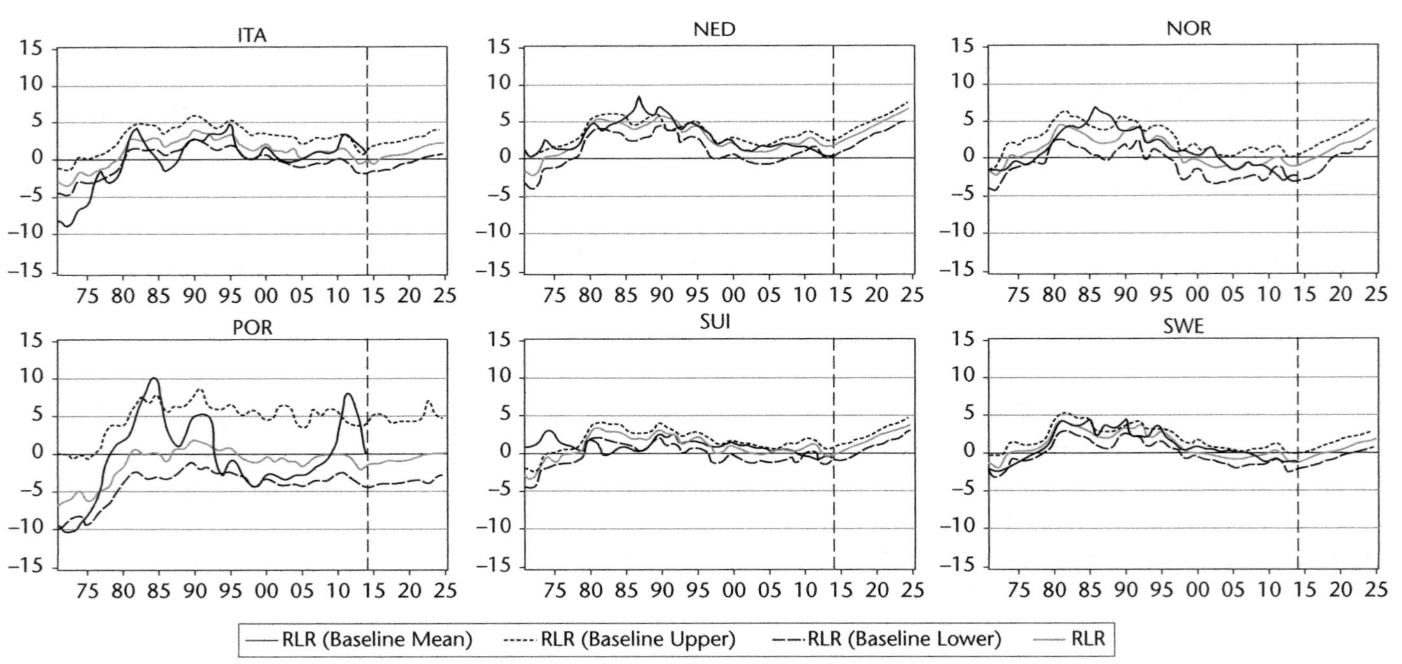


**Figure 5.5.** Continued

### 5.3.1. *Demographic Structure and Real Rates: Some Further Evidence*

The evidence reported on demographics and real rates so far for all countries in our sample is based only on domestic demographic factors. However, domestic debt is also held by foreign investors and therefore our results can be affected by the omission of demographic trends that are relevant to determine the share of domestic debt held by foreigners.

We address this issue by considering an alternative construction of our shares. Given the availability of data on foreign holdings of sovereign debt in advanced economies (Ali Abbas et al., 2014; Arslanalp and Tsuda, 2012), we have reconstructed the population of debt holders for each country as the weighted average of domestic and world population with time-varying weights determined by the share of domestic debt held abroad. Over the estimation sample we have adopted the sum of the population in Europe, USA and Japan as the relevant world population, while in the out-of-sample simulation we have also included China to determine the relevant world population aggregate. We have therefore implictly assumed that demographic changes in China have been so far less relevant than demographic changes in individual EU countries in the determination of bond prices, but we have removed this assumption for future projections. Importantly, although the composition of the relevant population changes from the estimation period to the out-of-sample simulation period, the share of domestic debt held abroad out-of-sample is kept fixed at the last within sample observation.

Table 5.2 shows that the patterns of the coefficients of the shares and of the stochastic mortality trends using the domestic population and the relevant world population are similar. Figure 5.6 illustrates that out-of-sample real

**Table 5.2.** Demographic-Based Projections for Real Interest Rates

| Real Interest Rate, Seemingly Unrelated Regression (SURE), 1971–2014 | | | | |
|---|---|---|---|---|
| | Coefficient | Std. Error | t-Statistic | Prob. |
| $a_{0-19}$ | 19.05117 | 1.873710 | 10.16762 | 0.0000 |
| $a_{20-39}$ | 24.50064 | 1.975536 | 12.40202 | 0.0000 |
| $a_{40-59}$ | 17.96599 | 2.017357 | 8.905707 | 0.0000 |
| $a_{60+}$ | 21.73423 | 1.525143 | 14.25062 | 0.0000 |
| $k_t$ | –0.139914 | 0.007949 | –17.60123 | 0.0000 |
| **Real Interest Rate, Seemingly Unrelated Regression (SURE), 1971–2013** | | | | |
| | Coefficient | Std. Error | t-Statistic | Prob. |
| $a_{0-19}$ | 44.71629 | 12.59162 | 3.551273 | 0.0004 |
| $a_{20-39}$ | 64.88732 | 12.14674 | 5.341952 | 0.0000 |
| $a_{40-59}$ | 24.03895 | 9.293653 | 2.586598 | 0.0100 |
| $a_{60+}$ | 32.71870 | 7.426528 | 4.405652 | 0.0000 |
| $k_t$ | –0.116852 | 0.007655 | –15.26486 | 0.0000 |

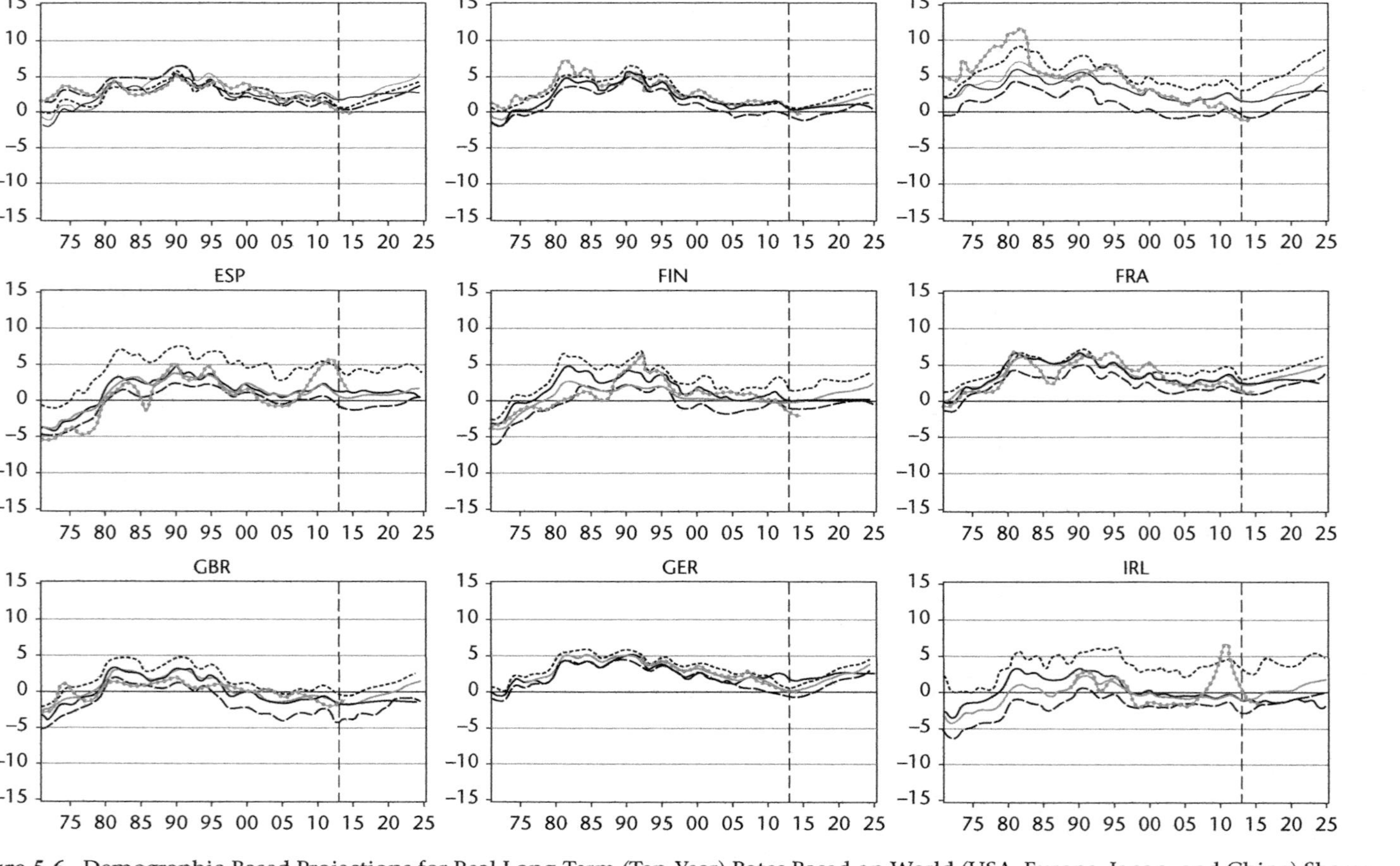


**Figure 5.6.** Demographic-Based Projections for Real Long-Term (Ten-Year) Rates Based on World (USA, Europe, Japan, and China) Shares.

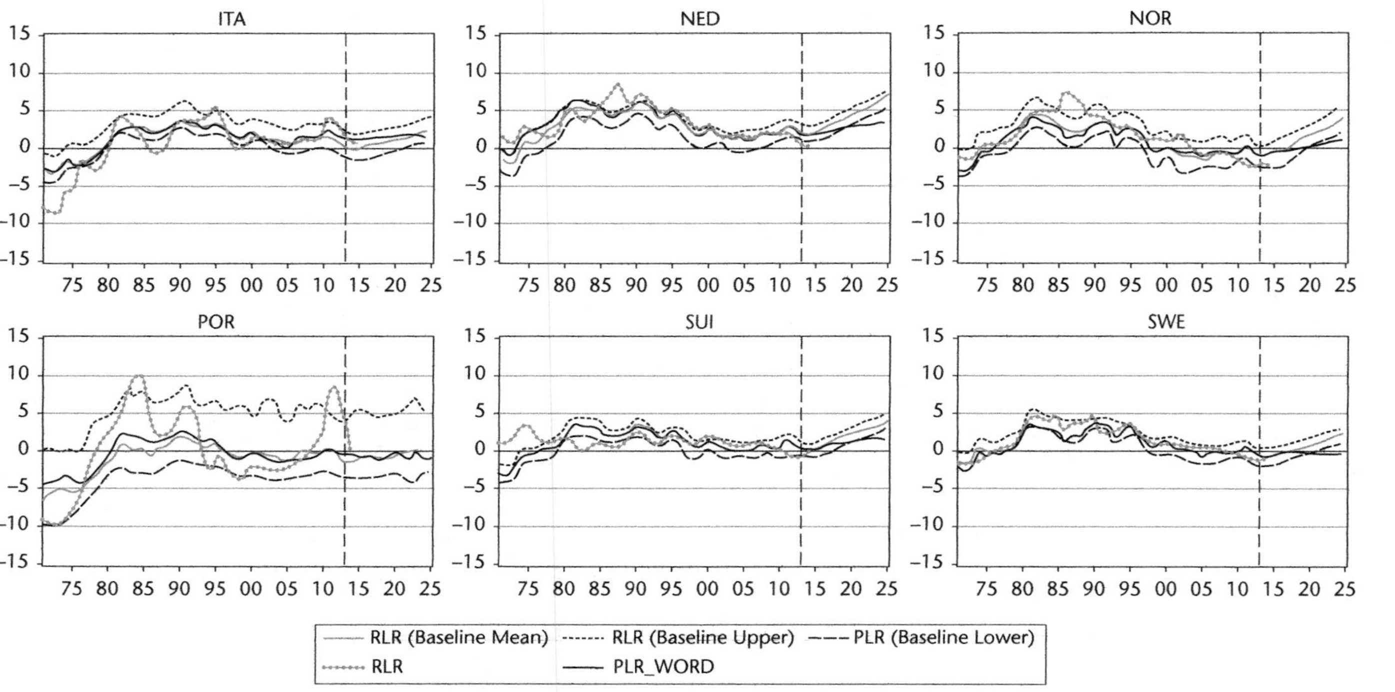


**Figure 5.6.** Continued

rates projected using the shares in the relevant world population (including China) are not very different from our baseline projections based on the domestic population shares, although in general real rates are projected at a positive but lower level than those in the baseline simulation.

## 5.4. Age Structure, Productivity, and Labour Markets

During the last few decades, particularly in Europe, the quest for more economic growth has often been associated with the need for structural reforms (see Eggertsson et al., 2014, for a critical review of this argument). Deep institutional changes took place in the nineties, such as the creation of the European Single Market or the adoption of the euro, which limited the role played by fiscal and monetary policy in accommodating national shocks. As a result, large emphasis has been attributed to more structural, microeconomic adjustments, needed to reduce the rigidities in the labour and product markets and ultimately to foster competition in output and input markets, and to increase economic efficiency (Nicoletti and Scarpetta, 2003). Several contributions discussed how structural reforms would have been incentivized by the introduction of the Euro (see Bean, 1998; Obstfeld, 1997), while others were more critical (Saint-Paul and Bentolila, 2000).

In the last two decades, a growing literature has analysed these structural reforms. Many contributions have highlighted the pattern of liberalization in product, labour, and financial markets in different countries. As shown in Figure 5.7, which displays the magnitude of the liberalization process between 1975 and 2013, product market regulations, as measured by the OECD index (see Conway and Nicoletti, 2006), have dropped, albeit to a different degree, in several countries. Besides the UK, which represented an early mover, most European countries began to liberalize their product market in the nineties following the introduction of the EU's internal market programme and of the Euro (see Alesina et al., 2009). Liberalization of the labour market, as measured by the Employment Protection Legislation (EPL) index (OECD, 2006) has instead proved to be more difficult to achieve. As shown in Figure 5.8, which displays the degree of EPL in 1985 and in 2013 for regular workers, few countries have reduced labour market rigidities for regular workers, although some liberalizations have instead taken place for the temporary workers.

Other contributions have focused on the economic and political determinants of the structural reforms.

Large emphasis has been given to the incentive provided by institutional changes, such as entrance into the European Single Market or the adoption of the euro. Alesina et al. (2009) found that the adoption of the Euro increased

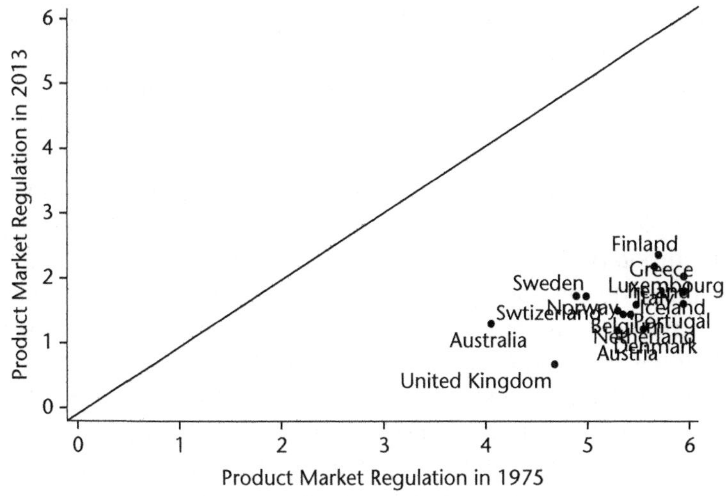


**Figure 5.7.** Convergence in Product Market Regulation.

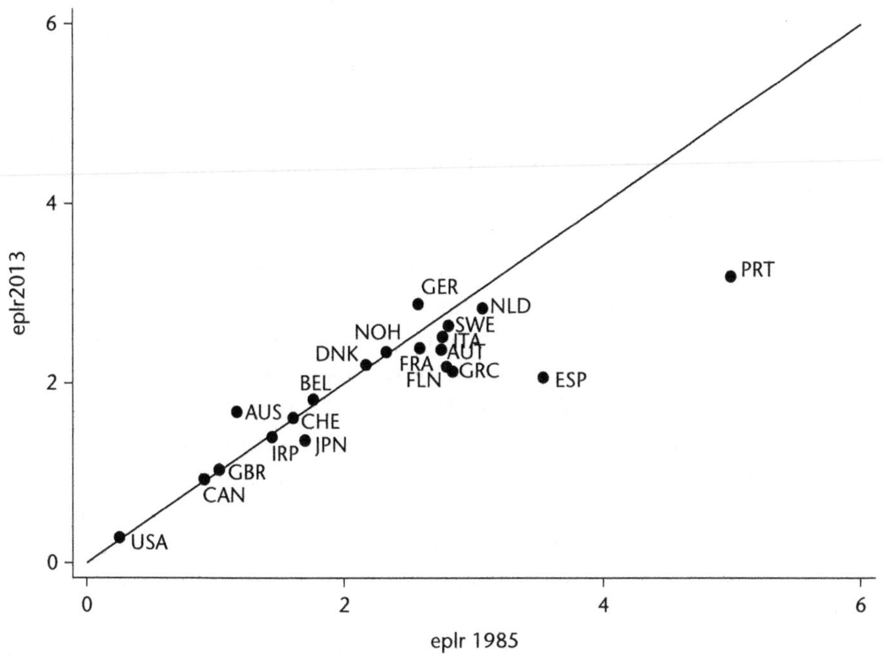


**Figure 5.8.** Labour Market Reforms.

the deregulations in the product market, particularly in countries such as France and Italy, and sectors such as energy and communication, which featured higher initial levels of regulation. The adoption of the euro was instead not associated with major reforms in the labour market.

Economic crises have been shown to lead to labour market reforms (IMF, 2004; Duval and Elmeskov, 2005; Høj et al., 2006), yet with opposite effects for labour market insiders and outsiders. In particular, increases in the long-term unemployment rates are associated with lower employment protection for temporary workers and more generous unemployment benefits, but have no effect on EPL for regular workers. Countries with more rigid labour markets enjoyed more reform efforts. Economic crises are also associated to deregulation in the product markets (Høj et al., 2006). Interestingly, also good fiscal positions have been shown to be beneficial for reforms in labour and product markets (Duval and Elmeskov, 2005; IMF, 2004), perhaps because they provide the fiscal capabilities to compensate the losers from the reforms.

Unsurprisingly, politics is crucial to reform. Ideology seems to matter, as right-wing governments are more active in reforming the labour market (IMF, 2004), adopt more liberalizations in the product market, and reduce generous unemployment benefits (Høj et al., 2006). However, during an economic crisis, right-wing parties refrain from promoting privatizations, whereas centre and left-wing governments are more keen on liberalizing and privatizing (Galasso, 2014). Finally, Buti et al. (2008) find no empirical support for the idea that reforming governments pay an electoral cost.

Little emphasis has instead been given to the role played by demographic variables, besides perhaps controlling for the share of the elderly in the empirical studies. In this chapter, we instead give a closer look at how demographic elements may affect structural reforms. We augment the standard panel regressions used in this literature (IMF, 2004; Høj et al., 2006) with two different types of demographic indicators. First, we include a trend to capture the aging process. In one set of regressions, we consider a simple linear time trend; in another set of regression, we instead use the mortality trend estimated in Section 5.2. While this latter trend is perhaps more accurate, it has the drawback of reducing the number of observations for the empirical analysis, as three countries are dropped from the sample. Second, we include a set of dummy variables to capture the age structure of the population. We consider the relative share of the population in four age groups: zero to nineteen, twenty to thirty-nine, forty to fifty-nine, and sixty plus, as displayed in Figure 5.3.

On a theoretical ground, there are at least two channels through which the age composition of the population may affect the structural reforms. An economic channel will consist of the impact that changes in the age composition may have on the (economic) costs and benefits of the status quo or of the reforms. A political channel will instead be given by how changes in the age composition affect the political representation, and thereby the political support for the status quo or the reforms. To see this, consider the PAYG pension systems. Population ageing induces an increase in the share of the elderly, and a contemporaneous drop in the share of the young workers. The economic channel would thus suggest pension generosity to be reduced, to secure the financial sustainability of a Pay As You Go (PAYG) pension scheme. Yet, in the political arena, a larger share of elderly increases the political support for generous pension schemes. In this case, ageing thus has opposite economic and political effects (see Galasso, 2006).

### 5.4.1. *Data Description*

In our empirical analysis, we examine the structural reforms in product and labour markets, and in the welfare state. We restrict the analysis to eighteen European countries, more specifically to Austria, Belgium, Denmark, Finland, France, Germany, Greece, Iceland, Ireland, Italy, Luxembourg, Netherlands, Norway, Portugal, Spain, Sweden, Switzerland, and UK.[4]

For the product market, reforms are measured as changes in the OECD indicators of sectoral product market regulation. These indicators were constructed by Conway and Nicoletti (2006) and later updated. We consider indicators for energy, communications, and transport from 1975 to 2013. These product market regulation indicators summarize information about entry regulation, public ownership, market structure, vertical integration, and price controls with reference to these three sectors, which are composed of seven industries: (i) energy (electricity, gas); (ii) communications (telecoms, post), and (iii) transport (rail, air transport, and road). A score, on a scale from 0 to 6, is attributed to each regulatory aspect, where the lowest possible score stands for the maximum deregulation. As in Høj et al. (2006), an overall regulation indicator that excludes public ownership index is used.

For labour market reforms, we use OECD indicators of strictness of employment protection. These indicators are intended to measure the legally envisaged constraints that employers face in hiring or firing workers. Data are available for the 1985–2013 period. On a scale from 0 to 6, they quantify three specific aspects of labour market regulation: (i) procedural inconveniences; (ii) notice and severance payment requirements; and (iii) difficulty of dismissal, such as litigation costs, restrictions on firing, due compensation for unfair dismissal. These indicators refer to permanent workers (EPLR), to temporary workers (EPLT), that is, those workers hired on fixed-term or temporary work agency contracts, and to an average of the two (EPL). The

[4] Greece, Iceland, and Luxembourg are dropped when we use the mortality trend.

OECD provides data also on union density, from 1975 to 2013, which we use in our regressions.

Unfortunately, OECD statistics do not provide long-series data on other labour market policies. We thus rely on the Comparative Welfare Entitlements Dataset assembled by Scruggs et al. (2014) to obtain comparable data on national welfare programmes for our sample of countries over 1970–2011. In particular, we have data on three social insurance programmes: Unemployment Insurance, Sick Pay Insurance, and Public Pension. Unemployment insurance consists only of national insurance provisions, and pensions include only mandatory public programmes. For the sick pay insurance, which consists of the benefits paid in case of temporary non-occupational illness or injury, we consider both public provisions and provisions for mandatory private benefits. For each of these three social insurance programmes, information on benefit replacement rates, qualifying conditions, and coverage are collected and aggregated into benefit generosity scores.

For product and labour markets, variations in the respective indicators denote structural reforms. A negative variation in indicator for product and labour market regulation represents deregulation. Our welfare state indicators denote instead generosity.

Consistently with previous empirical studies on structural reforms, we consider several control variables. We include in our regressions, economic crisis, measured as one standard deviation reduction in output gap, a dummy variable, respectively, for the adoption of the European Single Market (singlemkt) and of the euro (emu), a measure of the country openness, the logarithm of the real per-capita GDP, and a dummy variable for a right-wing government in power. Table 5.3 provides the summary statistics relative to our measures of labour and product market regulation, welfare state generosity, and to these control variables.

### 5.4.2. *Results*

Table 5.4 shows the results of our panel regression for the product market using year and country fixed effects, and, respectively, the linear and the mortality trend. The age composition of the population turns out to be an important determinant of reforms in the product market. In particular, a larger share of individuals of working age—namely aged twenty to thirty nine and even more forty to fifty-nine—is associated with a strong reduction in the overall product market regulator indicator. These results are robust to using linear or mortality trend.

Why would a larger share of the working population be associated with more product market reforms? Different interpretations can be provided. A first, static explanation hinges on the observation that the sectors measured

**Table 5.3.** Summary Statistics

| Variables | Num Obs | Mean | St. Deviation | Min | Max |
|---|---|---|---|---|---|
| pmr | 702 | 3.929957 | 1.619784 | 0.68 | 5.96 |
| transport | 612 | 3.55492 | 1.708931 | 0.6111111 | 6 |
| communication | 702 | 3.770726 | 1.802306 | 0.7 | 6 |
| energy | 344 | 3.576885 | 1.688385 | 0.7816667 | 6 |
| epl | 476 | 2.320998 | 0.9092663 | 0.64 | 4.19 |
| eplt | 476 | 2.223592 | 1.358306 | 0.25 | 5.25 |
| eplr | 476 | 2.418403 | 0.7766565 | 1.03 | 5 |
| tradeun | 679 | 43.94204 | 21.85163 | 7.55 | 99.07 |
| uegen | 577 | 10.24385 | 2.699466 | 2.6 | 14.5 |
| skgen | 576 | 11.74167 | 3.091419 | 5.3 | 18.2 |
| pgen | 540 | 12.17907 | 1.857389 | 7.2 | 17.1 |
| finreform | 465 | 14.65108 | 5.378197 | 1 | 21 |
| privatization | 465 | 1.647312 | 1.11239 | 0 | 3 |
| crisisgap | 614 | 0.0993485 | 0.2993733 | 0 | 1 |
| emu | 702 | 0.6666667 | 0.4717406 | 0 | 1 |
| single market | 700 | 0.4414286 | 0.4969126 | 0 | 1 |
| openess | 651 | 0.9070469 | 0.6702533 | 0.146074 | 4.43126 |
| GDP log | 651 | 26.38578 | 1.47732 | 22.13217 | 28.8467 |
| right | 646 | 0.3931889 | 0.4888367 | 0 | 1 |
| linear trend | 702 | 20 | 11.26265 | 1 | 39 |
| mortality trend | 585 | −13.01138 | 16.73193 | −54.13894 | 16.16084 |
| share 20–39 | 648 | 0.2913678 | 0.0197512 | 0.2424523 | 0.3325609 |
| share 40–59 | 648 | 0.2479392 | 0.0255655 | 0.1781538 | 0.3108268 |
| share 60+ | 648 | 0.1954618 | 0.0266706 | 0.1271392 | 0.2650315 |

in the OECD product market regulation index are all non-manufacturing sectors. Hence, the rents associated with the dominant positions in sectors such as energy or transportation translate into higher costs for other manufacturing industries, and perhaps to lower employment opportunities. Thus, a larger share of the working population, which is to some extent negatively affected by these higher costs, may put pressure for liberalizing on the non-manufacturing sectors. A second, more dynamic explanation relies on the idea that microeconomic adjustments induce long-term growth, although they have current costs for those employers and employees who benefit from the rents associated with the dominant market position. In this case, a larger share of workers—particularly the younger ones—may tilt the aggregate preferences more towards future growth perspectives.

The age composition of the population seems to matter also for the labour market reforms, as shown in Table 5.5. The overall employment protection drops as the share of the young individuals—aged twenty to thirty-nine—increases (columns 1 and 5). Unsurprisingly, this effect is mostly driven by the deregulation for the temporary contracts (columns 2 and 6). This evidence thus suggests that an increase in the share of young individuals, who represent potential entrants into the labour market, puts pressure on designing reforms that may indeed facilitate their entry. It is also interesting

**Table 5.4.** Product Market Regulation

| VARIABLES | (1) pmr | (2) transport | (3) communication | (4) energy | (5) pmr | (6) transport | (7) communication | (8) energy |
|---|---|---|---|---|---|---|---|---|
| lagged dependent | 0.793*** | 0.765*** | 0.832*** | 0.849*** | 0.799*** | 0.756*** | 0.827*** | 0.860*** |
| | (0.0383) | (0.0502) | (0.0340) | (0.0387) | (0.0383) | (0.0524) | (0.0374) | (0.0393) |
| L.crisisgap | −0.0512 | −0.00766 | −0.0804* | −0.0128 | −0.0649** | 0.000217 | −0.0961* | 0.00287 |
| | (0.0333) | (0.0467) | (0.0470) | (0.0696) | (0.0320) | (0.0468) | (0.0495) | (0.0690) |
| emu | 1.079*** | 1.399** | 0.474 | 2.202 | 1.084*** | 1.582*** | 0.293 | 2.618* |
| | (0.277) | (0.542) | (0.365) | (1.403) | (0.291) | (0.546) | (0.388) | (1.555) |
| single market | −0.0874** | −0.169** | 0.0304 | 4.398 | −0.129*** | −0.176** | 0.0520 | −0.475 |
| | (0.0427) | (0.0821) | (0.0579) | (3.549) | (0.0487) | (0.0834) | (0.0639) | (1.025) |
| L.openness | −0.0407 | 0.257** | −0.272** | −0.828*** | −0.163** | 0.173 | −0.311** | −0.816*** |
| | (0.0844) | (0.123) | (0.126) | (0.247) | (0.0827) | (0.125) | (0.130) | (0.265) |
| L.gdplog | 0.452*** | 0.623** | 0.184 | 0.737 | 0.435*** | 0.685*** | 0.0734 | 0.955 |
| | (0.137) | (0.258) | (0.184) | (0.749) | (0.142) | (0.261) | (0.194) | (0.855) |
| L.right | −0.0229 | −0.0148 | −0.00961 | 0.0312 | −0.00256 | 0.00900 | −0.000974 | 0.0160 |
| | (0.0165) | (0.0284) | (0.0241) | (0.0434) | (0.0165) | (0.0275) | (0.0277) | (0.0389) |
| linear trend | −0.0202*** | −0.0294*** | −0.00941* | −0.141 | | | | |
| | (0.00508) | (0.00820) | (0.00570) | (0.107) | | | | |
| mortality trend | | | | | 0.00444* | 0.00508 | 0.00606 | 0.00198 |
| | | | | | (0.00241) | (0.00410) | (0.00400) | (0.00788) |
| share 20–39 | −3.302*** | −4.070*** | −0.914 | −13.36*** | −3.109*** | −4.089*** | −0.465 | −14.44*** |
| | (0.650) | (1.244) | (0.813) | (4.722) | (0.646) | (1.229) | (0.856) | (5.124) |
| share 40–59 | −7.710*** | −8.778*** | −5.436*** | −10.23*** | −6.502*** | −8.675*** | −5.051*** | −10.30*** |
| | (1.615) | (2.521) | (1.961) | (3.349) | (1.442) | (2.541) | (1.916) | (3.551) |
| share 60+ | −0.623 | 0.817 | −2.199** | −3.485 | −0.295 | 1.008 | −2.317** | −3.260 |
| | (0.672) | (1.192) | (1.106) | (4.301) | (0.687) | (1.220) | (1.137) | (4.301) |
| constant | −8.773** | −13.34** | −2.295 | −12.75 | −8.783** | −15.18** | 0.526 | −18.84 |
| | (3.429) | (6.468) | (4.792) | (20.63) | (3.647) | (6.583) | (5.112) | (23.91) |
| number of countries | 18 | 18 | 18 | 18 | 15 | 15 | 15 | 15 |
| country fixed effects | yes | yes | yes | yes | yes | yes | yes | yes |
| year fixed effects | yes | yes | yes | yes | yes | yes | yes | yes |
| observations | 509 | 445 | 509 | 235 | 453 | 430 | 453 | 220 |
| R-squared | 0.990 | 0.979 | 0.983 | 0.987 | 0.991 | 0.980 | 0.983 | 0.989 |

Robust standard errors in parentheses

*** p<0.01, ** p<0.05, * p<0.1

**Table 5.5.** Labour Market Regulation

| VARIABLES | (1)<br>epl | (2)<br>eplt | (3)<br>eplr | (4)<br>tradeun | (5)<br>epl | (6)<br>eplt | (7)<br>eplr | (8)<br>tradeun |
|---|---|---|---|---|---|---|---|---|
| lagged dependent | 0.891*** | 0.909*** | 0.851*** | 0.923*** | 0.886*** | 0.903*** | 0.848*** | 0.942*** |
| | (0.0389) | (0.0366) | (0.0986) | (0.0166) | (0.0431) | (0.0409) | (0.0992) | (0.0114) |
| L.crisisgap | 0.0101 | −0.00183 | 0.0207 | −0.0321 | 0.00936 | −0.00388 | 0.0207 | 0.0839 |
| | (0.0225) | (0.0414) | (0.0142) | (0.154) | (0.0226) | (0.0411) | (0.0144) | (0.148) |
| emu | 0.526* | 0.669 | 0.251 | −2.735 | 0.900** | 1.416** | 0.191 | −2.066 |
| | (0.274) | (0.486) | (0.218) | (2.719) | (0.394) | (0.709) | (0.255) | (2.142) |
| single market | 0.00930 | 0.0323 | −0.00683 | −0.0281 | 0.00850 | 0.0312 | −0.00791 | −0.259 |
| | (0.0319) | (0.0610) | (0.0116) | (0.322) | (0.0321) | (0.0614) | (0.0120) | (0.195) |
| L.openness | −0.0103 | 0.0240 | −0.0204 | −0.00858 | −0.0758 | −0.103 | −0.0101 | −0.326 |
| | (0.0523) | (0.0892) | (0.0356) | (0.813) | (0.0614) | (0.101) | (0.0386) | (0.549) |
| L.gdplog | 0.201* | 0.300 | 0.0106 | −1.456 | 0.392** | 0.689** | −0.0237 | −1.016 |
| | (0.122) | (0.229) | (0.0916) | (1.361) | (0.183) | (0.348) | (0.103) | (1.090) |
| L.right | 0.00732 | 0.0197 | −0.00353 | −0.0322 | 0.00112 | 0.00561 | −0.00373 | −0.250** |
| | (0.0152) | (0.0285) | (0.00908) | (0.147) | (0.0140) | (0.0254) | (0.00892) | (0.109) |
| linear trend | −0.00666** | −0.0115* | 0.00172 | −0.0864** | | | | |
| | (0.00315) | (0.00594) | (0.00272) | (0.0341) | | | | |
| mortality trend | | | | | −0.00381 | −0.00830 | 0.000977 | −0.00207 |
| | | | | | (0.00330) | (0.00637) | (0.00147) | (0.0185) |
| share 20–39 | −1.372** | −1.857 | −0.830 | 6.170 | −1.919** | −2.960* | −0.739 | 7.732 |
| | (0.694) | (1.209) | (0.582) | (5.715) | (0.898) | (1.661) | (0.660) | (5.309) |
| share 40–59 | −0.350 | −0.110 | −0.993 | 17.06 | −0.900 | −1.290 | −0.921 | 20.08** |
| | (1.445) | (2.636) | (0.670) | (10.35) | (1.682) | (3.187) | (0.736) | (8.549) |
| share 60+ | −1.467* | −1.992 | −1.531 | 19.97*** | −1.380* | −1.786 | −1.548 | 23.08*** |
| | (0.804) | (1.348) | (1.307) | (5.852) | (0.782) | (1.293) | (1.344) | (5.276) |
| constant | −4.628 | −7.174 | 0.659 | 35.44 | −9.734** | −17.55** | 1.598 | 20.77 |
| | (3.020) | (5.746) | (2.474) | (36.47) | (4.587) | (8.753) | (2.715) | (28.63) |
| number of countries | 18 | 18 | 18 | 18 | 15 | 15 | 15 | 15 |
| country fixed effects | yes | yes | yes | yes | yes | yes | yes | yes |
| year fixed effects | yes | yes | yes | yes | yes | yes | yes | yes |
| observations | 360 | 360 | 360 | 507 | 343 | 343 | 343 | 452 |
| R-squared | 0.985 | 0.975 | 0.993 | 0.998 | 0.987 | 0.978 | 0.993 | 0.999 |

Robust standard errors in parentheses

*** $p<0.01$, ** $p<0.05$, ** $p<0.1$

**Table 5.6.** Welfare State

| VARIABLES | (1)<br>uegen | (2)<br>skgen | (3)<br>pgen | (4)<br>uegen | (5)<br>skgen | (6)<br>pgen |
|---|---|---|---|---|---|---|
| lagged dependent | 0.838*** | 0.860*** | 0.931*** | 0.837*** | 0.856*** | 0.933*** |
| | (0.0319) | (0.0475) | (0.0211) | (0.0318) | (0.0482) | (0.0212) |
| L.crisisgap | 0.210** | 0.0431 | 0.0136 | 0.205** | 0.0412 | 0.00985 |
| | (0.0911) | (0.0606) | (0.0626) | (0.0890) | (0.0609) | (0.0629) |
| emu | 0.886 | 1.206* | 0.693 | 1.161 | 1.536* | 0.656 |
| | (0.957) | (0.722) | (0.861) | (1.064) | (0.800) | (0.786) |
| single market | −0.318*** | −0.107 | −0.166* | −0.312*** | −0.104 | −0.165* |
| | (0.106) | (0.0718) | (0.0849) | (0.105) | (0.0721) | (0.0849) |
| L.openness | −0.198 | −0.0913 | −0.0908 | −0.184 | −0.0976 | −0.116 |
| | (0.277) | (0.261) | (0.195) | (0.278) | (0.264) | (0.198) |
| L.gdplog | 0.343 | 0.515 | 0.279 | 0.502 | 0.695 | 0.254 |
| | (0.489) | (0.390) | (0.435) | (0.559) | (0.441) | (0.393) |
| L.right | −0.00762 | 0.0517 | −0.0951** | −0.00956 | 0.0522 | −0.0895** |
| | (0.0518) | (0.0502) | (0.0380) | (0.0545) | (0.0524) | (0.0391) |
| linear trend | −0.0264* | −0.0226** | 0.00219 | | | |
| | (0.0142) | (0.0111) | (0.00933) | | | |
| mortality trend | | | | −0.00808 | −0.00643 | 0.00244 |
| | | | | (0.00772) | (0.00617) | (0.00676) |
| share 20–39 | 2.419 | 0.992 | 0.105 | 1.738 | 0.393 | 0.228 |
| | (1.884) | (2.151) | (2.039) | (1.912) | (2.073) | (1.941) |
| share 40–59 | 10.20*** | 2.475 | −1.288 | 10.20*** | 2.522 | −0.996 |
| | (3.886) | (2.911) | (3.688) | (3.870) | (2.879) | (3.751) |
| share 60+ | 10.47*** | 5.695** | 0.159 | 10.29*** | 5.684** | 0.135 |
| | (2.398) | (2.520) | (2.164) | (2.368) | (2.490) | (2.145) |
| constant | −12.91 | −14.86 | −6.638 | −17.03 | −19.61 | −6.065 |
| | (12.99) | (10.50) | (11.17) | (14.90) | (11.92) | (10.12) |
| number of countries | 18 | 18 | 18 | 15 | 15 | 15 |
| country fixed effects | yes | yes | yes | yes | yes | yes |
| year fixed effects | yes | yes | yes | yes | yes | yes |
| observations | 464 | 463 | 450 | 449 | 448 | 435 |
| R-squared | 0.981 | 0.989 | 0.960 | 0.980 | 0.988 | 0.958 |

Robust standard errors in parentheses
*** $p<0.01$, ** $p<0.05$, * $p<0.1$

to notice that the degree of union density (columns 4 and 8) is increasing in the share of the elderly—aged sixty plus, most of whom are indeed retired—and thereby out of the labour force. This evidence is, however, consistent with the drop in union density among the current young workers, and may indeed be driven by a cohort effect, with past generations of workers being more heavily unionized. As before, these results are robust to using a linear or mortality trend.

Table 5.6 presents our evidence on the generosity of three social insurance programmes, namely unemployment insurance, sick pay insurance, and public pensions. An increase in the share of the 'older' working population, aged forty to fifty-nine, is associated with more generous unemployment benefits. Indeed, even a larger share of the elderly—aged sixty years old or more—

is correlated with more unemployment benefits. This is, however, not very surprising, as many elderly workers have used unemployment insurance as an early pathway out of the labour market. All these individuals, albeit to different degrees, thus seem to support more generous unemployment insurance system. The support for more generous sick pay insurance is instead stronger among the elderly. Perhaps surprisingly, the generosity of the pension system—a programme clearly targeted at the elderly—is not affected by the age composition. This may well be because of the opposite economic and political effects of ageing. In other words, while the elderly would support a more generous pension scheme, the ageing process makes it financially impossible to sustain such a system.

## 5.5. The Political Economy of the Age Structure of Population

Two different schools of thought have recently emerged on how to exit from the current economic crisis and on the determinants of growth. Several scholars and institutions—including the Governor of the European Central Bank, Mario Draghi—have emphasized the crucial role of structural reforms in fostering competition in the product and labour markets. These microeconomic adjustments are deemed to be necessary to increase economic efficiency (Nicoletti and Scarpetta, 2003). This is particularly the case in the southern European countries strongly hit by the crisis, in which larger price adjustments are needed. Other scholars have instead argued that the current crisis needs to be addressed with macroeconomic adjustments. Eggertsson et al. (2014) go even further to suggest that structural reforms may indeed prove detrimental in the short run, if decreases in wages lead to deflationary policies that cannot be accommodated by the central bank with a reduction in the interest rate. Gali and Monacelli (2014) have remarked that structural reforms, when asymmetric across countries, require asymmetric monetary policy to accompany them. Such policies cannot be implemented in a common currency area.

Regardless of the relative merits of these two arguments, however, Section 5.4 suggests that there may be political economy motivations to support one school of thought or the other. And these motivations are likely to differ mainly across generations.

To address this intergenerational issue, we use data from the Eurobarometer, a survey run by the European Commission, to learn the opinions of the citizens in the EU countries on several issues. We exploit the 2014 Eurobarometer survey for the seventeen countries examined in the analysis in Section 5.4 (we have no data for Switzerland) on three broad issues: reforms, competition, and globalization. The questions asked in the Eurobarometer

**Table 5.7.** Reforms

| VARIABLES | (1) need of reforms | (2) preference for reform | (3) preference for liberalization | (4) preference for flexibility |
|---|---|---|---|---|
| male | −0.0506*** | −0.0286** | −0.167*** | −0.0579*** |
| | (0.0116) | (0.0128) | (0.0185) | (0.0167) |
| single | 0.0177 | 0.0125 | 0.0605*** | 0.0510*** |
| | (0.0120) | (0.0133) | (0.0194) | (0.0176) |
| manager | 0.000458 | −0.0834*** | −0.0954*** | −0.133*** |
| | (0.0203) | (0.0216) | (0.0301) | (0.0268) |
| employed | 0.0229 | −0.0244 | −0.0750*** | −0.0889*** |
| | (0.0153) | (0.0172) | (0.0247) | (0.0224) |
| self-employed | −0.0516** | −0.0981*** | −0.101*** | −0.152*** |
| | (0.0245) | (0.0265) | (0.0356) | (0.0326) |
| middle age | −0.0141 | 0.0420** | 0.102*** | 0.119*** |
| | (0.0149) | (0.0168) | (0.0238) | (0.0214) |
| old | −0.0145 | −0.0146 | 0.196*** | 0.232*** |
| | (0.0163) | (0.0180) | (0.0266) | (0.0241) |
| left | −0.0273* | 0.0113 | 0.0367 | 0.0382* |
| | (0.0153) | (0.0171) | (0.0242) | (0.0223) |
| right | −0.0126 | 0.0459** | −0.162*** | 0.00767 |
| | (0.0196) | (0.0208) | (0.0285) | (0.0265) |
| middle class | −0.0905*** | −0.152*** | −0.278*** | −0.200*** |
| | (0.0133) | (0.0146) | (0.0209) | (0.0188) |
| upper class | −0.148** | −0.391*** | −0.372*** | −0.339*** |
| | (0.0718) | (0.0716) | (0.104) | (0.0900) |
| constant | 1.861*** | 2.367*** | 2.834*** | 2.250*** |
| | (0.0380) | (0.0455) | (0.0744) | (0.0488) |
| number of countries | 17 | 17 | 17 | 17 |
| country FE | yes | yes | yes | yes |
| observations | 14927 | 14691 | 16105 | 15605 |
| R-squared | 0.093 | 0.078 | 0.054 | 0.112 |

Robust standard errors in parentheses
*** p<0.01, ** p<0.05, * p<0.1

allow us to obtain information on the individual perceptions about the relevance of reforms, competition, and globalization for economic growth, as well as on their preferences for reforms, free trade, liberalization, and competition. We regress the individual responses to these questions on several individual characteristics, such as gender, marital status, employment status, self-declared social status, and political orientation, and of course on an age indicator. In particular, in all regressions, we identify the individuals younger than forty years old as our reference group, and include middle aged (forty to fifty-nine) and old (sixty plus) among the regressors. We always use country fixed effects to exploit only within country variation.

Table 5.7 presents the results of our empirical analysis on the reforms. In column (1), we consider as dependent variable the individual responses to a question in which individuals assign a value between 1 (totally agree) and 4 (totally disagree) to the following statement 'Our country needs reforms to face the future.' Awareness of the need for reforming is higher among males,

**Table 5.8.** Competition

| VARIABLES | (1) industrial competition | (2) preference for competition |
|---|---|---|
| male | 0.0266 | −0.163*** |
| | (0.0295) | (0.0153) |
| single | −0.143*** | 0.0534*** |
| | (0.0308) | (0.0161) |
| manager | −0.0212 | −0.0656*** |
| | (0.0521) | (0.0244) |
| employed | 0.0615 | −0.0760*** |
| | (0.0392) | (0.0207) |
| self-employed | 0.190*** | −0.119*** |
| | (0.0628) | (0.0298) |
| middle age | 0.168*** | 0.0595*** |
| | (0.0388) | (0.0196) |
| old | 0.298*** | 0.109*** |
| | (0.0414) | (0.0223) |
| left | −0.121*** | 0.0968*** |
| | (0.0418) | (0.0203) |
| right | 0.155*** | −0.110*** |
| | (0.0492) | (0.0237) |
| middle class | 0.279*** | −0.187*** |
| | (0.0334) | (0.0173) |
| upper class | 0.535*** | 0.306*** |
| | (0.148) | −(0.0859) |
| constant | 7.272*** | 2.289*** |
| | (0.0969) | (0.0643) |
| number of countries | 17 | 17 |
| country FE | yes | yes |
| observations | 14912 | 16105 |
| R-squared | 0.054 | 0.066 |

Robust standard errors in parentheses
*** p<0.01, ** p<0.05, * p<0.1

the self-employed, and among middle and upper class individuals, while no difference emerges across age groups. Columns (2), (3), and (4) show instead the results related to individual preferences for reforms, liberalization, and flexibility. For these questions, individuals assign a value between 1 (very positive) and 4 (very negative) to the following statement: 'Could you please tell me whether the following term—respectively *reforms* for column (2), *liberalization* for column (3), and *flexibility* for column (4)—brings to mind something very positive, fairly positive, fairly negative, or very negative?' In all three cases, males, managers, self-employed, and middle and upper class individuals tend to have a more positive view. Preferences strongly differ by age groups. For middle age individuals, reforms, liberalization, and flexibility are considered strongly more negatively than for the young. And the same holds true for the old, except for the case of reforms.

In Table 5.8, we show the results for our empirical analysis on competition. Column (1) reports the results related to the question in which individuals assign a value between 1 (not at all important) and 10 (very important) to the following statement 'Please tell me how important or not you think in order for the EU to exit the present financial and economic crisis and prepare for the next decade is to help the EU's industrial base to be more competitive by promoting entrepreneurship and developing new skills.' Unsurprisingly, self-employed, middle and upper class individuals endorse the relevance of competition to exit the crisis. Individuals with right-wing political views also believe competition to be important, while left-wing individuals do not. A, perhaps surprising, difference emerges also across age groups: middle age, and even more elderly individuals deem competition to be relevant more than young individuals do. This awareness by the elderly, however, does not translate into more preference for competition. Column (2) shows the results related to individual responses to the following statement: 'Could you please tell me whether *competition* brings to mind something very positive, fairly positive, fairly negative or very negative?', where 1 indicates very positive and 4 very negative. Consistently with the answer to the previous question (column 1), self-employed, right-wing, and middle and upper class individuals tend to have a more positive view of competition. Middle aged and elderly individuals instead have a more negative view of competition than the young, despite the fact that they seem to be aware of its relevance for economic growth.

Finally, in Table 5.9, we concentrate our empirical analysis on globalization. Column (1) reports the results related to the Eurobarometer question in which individuals assign a value between 1 (totally agree) and 4 (totally disagree) to the following statement 'Globalization is an opportunity for economic growth'. Males, managers, and middle and upper class individuals are more likely to agree with this statement; left-wing and singles to disagree. A strong difference about the merit of globalization emerges also by age group, as middle aged and elderly individuals strongly disagree with the above statement. Columns (2) and (3) report the results of the individual responses to the following statement: 'Could you please tell me whether *globalization* (column 2) or *free trade* (column 3) bring to mind something very positive, fairly positive, fairly negative, or very negative?', where 1 indicates very positive and 4 very negative. Consistently with the previous answers, middle aged and elderly individuals view globalization and free trade more negatively than the young.

In a nutshell, our analysis with Eurobarometer data suggests that, regardless of their awareness on the relevance of reforms, competitiveness, and globalization for economic growth, middle aged and elderly individuals have much stronger views against reforms, liberalization, flexibility, competitiveness, globalization, and free trade than the young may have. These findings are consistent with the idea that structural reforms in the labour and product

**Table 5.9.** Globalization

| VARIABLES | (1) globalization | (2) preference for globalization | (3) preference for free trade |
|---|---|---|---|
| male | 0.0564*** | 0.154*** | 0.233*** |
| | (0.0135) | (0.0176) | (0.0173) |
| single | 0.0502*** | 0.0844*** | 0.0757*** |
| | (0.0141) | (0.0185) | (0.0182) |
| manager | 0.0716*** | 0.132*** | 0.0607** |
| | (0.0225) | (0.0287) | (0.0287) |
| employed | 0.00276 | 0.0571** | 0.0437* |
| | (0.0181) | (0.0236) | (0.0232) |
| self-employed | 0.0125 | 0.0983*** | 0.0775** |
| | (0.0284) | (0.0343) | (0.0332) |
| middle age | 0.177*** | 0.226*** | 0.0971*** |
| | (0.0174) | (0.0228) | (0.0223) |
| old | 0.170*** | 0.332*** | 0.185*** |
| | (0.0189) | (0.0252) | (0.0250) |
| left | 0.0836*** | 0.00705 | 0.0464** |
| | (0.0185) | (0.0229) | (0.0228) |
| right | 0.0312 | 0.0492* | 0.156*** |
| | (0.0224) | (0.0284) | (0.0274) |
| middle class | 0.194*** | 0.286*** | 0.233*** |
| | (0.0156) | (0.0200) | (0.0197) |
| upper class | 0.220** | 0.509*** | 0.366*** |
| | (0.0953) | (0.109) | (0.106) |
| constant | 2.216*** | 2.965*** | 2.558*** |
| | (0.0527) | (0.0540) | (0.0522) |
| number of countries | 17 | 17 | 17 |
| country FE | yes | yes | yes |
| observations | 14,110 | 15,605 | 15,605 |
| R-squared | 0.145 | 0.091 | 0.064 |

Robust standard errors in parentheses
*** p<0.01, ** p<0.05, * p<0.1

markets, as well as the retrenchment of the welfare state, have clear redistributive consequences. Labour market liberalizations may increase hiring, but they reduce the degree of production of the insiders. Analogously, less generous unemployment benefits reduce the degree of insurance for those workers who were initially protected. As a clear age cleavage emerges among labour market insiders and outsiders, these labour market policies may benefit the younger generation but they tend to impose a cost on the elderly workers. Our empirical results on both aggregate outcome and individual perceptions are in line with this interpretation. Product market deregulations instead reduce the economic rents enjoyed in these protected markets. Economic theory suggests that these rents are shared between employees and employers active in the protected sectors. Also product market liberalizations thus have redistributive consequences. To the extent that elderly workers in these protected sectors are able to extract more rents, again an age cleavage may emerge. The same age divide would emerge in the preferences for welfare state retrenchment, as in most countries—particularly in Southern Europe—current social spending is massively targeted to the elderly. Finally, to the extent that structural reforms are able to spur future growth, the main beneficiaries of this economic growth would still be the young generations. As a result, structural reforms may obtain the political support of the young generations, but they most likely get the opposition of the elderly (insiders).

Neo-Keynesian macroeconomic adjustments, on the other hand, may be less divisive, to the extent that all generations are allowed to benefit from more public spending and easier access to credit. However, given the large influence that elderly and insiders have on the political process that allocates public resources, these macroeconomic adjustments would most likely benefit the older generations, rather than the younger ones. Moreover, our evidence on real rates and demographic structure does not support the concern of the existence of a negative equilibrium for real rates that cannot be achieved in the presence of a zero lower bound on policy rates.

## 5.6. Conclusions

The main tenet of secular stagnation is that negative real interest rates are needed to equate saving and investment with full employment. Demographics is often referred to as one of the potential causes of secular stagnation. In this chapter we have addressed the relationship between the age structure of population and long-term growth and real rates. We have estimated a standard model of mortality, the Lee–Carter model, to generate a mortality trend for fifteeen European countries and combine it with the projected age structure of population to generate long-term projections for the trend in output per capita and real interest rates for euro area economies. Our evidence shows that demographic-based projections deliver for the next twenty years a lower long-run potential growth rate but a reversion of real interest rates to their historical mean. Within this framework, policies for growth become of crucial importance and we therefore address the debate on structural reforms versus macroeconomic adjustment.

On the basis of this evidence, we have assessed the role of the age structure in promoting or hindering reforms in labour and product markets, which have been advocated to increase long-term growth. Our results suggest that the implementation of such reforms will not be facilitated by the age structure of population. In a world of ageing population, structural reforms should obtain the political support of the young generations, but they will most likely get the opposition of the elderly.

Our evidence on the feasibility of Neo-Keynesian macroeconomic adjustment given projected positive real rates paired with the projection for an increasing share of the old age bracket leads us to conclude that, given the large influence that elderly and insiders have on the political process that allocates public resources, these macroeconomic adjustments would most likely benefit the older generations, rather than the younger ones. Different policy recipes may have different intellectual and academic backgrounds, but they also seem to have different redistributive consequences. It should thus not be surprising if the older countries—in terms of share of elderly people—lean more towards macroeconomic adjustments, whereas younger nations—again in terms of population share—are more supportive of structural reforms.

*Acknowledgements*

Gualtiero Azzalini and Vito Gervasi provided excellent research assistance. Vincenzo Galasso acknowledges financial support from Progetto MIUR-PRIN year 2010–11 protocol number 2010T8XAXB_008.

## 5.7. Appendix

### A.5.1. Data Sources

Series for Expenditure-side Real GDP at Chained PPP (Millions of 2005 US$) and Total Population (Millions) were downloaded from the Penn World Table 8 database. Data for Long-Term Nominal Interest Rates, Nominal and Real GDP (OECD base year i.e. 2005) in national currencies were downloaded from the databases in OECD Statistics. Data on GDP from OECD were used to compute the GDP deflator. Series for population's age structure were obtained by combining databases from the U.N. Population Division and the US Census Bureau. Data on mortality were downloaded from The Human Mortality Database.

### A.5.2. Identification and Estimation of the Lee–Carter Model

The Lee–Carter (1992) model consists of a system of equations for logarithms of mortality rates for age cohort $x$ at time $t$, $\ln[m_{x,t}]$, and a time-series equation for an unobservable time-varying mortality index $k_t$:

$$
\begin{aligned}
\ln\left(m_{x,t}\right) &= a_x + b_x k_t + \epsilon_{x,t} \\
k_t &= c_0 + c_1 k_{t-1} + e_t \\
\epsilon_{x,t} &\sim NID\left(0, \sigma_\epsilon^2\right) \\
e_t &\sim \text{MeanZero - Stationary Process}
\end{aligned}
\tag{5.3}
$$

where $a_x$ and $b_x$ are age-specific constants. The error term $\epsilon_{x,t}$ captures cross-sectional errors in the model based prediction for mortality of different cohorts, while the error term $e_t$ captures random fluctuations in the time series of the common factor $k_t$ driving mortality at all ages. Identification of the parameters of interest is achieved by imposing the restrictions $\sum_t k_t = 0$ and $\sum_x b_x = 1$, so that the unobserved mortality index $k_t$ is estimated through Singular Value Decomposition (S.V.D.). S.V.D. is a technique based on a theorem of linear algebra stating that a $(m \times n)$ rectangular matrix $M$ can be broken down into the product of three matrices - an $(m \times m)$ orthogonal matrix $U$, a diagonal $(m \times n)$ matrix $S$, and the transpose of an orthogonal $(n \times n)$ matrix $V$. The S.V.D. of the matrix $M$ will be therefore be given by $M = USV'$ where $U'U = I$ and $V'V = I$. The columns of $U$ are orthonormal eigenvectors of $AA'$, the columns of $V$ are orthonormal eigenvectors of $A'A$, and $S$ is a diagonal matrix whose elements are the square roots of eigenvalues from $U$ or $V$ in descending order. The restriction $\sum_t k_t = 0$ implies that $a_x$ is the average across time of $\ln(m_{x,t})$, and Equation 5.3 can be rewritten in terms of the mean-centered log-mortality rate as

$$m_{x,t} - \overline{m}_{x,t} \equiv \tilde{m}_{x,t} = b_x k_t + \epsilon_{x,t}. \tag{5.4}$$

Grouping all the $\tilde{m}_{x,t}$ in a unique $(X \times T)$ matrix $\tilde{m}$ (where the columns are mortality rates at time-$t$ ordered by age groups and the rows are mortality rates through time for a specific age-group $x$), leads naturally to use S.V.D. to obtain estimates of $b_x$ and $k_t$. In particular, if $\tilde{m}$ can be decomposed as $\tilde{m} = USV'$, $b = [b_0, b_1, \ldots, b_X]$ is represented by the normalized first column of U, $u_1 = [u_{0,1}, u_{1,1}, \ldots, u_{X,1}]$, so that

$$b = \frac{u_1}{\sum_{x=0}^{X} u_{x,1}}.$$

On the other hand the mortality index vector $k = [k_1, k_2, \ldots, k_T]$ is given by

$$k = \lambda_1 (\sum_{x=0}^{X} u_{x,1}) v_1$$

where $v_1 = [v_{1,1}, v_{1,2}, \ldots, v_{1,T}]'$ is the first column of the V matrix and $\lambda_1$ is the highest eigenvalue of the matrix $S$ (see Girosi and King, 2007; Giacometti et al., 2010) where $v_1 = [v_{1,1}, v_{1,2}, \ldots, v_{1,T}]'$ is the first column of the V matrix and $\lambda_1$ is the highest eigenvalue of the matrix $S$.

## 5.8. References

Aksoy, Y., H. S. Basso, T. Grasl, and R. P. Smith (2015), 'Demographic Structure and Macroeconomic Trends', mimeo Birkbeck College, University of London.

Alesina, A., S. Ardagna, and V. Galasso (2009), 'The Euro and Structural Reforms', in A. Alesina and F. Giavazzi (eds.) *Europe and the Euro*, University of Chicago Press and NBER.

Bean, C. (1998), 'The Interaction of Aggregate-Demand Policies and Labour-Market Reform'. *Swedish Economic Policy Review* 5: 353–82.

Bloom, D. E., D. Canning, and J. Sevilla (2003), 'The Demographic Dividend: a new perspective on the economic consequences of population change', RAND.

Buti, M., A. Turrini, P. van den Noord, and P. Biroli (2008), 'Defying the Juncker Curse: Can Reformist Governments Be Re-Elected?' *European Economy Economic Papers* 324.

Conway, P. and G. Nicoletti (2006), 'Product Market Regulation in the Non-Manufacturing Sectors of OECD Countries: Measurement and Highlights', *OECD Economics Department Working Paper* No. 530.

Duval, R. and J. Elmeskov (2005), 'The Effects of EMU on Structural Reforms in Labour and Product Markets', *OECD Economics Department Working Papers* No. 438.

Eggertsson, G., A. Ferrero, and A. Raffo (2014), 'Can structural reforms help Europe?', *Journal of Monetary Economics* 61: 2–22.

Galasso, V. (2006), *The Political Future of Social Security in Aging Societies*, The MIT Press.

Galasso, V. (2014), 'The role of political partisanship during economic crises', *Public Choice* 158: 143–65.

Gali, J. and T. Monacelli (2014), 'Understanding the Gains from Wage Flexibility: the Exchange Rate Connection', available at www.igier.unibocconi.it/monacelli.

Giacometti R., M. Bertocchi, S. T. Rachev, and F. J. Fabbozzi (2010), 'A comparison of the Lee-Carter model and AR-ARCH model for forecasting mortality rates', Working Paper.

Girosi, F. and G. King (2007), 'Understanding the Lee-Carter mortality forecasting method', Working paper.

Hansen, A. H. (1939), 'Economic Progress and Declining Population Growth', *American Economic Review* 29: 1–15.

Høj J., V. Galasso, G. Nicoletti, and T. Dang (2006), 'The Political Economy of Structural Reform: Empirical Evidence from OECD Countries', *OECD Economics Department Working Papers* No. 501.

IMF (2004), 'Fostering Structural Reforms in Industrial Countries', chapter III of World Economic Outlook: Advancing Structural Reforms, *International Monetary Fund*, Washington DC.

Lee, R. D. and R. L. Carter (1992), 'Modeling and Forecasting U.S. Mortality', *Journal of the American Statistical Association* 87: 659–71.

Nicoletti, G. and S. Scarpetta (2003), 'Regulation, Productivity and Growth: OECD Evidence', *Economic Policy* 18, No. 36.

Obstfeld, M. (1997), 'Europe's Gamble', *Brookings Papers on Economic Activity*, The Brookings Institution, Washington DC.

OECD (2006), *OECD Employment Outlook* 2006, OECD, Paris.

Robine, J., J. P. Michel, and S. Institut (2008), 'Has there been a compression of morbidity in countries with low mortality?', *Prevention of Functional Dependency*: 139–48.

Saint-Paul, G. and S. Bentolila (2000), 'Will EMU Increase Eurosclerosis?', CEPR Discussion Paper No. 2423.

Scruggs, L., D. Jahn, and K. Kuitto (2014), 'Comparative Welfare Entitlement Dataset 2, Version 2014-03. Codebook', available at http://cwed2.org/.

Teulings, C. and R. Baldwin (2014), 'Secular Stagnation: Facts, Causes and Cures', CEPR Press, A Voxeu.org ebook.

# 6

# The Crisis, the Public, and the Future of European Integration

*Jeffry Frieden*

The crisis in the Eurozone has been the greatest failure in the history of European integration. Trillions of dollars in accumulated debts have confronted the member states with a difficult set of inter-state and domestic problems, largely to do with the distribution of the burden of economic adjustment in the light of a decade of ill-advised lending and borrowing. To the discredit of both national governments and European institutions, conflict has dragged on for years—and still continues—with no real resolution. Possible Pareto improvements have fallen by the wayside as countries manoeuvre to shunt as much of the adjustment burden as possible onto their partners, and as groups within countries do the same domestically.

The dismal experience of the past several years raises fundamental questions about the future of the European Union (EU). The region's progress in economic integration, and in the creation of joint decision-making in a number of issue areas, was predicated on the willingness and ability of national governments to compromise, and to trade off concessions on some dimensions for countervailing concessions on other dimensions. In turn, these compromises were possible because domestic political conditions in the main member states were permissive. National governments can only make international compromises if there is enough domestic political support for the compromises, and for the ultimate goals of the enterprise.

European integration has been generally popular among powerful interest groups, and the mass public, for most of the time since the process began. Certainly there have been periods of greater and lesser enthusiasm, countries that are more and less positive, and groups within countries that are more Europtimistic or Eurosceptical. By the same token, the future of the EU depends on the willingness and ability of national governments, and groups within countries, to accept further compromises on a wide range of policy issues.

This chapter assesses aspects of the state of play in the politics of European integration. It focuses on the preferences of European citizens, on the principle that the domestic politics of European issues is the foundation-stone of whatever progress can be made among the member states. The emphasis is on general attitudes toward the process of economic and monetary integration; this includes trust in the institutions of the EU, and on the impact of the crisis on these attitudes.

Public opinion toward the broad process of economic integration is of central importance to the future of the EU. Although the completion of the single market made the EU a functioning economic unit on many dimensions, there is still some distance to go before the Union allows the completely free movement of goods, capital, and people. And there is always the possibility of a reversal of the levels of integration achieved to date, whether with the withdrawal of some countries or the imposition of new barriers. In addition, some would argue that the completion of the Economic and Monetary Union (EMU) requires the adoption of the euro by all, or almost all, member states. A fully integrated market is still an issue of some contention; and, perhaps just as important, attitudes toward full economic integration are closely related to attitudes toward European integration more generally. I start by looking at factors that affect preferences over economic integration, and within it monetary union; this includes the extent to which citizens trust both European and national democratic institutions. I also look at trends in popular attitudes, and in particular at how the crisis and its aftermath has affected these attitudes.

There are many theoretical perspectives on determinants of preferences toward economic integration (or globalization more generally), based on everything from factors of production or industry of employment through to levels of education. Constrained by the availability of data, I look at public opinion surveys and find that some basic economic variables—primarily educational and occupational categories—have powerful effects on these preferences. Throughout the union—more or less without regard to the country in question—those with more education, and in more skilled and professional economic activities, are more favourable to integration. There are also important differences across countries, especially in the extent to which individuals trust the EU and their own national governments.

In addition to such general findings, we are also interested in how the crisis that began in 2008 has affected the politics of European integration. I also explore the evolution of attitudes over the course of the crisis, in particular inasmuch as it differs among groups of countries. Here it is clear that the crisis has severely eroded popular faith in both national governments and the EU. Again, there is variation among groups and across countries. Less educated and less skilled citizens, along with the unemployed, are particularly disenchanted; and those in the Eurozone debtor nations are uniformly disappointed with the functioning of both their national political institutions and the institutions of the EU.

The chapter is organized as follows. In Section 6.1 I present general theoretical principles that guide the analysis, focusing on how socio-economic characteristics of individuals might affect attitudes toward European integration. Section 6.2 looks at popular attitudes toward European economic integration generally, and monetary union in particular; as well as levels of trust in the institutions of the EU. Section 6.3 focuses specifically on developments over the past decade, and in particular on the evolution of attitudes since the crisis began. Section 6.4 draws some broader implications and concludes.

## 6.1. Analytical Perspectives and Expectations

Virtually all policies have a differential impact on groups and individuals, and create both winners and losers. These distributional patterns can have a powerful impact on politics. In considering the future of European integration, and of the euro, it is important to attempt to understand patterns of expected costs and benefits—and hence support and opposition—that are likely to develop. In this section, I attempt to outline some analytical principles that can help us think about the future course of European politics.

I consider a variety of factors that may explain variation in support for European integration, largely focusing on socio-economic considerations. These are hardly exhaustive of all the complex considerations that affect national, class, group, and individual attitudes towards the EU, but they do play an important role, particularly with respect to economic policy.

Much of the debate over European integration is, like similar debates elsewhere over globalization, about the reduction of barriers to the movement of goods, capital, and people across borders.[1] In the European case, this has to do with the creation and completion of the single market, a process that goes back to the earliest years of the EU. In many ways the single market is now complete, but there are still areas in which it is a work in progress; and there are continuing concerns in some sections of the population about the single market itself. Migration is not free throughout the EU, although policy has been moving in that direction. While capital flows freely throughout the union, the fragmentation of financial regulation can be seen as a regulatory barrier of sorts, although again the EU is moving in the direction of more centralized and harmonized financial regulation. In addition, citizens of the

[1] Of course, it also has to do with the delegation of policies from the national to the European level, an issue that I do not address directly here.

member states have to form judgements as to how the institutions of the monetary union and of the EU more generally are functioning.

The broader point is that for many, attitudes toward the EU are closely related to attitudes toward the greater integration of the member economies, and toward the functioning of the institutions that manage the Union. To understand the sources of these attitudes, we can rely upon an enormous literature that analyses sources of preferences over trade, finance, investment, and immigration.

The simplest starting point is the enormous literature on trade policy, which suggests factors that would lead individuals and groups to support (or oppose) more openness to international trade. As trade is a substitute for factor movements, we can assume that similar distributional considerations apply to the broader issue of economic integration more generally—and, in this case, of European economic integration.

The predominant trade-theoretic approach to explaining cleavages on this issue emphasizes how close the individual, firm, or group is to the country's comparative advantage. Leaving aside debates within the literature, and simplifying wildly, this would tend to suggest a simple division. Industries in rich (core) countries that make intensive use of capital and skilled labour are expected to be pro-integration, while industries in poorer (peripheral) countries that make intensive use of unskilled and semi-skilled labour should also be pro-integration (and vice versa, in both cases).[2]

However, analyses of support for 'globalization', or economic integration more generally, have tended to gravitate toward a somewhat different distributional cleavage. Some combination of economic integration and skill-biased technological change appear to have advantaged higher-skilled workers in virtually all countries. There is substantial evidence for this even in developing countries, and certainly within the EU—indeed, the fact that economic integration does not appear to have benefited low-skill workers in quite a few poorer countries is one troublesome feature of the modern international economy. In the European context, this tendency is probably heightened by the fact that high-skill workers have, or may come to have, the option of migrating to core countries where there is substantial demand for their services. Its relevance is similarly accentuated by the relatively small differences among EU member states (compared with between developed and developing countries) and by the extremely high level of intra-industry and intra-firm trade within the EU.

[2] This skips over the debate between Stolper-Samuelson and specific-factors approaches. For our purposes, they both imply, in one way or another, that there should be a fundamental difference between rich and poor countries with respect to the patterns of policy preferences. It also abstracts from the impact of factor supply on the EU's trade with the rest of the world, which adds another layer of complexity—also ignored here.

A related, but more detailed, approach is to look specifically at the activities and interests of particular industries and firms rather than at broad trends in factor supply. In this light, those industries, firms, and employees whose activities are strongly oriented toward, and depend on, cross-border (intra-EU) trade and investment are likely to be the strongest supporters of continued and deepened European economic integration. This is almost certainly accurate; however, finding evidence along these lines is particularly difficult, given that the variation is often at the level of the firm. Nonetheless, this provides an additional way to understand the sources of preferences toward European economic integration.

So one set of expectations is that high-skill, high-education individuals will anticipate net benefits from European integration, as will those whose activities are closely tied to intra-European trade and investment. On the other hand, low-skilled and low-education citizens will be less enthusiastic about economic integration. Virtually all survey and electoral analyses point in this direction (e.g. Gabel and Palmer, 1995; Anderson and Reichert, 1995; Gabel, 1998; Tucker et al., 2002; see also Guiso et al. 2014).

Attitudes toward European integration generally are likely to be closely related to attitudes toward monetary integration more specifically. The single currency was expected to—and, by most accounts, did—facilitate cross-border trade, finance, investment, and migration among members of the Eurozone. At this very general level, and leaving aside the few countries (the UK, Sweden, Denmark) that have definitively decided against joining EMU, support for monetary integration can be regarded as a subset of support for economic integration more generally. We return to this point below, to sharpen the analysis.[3]

All of these general perspectives almost certainly need to be tempered by the impact of the crisis that began in 2008, and that entered into its most critical phase with the eruption of the Eurozone sovereign debt crises in 2010. Especially among countries in the Eurozone, the crisis may have changed perceptions of the impact of the EU, and especially of the euro. This is an extraordinarily complex topic, and for our purposes we focus only on one aspect of it—albeit a prominent one. Among many core Eurozone member states, which are largely the creditor countries in the Eurozone debt relationship, the single currency has come to be associated with a bail-out of troubled financial institutions and troubled debtors. Among peripheral Eurozone member states, largely the debtor countries, the single currency has come to be associated with a very deep depression and the imposition

[3] The literature on public opinion toward monetary integration is far too vast to cite here; for some examples see Banducci et al. (2009) and Kaltenthaler and Anderson (2001).

of austerity measures.[4] It can certainly be expected that dissatisfaction with the euro, and perhaps with the EU more generally, will be greater on both sides—those who feel they have been paying too much to bail out reckless banks and reckless borrowers, and those who feel they have been forced to suffer too much to atone for the sins of others. It can also be expected that reactions to the crisis will vary among groups within countries: especially in the hardest-hit countries, the burden has fallen more heavily on the unskilled and unemployed than on other categories (see, for example, Fernández-Albertos et al., 2013, and Magalhães, 2012).

In what follows I attempt to assess the correlates of support for and opposition to the general process of European economic integration. I also assess attitudes toward the euro. In both instances, I explore how the ongoing Eurozone crisis has affected preferences on both issues. I start by summarizing some of the existing literature, but rely primarily on my own analysis of survey data.

## 6.2. Views on European Integration: An Overview

Attitudes toward the broad project of European economic integration vary among countries and groups within countries. Many studies have documented the socio-economic and other attributes associated with greater or less support for economic integration. For our purposes, I emphasize material factors, recognizing that there is substantial evidence that such non-material considerations as nationalism and culture are important.[5] This is not to downplay these considerations, but to indicate that for present purposes I focus on socio-economic correlates of attitudes toward European economic integration.

A number of socio-economic factors recur in the literature. Professionals and more highly skilled workers are typically more pro-integration than unskilled workers. So too are higher levels of education correlated with more integrationist sentiment. Broad public opinion surveys typically are not detailed enough to permit investigation of the impact of the specific industry of employment, but there are some more in-depth studies of national referendums on European issues that shed light on the issue. These usually find that those in industries that are heavily oriented toward exports, foreign direct investment, as well as in the financial services sector, are most supportive

[4] I exclude from this generalization those Eurozone member states that were not directly caught up in the debt crisis (such as Malta), or that joined after the crisis had begun (e.g. the Baltic states).

[5] Jupille and Leblang (2007) provide one of the more convincing indications that even where economic factors matter, so do nationalist sentiments.

of greater economic integration.[6] These findings are consistent with broader studies of attitudes toward international economic integration writ large. The sectoral findings are largely encouraging in the sense that they tend to imply that economic integration reinforces support for itself: the more tightly tied together are the region's economies, the greater the extent of support for further integration from those who have already benefited from it.

There is plenty of country-level evidence for the important role of organized interests both in the process of European integration generally, and in movement toward Economic and Monetary Union (EMU) more specifically.[7] There have also been attempts to find generalizable proxies for such particularistic interest groups that would allow for cross-national and over-time analyses, but such proxies are not particularly convincing.[8] The consequence is that it is very difficult to carry out systematic analyses, across countries and over time, of the role of particularistic interests in the process of European integration.

As a result, in this study I rely on twenty-four Eurobarometer surveys taken since 2004. These have the advantages of asking consistent questions over time, of covering all members of the EU, and of (for most questions) covering the period up to and including the crisis years. The analytical conclusions we draw from these recent Eurobarometer surveys are well within the lines of the existing literature, especially in tending to confirm the general conclusions of prior studies about the socio-economic correlates of views on European integration. Analysis also shows that there are important nuances among groups and across countries, as well as striking trends in attitudes with the onset and course of the Eurozone sovereign debt crisis, with significant differences among groups and countries.

I start with some figures to describe the patterns and trends in attitudes toward European integration generally, and EMU specifically. Although the individual-level responses to the most general questions about support for the EU were not reported for every wave, the responses from sixteen of twenty-four waves for the membership question and fifteen of twenty-four waves for the benefit question provide sufficient information to identify general trends. I start with some descriptive figures to indicate trends, and then, in the next section, move on to more systematic statistical analysis.

[6] See especially Gabel and Palmer (1995), Gabel (1998), and Gabel (2001); Moses and Jenssen (1998) use referendum data.

[7] Moravcsik (1998) is the classic general statement; on EMU see, for example, Hefeker (1997), Duckenfield (2006), and Eglene (2011).

[8] So as not to implicate others, I can cite my own work in, for example, Frieden (2002) and Frieden (2015). Although I stand by the results, I have no doubt that the measures I use to approximate the preferences and power of special interest groups are highly suspect.

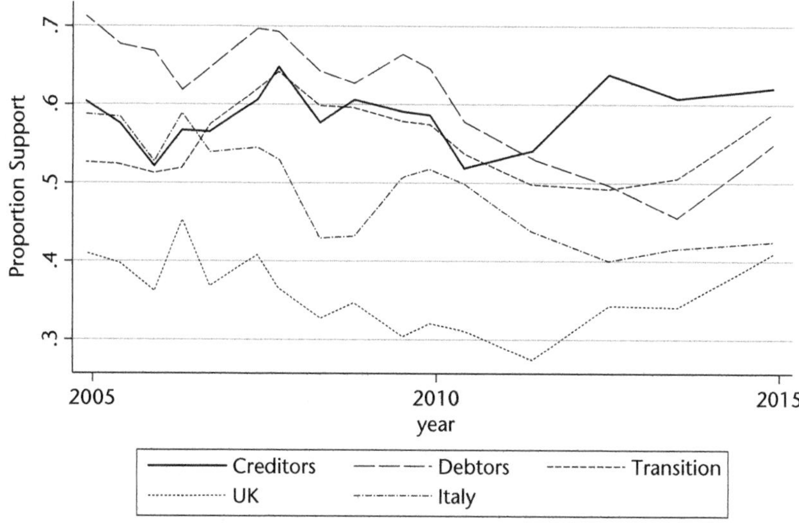


**Figure 6.1.** Support for EU Membership, by Region.
*Source*: Eurobarometer 2004–14. Weighted proportions.

Figure 6.1 shows trends between 2004 and 2014 in responses to a question about the desirability of EU membership in general, divided by country group. The question asks, specifically, 'Generally speaking, do you think that (your country's) membership of the European Union is . . . a good thing, bad thing, neither, or don't know?' Figure 6.1 indicates the percentage of respondents indicating 'a good thing'. Support for the EU is quite high outside of the UK and quite stable within creditor and newly acceded countries. Although there is a sizable decline in countries hit hard by the crisis beginning in 2010, support in debtor countries ticks up slightly in 2014. Figure 6.2 illustrates the proportion of pro-EU answers to a related question: 'Taking everything into consideration, would you say that (your country) has on balance benefited or not from being a member of the European Union?' Again, perceptions of benefit are quite high everywhere outside of the UK and quite stable within creditor and Eastern European countries. But in Italy, Greece, Spain, Portugal, and Ireland, the proportion of respondents perceiving benefit from the EU declines approximately twenty percentage points. Nonetheless, even in debtor countries a majority of respondents regard the EU as beneficial.

Surveys about attitudes toward EMU tell a related story. Figure 6.3 shows affirmative responses to a question that asks about support for 'an European economic and monetary union with one single currency, the Euro'; it demonstrates that support for monetary union has remained quite high, although gradually declining, among both debtor and creditor countries in

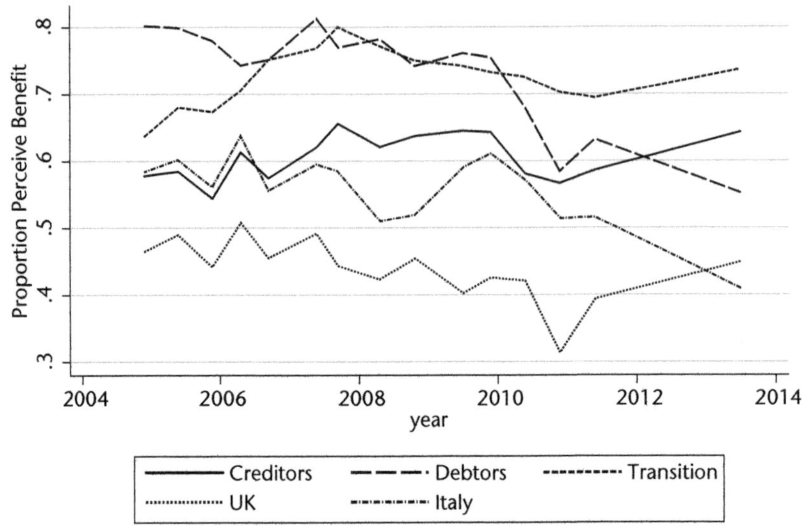


**Figure 6.2.** Benefit of EU Membership, by Region.
*Source*: Eurobarometer 2004–14. Weighted proportions.

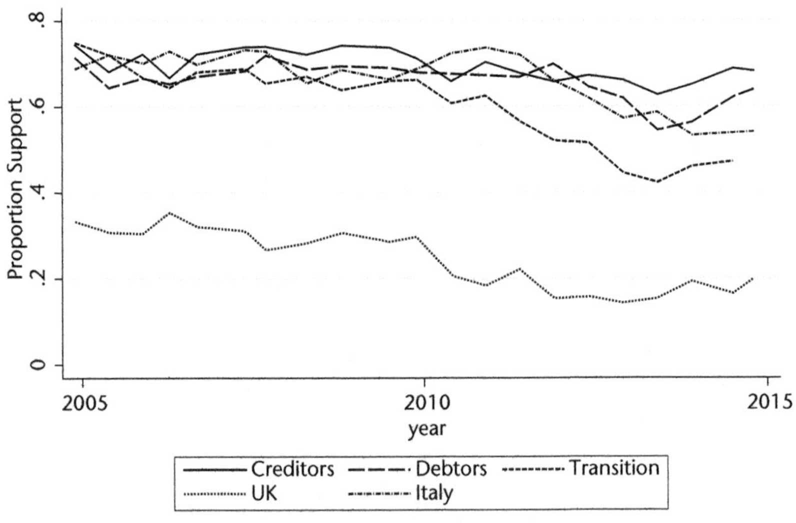


**Figure 6.3.** Support for EMU.
*Source*: Eurobarometer 2004–14. Weighted proportions.

the Eurozone; in the UK and the transition economies support has declined more rapidly.[9]

[9] Eurozone debtor countries are Ireland, Spain, Portugal, Greece, and Cyprus; Eurozone creditor countries are Germany, France, Sweden, the Netherlands, Luxembourg, Finland, Belgium, Denmark, and Austria.

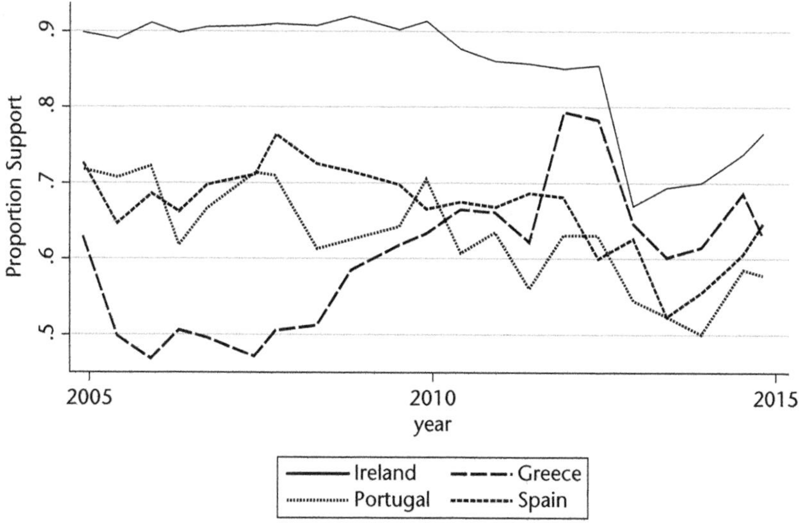


**Figure 6.4.** Support for EMU, by Eurozone Debtor Country.
*Source*: Eurobarometer 2004–14. Weighted proportions.

Figure 6.4 looks specifically at the four principal Eurozone debtor countries, and shows that support remains high. Irish support has dropped from extremely high levels, but never went below two-thirds of the population. Support in the Iberian countries also fell a bit, but remains strong; and in Greece, surprisingly, support for the euro has actually increased. These figures—the broad outlines of which are confirmed by more systematic statistical analysis below—indicate that Europeans in the Eurozone remain, despite the crisis, quite supportive of the project of monetary union. Later in this section I will show, however, that this general support for the euro is countered by deepening dissatisfaction with how the monetary union has been managed.

First, however, it is useful to illustrate some of the socio-economic divisions that are masked by broad national trends. Figure 6.5 shows attitudes toward monetary union, divided both between debtor and creditor countries and between high-education and low-education respondents. It is readily apparent that there are far more differences across educational categories than between debtor and creditor countries: that is, those with advanced education in both debtor and creditor nations are very similar in their support for EMU, whereas those with much less education are also very similar and far less supportive. In both cases, there has been a gradual decline in support, but it is not dramatic and both groups remain, on balance, positive about the euro. Figure 6.6 shows similar patterns across occupational categories.

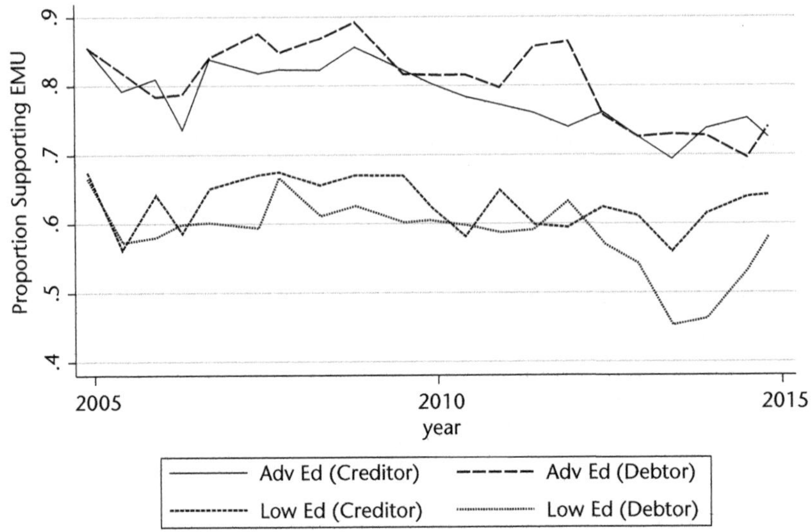


**Figure 6.5.** Support for EMU, Groups of Countries and Educational Categories.
*Source*: Eurobarometer 2004–14. Weighted proportions.

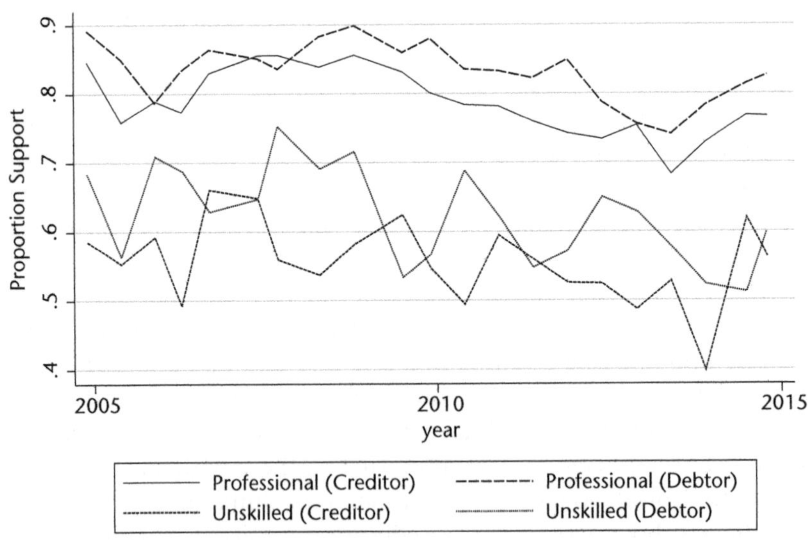


**Figure 6.6.** Support for EMU, Groups of Countries and Occupational Categories.
*Source*: Eurobarometer 2004–14. Weighted proportions.

Professionals in both creditors and debtors have been, and remain, positive about EMU; unskilled workers are much less enthusiastic, and increasingly sceptical. Whether educational levels or occupational categories are used, in any event, it is evident that attitudes toward the EU and EMU are more similar among similarly situated socio-economic groups than they are among citizens of the same country. Specifically, more educated and skilled workers are substantially more favourable to European integration than are less educated and less skilled workers.

The generally positive and relatively stable attitudes toward the EU and EMU, however, mask some more troubling trends. Eurobarometer asks respondents to indicate how much they trust the institutions of the EU, and of their national governments, and how they feel about the functioning of democracy at the EU and national level. And here the story is very different: there has been a dramatic loss of confidence in the EU, and in many national governments; this loss has been particularly concentrated among debtor nations, and among poorer, less educated, and less skilled workers.

Figure 6.7 shows the breakdown of responses to questions that ask whether individuals trust the EU and their respective national governments. There are

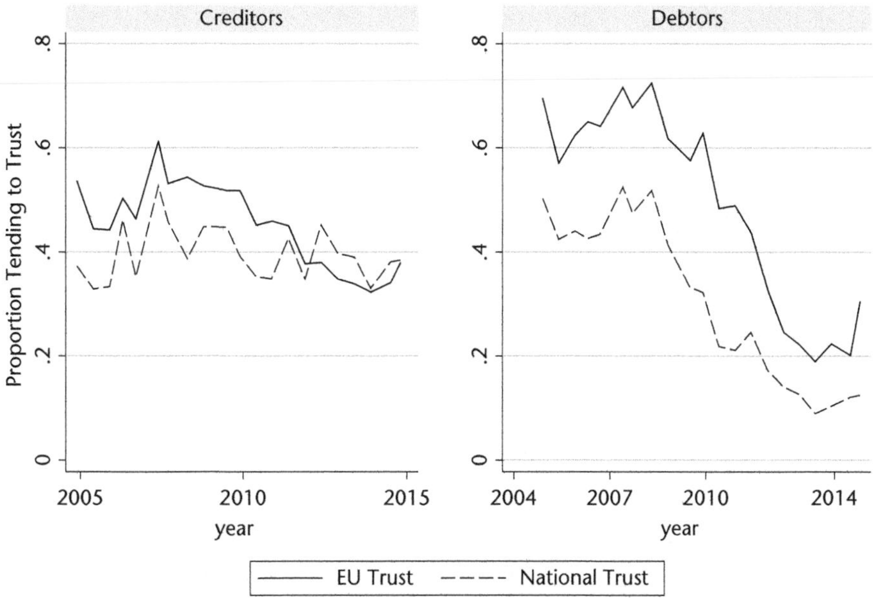


**Figure 6.7.** Trust in the EU and National Governments, by Eurozone Country Group.
*Source*: Graphs by Region.

very similar questions about attitudes toward the functioning of democracy in the EU and their respective countries; as the responses are nearly identical, I focus only on the 'trust' questions. And the results are striking.

Before the crisis, people in the Eurozone debtor economies had a great deal of trust in the EU—substantially more than in their own national governments. Even in the creditor countries, trust in the EU was a bit higher than in national governments. But matters changed dramatically with the crisis. While trust in both EU and national institutions has declined with the crisis, the collapse is remarkable in the debtor countries. In 2004, some 70% of debtor-country citizens trusted the EU and some 50% trusted their national governments; by 2014, the respective proportions hovered around 30% and 10%, respectively. This is a stunning loss of confidence in European and national institutions.

Figures 6.8–6.11 look in more detail at the loss of confidence in EU and national institutions. They confirm that, generally speaking, there is a gap between more and less educated citizens, with the less educated trusting both the EU and their national governments less (the occupational differences are less clear). And there is a general trend in creditor countries for people to trust both EU and national governments less as the crisis hits and persists. But the most striking trend is that in debtor countries, the crisis has led citizens to almost completely lose faith in the EU and their national governments. This loss of trust cuts across socio-economic and educational groups and is almost

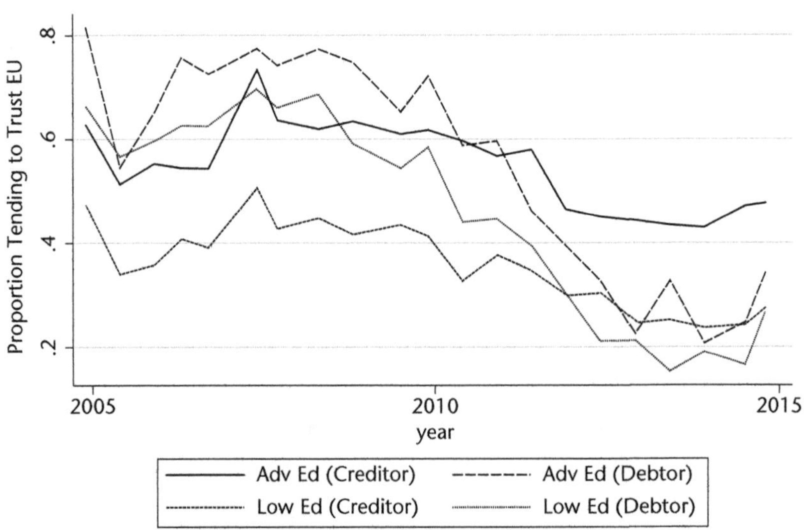


**Figure 6.8.** Trust in the EU, by Country Group and Educational Level.
*Source*: Eurobarometer 2004–14. Weighted proportions.

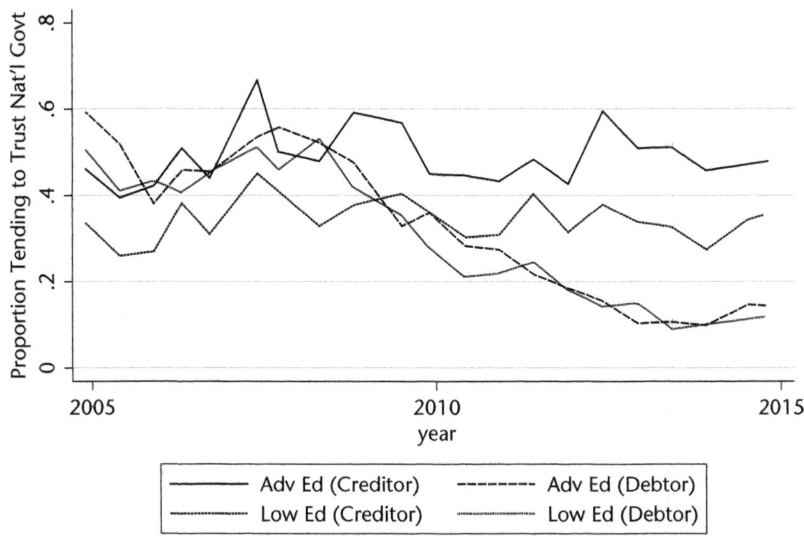


**Figure 6.9.** Trust in National Governments, by Country Group and Education Level.
*Source*: Eurobarometer 2004–14. Weighted proportions.

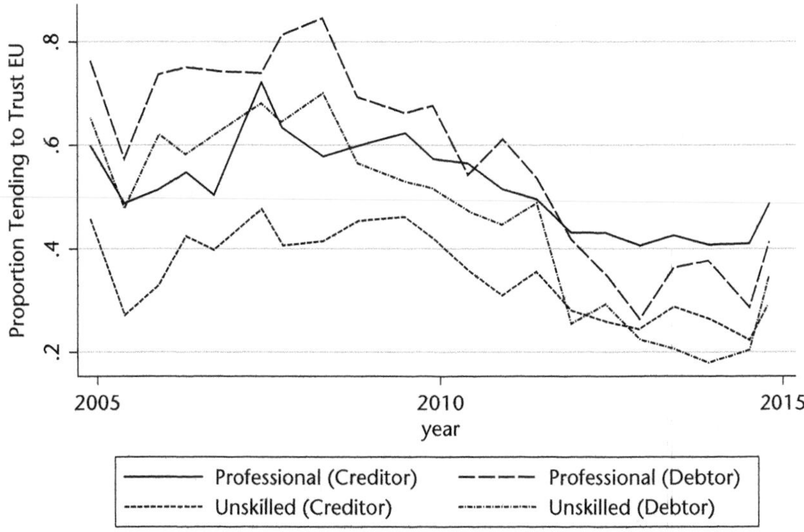


**Figure 6.10.** Trust in the EU, by Country Group and Occupational Category.
*Source*: Eurobarometer 2004–14. Weighted proportions.

complete—only small fractions of the populations have faith in the EU or their government. This is, of course, deeply disturbing for the future of both European integration and the stability of governments in the more troubled members of the Eurozone.

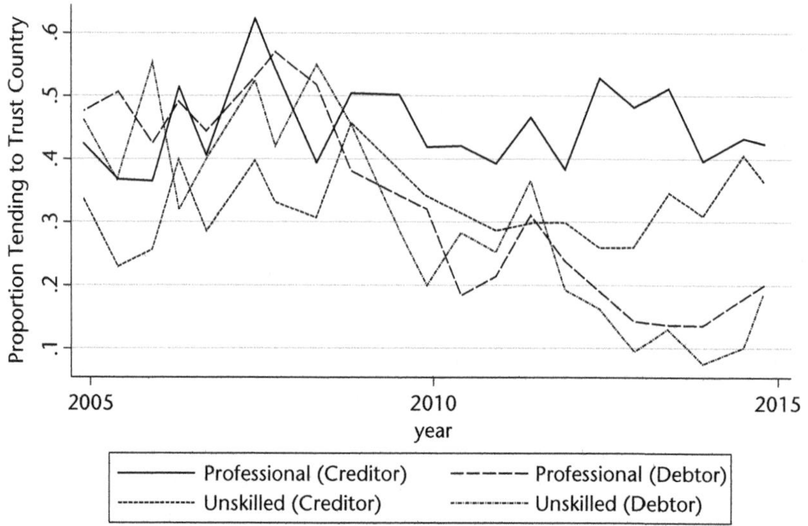


**Figure 6.11.** Trust in National Governments, by Country Group and Occupational Category.
*Source*: Eurobarometer 2004–14. Weighted proportions.

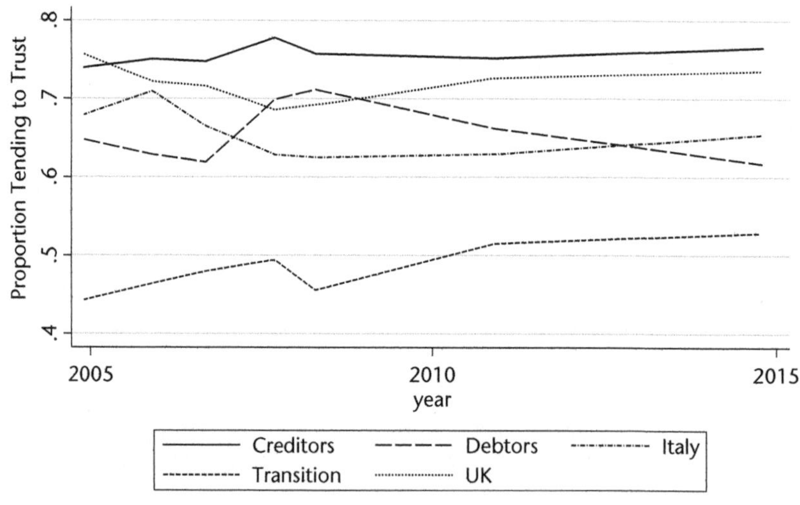


**Figure 6.12.** Trust in the Local Police, by Region.
*Source*: Eurobarometer 2004–14. Weighted proportions.

One might wonder whether the crisis has simply reduced trust in all national institutions across the board. Figures 6.12 and 6.13 indicate that this is not really the case. Trust in national police forces has remained roughly constant throughout the crisis; there is a mild decline in debtor countries, but

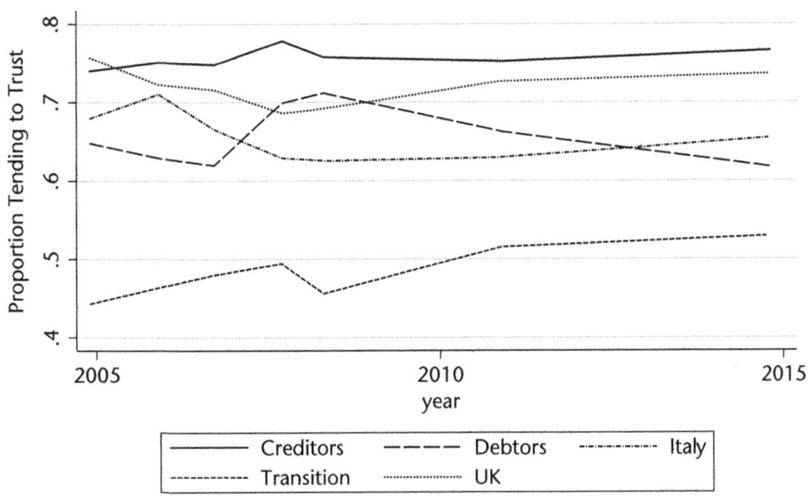


**Figure 6.13.** Trust in the National Army, by Region.
*Source*: Eurobarometer 2004–14. Weighted proportions.

trust still remains at very high levels (over 60% for the debtor countries). As Figure 6.13 shows, trust in national armies has been on a gradual decline—although, in the context of some of the region's geopolitical problems, such as Libya and Ukraine, this may not be related to the financial crisis. Nonetheless, the decline has been small and, again, levels of trust remain very high, well above 60% even in the debtor countries. This indicates that the collapse in trust in EU and national institutions is not part of a broader collapse in trust in all official institutions.

It is also worth noting that this loss of confidence has not been associated with any substantial change in the ideological self-identifications of respondents. In other words, the divisions of electorates among Right, Left, and Centre have not changed appreciably—that is, in terms of how the voters identify themselves. However, in some countries, as we know, there have been changes in voting behaviour, largely reflected in substantial increases in voting for more extreme parties of the Right or Left in troubled debtor nations, and some others as well. The fact that self-reported ideologies have not changed while voting for more extreme parties has, implies that more and more Europeans, especially in the more crisis-ridden nations, are expressing serious protests with their electoral behaviour. And this in turn can bode ill for the future of existing political parties and institutions.

These figures show simple relationships, without attempting to account for other considerations. In Section 6.3, I subject the data to more systematic analysis, which provides more insight into the nature and sources of these attitudes. However, the more detailed analysis does not substantially alter the message that comes through quite clearly from the simpler figures. While there is substantial popular support for both European integration and EMU, populations are divided, with better educated and more skilled citizens much more positive than others. And the general support for the EU and EMU has been deeply compromised by the performance of both EU and national political institutions since the crisis began in 2007. This is especially the case among the more troubled debtor nations, where there has been an almost complete evaporation of previously high levels of trust in EU and national politicians, across the board and among all groups. I now turn to a more detailed analysis of the survey data.

## 6.3. Views on European Integration: A Statistical Analysis

The Eurobarometer surveys are extensive face-to-face interviews asking hundreds of questions in a respondent's native language. They cover a number of features of respondents, which allows for a fairly detailed analysis of the correlates of the views expressed by respondents. I have compiled data from 24 Eurobarometer waves, each of which surveyed approximately 26,700 people living in the EU-27 (500–1600 per country) during the autumn and spring of each year from November 2004 through November 2014. Using these data, I run logistic regression models to predict the likelihood of a pro-EU response based on the presence of a range of co-variates, from individual socio-economic characteristics to country. I address concerns about unobserved intra-country correlations between respondents by using robust standard errors, clustered by country. In this section I look in more detail at the relationships among socio-economic and other factors and attitudes toward European integration, and toward EU and national institutions.

Table 6.1 looks at responses to the two questions about overall attitudes to European integration, for which we have approximately 350,000–400,000 responses from autumn 2004 to autumn 2014. Column 1 shows results regarding responses to whether membership in the EU is a good or bad thing for the country, while column 2 uses data from responses to the question about whether membership has, on balance, benefited the country in question. The very large number of responses, over a relatively long period allows us to look in some detail at the data.[10]

[10] We analyse 348,681 responses from 2004–13 to the question 'Taking everything into account, would you say that (OUR COUNTRY) has on balance benefited or not from being a member of the European Union?', with the dependent variable being the proportion who said their country had 'benefited'. We analyse 404,943 responses from 2004–14 to the question 'Generally speaking, do you think that (OUR COUNTRY)'s membership of the European Union is...?', with the dependent variable being the proportion of people who responded 'a good thing' given the choices of 'a good thing', 'a bad thing', 'neither', or 'don't know'.

**Table 6.1.** Odds of Support for European Integration

| | EU Membership | | EU Benefit | |
|---|---|---|---|---|
| | Odds Ratio | Z-Statistic | Odds Ratio | Z-Statistic |
| ideology | 0.994 | −0.35 | 0.988 | −0.71 |
| age | 0.997 | −1.85 | 0.995 | −4.06*** |
| gender | 0.803 | −7.05*** | 0.844 | −6.62*** |
| loweducation | 0.496 | −10.68*** | 0.490 | −10.23*** |
| mededucation | 0.678 | −7.4*** | 0.683 | −7.56*** |
| advancededucation | 1.359 | 8.56*** | 1.245 | 6.62*** |
| unskilled | 0.782 | −5.74*** | 0.833 | −6.3*** |
| unemployed | 0.744 | −4.52*** | 0.715 | −5.56*** |
| professional | 1.404 | 8.53*** | 1.310 | 6.36*** |
| Belgium | 1.952 | 180.11*** | 1.608 | 14.05*** |
| Netherlands | 2.309 | 185.51*** | 1.779 | 124.4*** |
| Germany | 1.855 | 45.31*** | 1.624 | 108.91*** |
| Italy | 0.974 | −4.2*** | 1.124 | 8.43*** |
| Austria | 0.639 | −47.16*** | 0.900 | −16.03*** |
| Luxembourg | 3.056 | 83*** | 0.730 | −29.13*** |
| Denmark | 1.281 | 11.94*** | 2.607 | 61.4*** |
| Ireland | 3.358 | 55.53*** | 2.401 | 49.66*** |
| UK | 0.581 | −42.76*** | 7.513 | 84.11*** |
| Greece | 1.056 | 3.51*** | 0.615 | −34.22*** |
| Spain | 2.361 | 70.37*** | 1.815 | 30.2*** |
| Portugal | 1.359 | 16.47*** | 2.464 | 87.68*** |
| Finland | 0.668 | −24.67*** | 2.040 | 35.2*** |
| Sweden | 0.858 | −9.84*** | 0.767 | −19.78*** |
| Cyprus | 0.958 | −2.63** | 0.661 | −32.71*** |
| Czech Republic | 0.671 | −35.31*** | 0.709 | −22.3*** |
| Estonia | 1.279 | 17.42*** | 1.252 | 19.29*** |
| Hungary | 0.772 | −11.39*** | 2.675 | 62.21*** |
| Latvia | 0.525 | −33.24*** | 0.837 | −8.33* |
| Lithuania | 1.648 | 54.23*** | 1.045 | 2.19*** |
| Malta | 1.208 | 6.82*** | 4.286 | 117.65*** |
| Poland | 1.455 | 24.7*** | 3.088 | 71.28*** |
| Slovakia | 1.233 | 24.37*** | 2.528 | 113.73*** |
| Slovenia | 1.036 | 5.76*** | 1.816 | 76.58*** |
| Bulgaria | 1.106 | 16.63*** | 1.332 | 40.57*** |
| Romania | 1.968 | 36.66*** | 2.362 | 48.11*** |

* = .05, ** = .01, *** = .001.

Table 6.1 shows differences both across countries and among groups, with one column for each of the two questions; results are very similar between them. Country fixed effects are included, and the countries are labelled. Because the responses are binary, as are the explanatory variables, I present results expressed in odds ratios, that is, the odds of the response given a particular condition (such as being highly educated or unskilled), compared with the odds of the response in the absence of that condition.[11] So in the first column of Table 6.1, being a professional increases the odds that an individual thinks EU membership is a good thing by 40%; being an

[11] Several of the variables had three or four categories, and we converted them to binary variables for comparability. Note also that age and ideology are continuous rather than binary.

unskilled worker reduces the odds by 22%. Odds ratios above 1 indicate positive responses (i.e. trust in government, support for EMU); those below 1 indicate negative responses.

The country dummies provide some interesting information. Generally, EU membership is popular; but some countries are much less favourable than others—notably Austria, Finland, Sweden, and the UK. These inter-country differences are more interesting in results, presented below, that look at trends once the crisis hits.

The impact of socio-economic factors is striking: less educated and less skilled workers, as well as the unemployed, are much less favourable to the EU, while more educated and professional workers are much more favourable.[12] Older people and women are also more sceptical of the benefits of EU membership. These results begin—like the figures presented above—to give us a sense of the substantial impact of socio-economic factors on attitudes toward the EU.

We have responses to the question about support for EMU and the euro through 2014. Table 6.2 presents results of an evaluation of these responses. The first column shows the basic results. Not surprisingly, people in the Eurozone are much more favourable; people in debtor countries are less positive than those in creditor nations. On educational and occupational dimensions, once again, the less skilled and less educated are much more negative about the euro than are the more educated and professional workers. And, once more—for reasons we do not explore—older people and women are substantially more negative about EMU.

The questions about EMU, as well as about trust in the EU and national governments, allow us to look in much greater detail at the impact of the crisis on attitudes, both among countries and among groups within and across countries. The message that comes through is quite clear: the crisis has seriously eroded confidence in the management of the euro, of the EU more generally, and of national governments. This erosion is especially notable among the debtor nations, and among the less educated and skilled groups in society.

[12] 'Low education' refers to individuals who have some school but stopped attending school before the age of 18, and constitute 34% of the sample overall. 'Medium education' refers to individuals who have exactly 18 years of school, constituting 18% of the sample. 'High education' refers to individuals who stopped school between the ages of 19 and 23, and constitute 26% of the sample; 'Advanced education' refers to individuals who stopped school between the ages of 24 and 33, and constitute 11% of the sample. In the occupational categories, the unskilled and unemployed are 11% of the sample, while professionals are 12%. Professionals include categories defined as 'Employed professional', 'General management, director or top management', 'Middle management', 'Other management', and 'Professional'. Many of the intermediate occupational categories are quite ambiguous (such as 'Employed position, not at a desk but travelling (salesmen, driver, etc.),' and 'Employed position, not at a desk, but in a service job (hospital, restaurant, police, fireman, etc.)'). The three I use are, I think, unambiguous as to skill and employment level.

**Table 6.2.** Odds of Support for Economic and Monetary Union

| | Column 1 | | Column 2 | | Column 3 | |
|---|---|---|---|---|---|---|
| | Odds Ratio | Z-Statistic | Odds Ratio | Z-Statistic | Odds Ratio | Z-Statistic |
| creditor | 1.011 | 0.05 | | | | |
| debtor | 0.867 | −0.65 | | | | |
| eurozone | 2.162 | 2.77** | 2.305 | 6.13*** | 2.384 | 6.16*** |
| aftersovcrisis | 0.630 | −5.19*** | 0.620 | −5.08*** | 0.594 | −4.73*** |
| age | 0.998 | −1.26 | 0.998 | −1.01 | 0.998 | −1.01 |
| gender | 0.763 | −9.47*** | 0.759 | −9.3*** | 0.759 | −9.29*** |
| loweducation | 0.606 | −7.59*** | 0.570 | −14.83*** | 0.569 | −15.03*** |
| mededucation | 0.840 | −2.73** | 0.782 | −5.03*** | 0.780 | −5.13*** |
| adveducation | 1.288 | 5.60*** | 1.338 | 9.44*** | 1.339 | 9.56*** |
| unskilled | 0.833 | −2.63** | 0.818 | −3.07** | 0.817 | −3.05** |
| unemployed | 0.825 | −2.92** | 0.809 | −3.15** | 0.801 | −3.42** |
| professional | 1.304 | 6.96*** | 1.309 | 6.81*** | 1.310 | 6.81*** |
| Belgium | | | 1.618 | 141.29*** | 1.617 | 139.32*** |
| Netherlands | | | 1.088 | 17.73*** | 1.086 | 19.06*** |
| Germany | | | 0.968 | −5.63*** | 0.968 | −5.51*** |
| Italy | | | 0.756 | −133.28*** | 0.755 | −112.79*** |
| Austria | | | 0.937 | −6.42*** | 0.935 | −5.86*** |
| Luxembourg | | | 1.646 | 29.27*** | 1.631 | 24.51*** |
| Denmark | | | 0.554 | −4.4*** | 0.568 | −4.11*** |
| Ireland | | | 2.391 | 55.94*** | 3.103 | 18.19*** |
| UK | 0.285 | −5.61*** | 0.291 | −9.54*** | 0.300 | −9.12*** |
| Greece | | | 0.578 | −42.83*** | 0.399 | −16.44*** |
| Spain | | | 0.868 | −10.47*** | 0.806 | −3.5*** |
| Portugal | | | 0.774 | −15.69*** | 0.733 | −4.92*** |
| Finland | | | 1.178 | 21.63*** | 1.175 | 24.39*** |
| Sweden | | | 0.444 | −5.96*** | 0.456 | −5.61*** |
| Cyprus | | | 0.640 | −7.48*** | 0.688 | −4.52*** |
| Czech Republic | | | 0.659 | −3.14** | 0.679 | −2.86** |
| Estonia | | | 0.922 | −0.88 | 0.935 | −0.72 |
| Hungary | | | 1.942 | 5.07*** | 2.006 | 5.19*** |
| Latvia | | | 0.830 | −1.73 | 0.847 | −1.51 |
| Lithuania | | | 0.970 | −0.24 | 0.997 | −0.02 |
| Malta | | | 1.111 | 1.34 | 1.067 | 0.67 |
| Poland | | | 0.753 | −2.13* | 0.777 | −1.85 |
| Slovakia | | | 1.638 | 8.44*** | 1.656 | 8.56*** |
| Slovenia | | | 2.123 | 44.88*** | 2.121 | 43*** |
| Bulgaria | | | 1.672 | 3.85*** | 1.727 | 3.99*** |
| Romania | | | 2.731 | 7.47*** | 2.825 | 7.49*** |
| crisis*Greece | | | | | 2.797 | 9.24*** |
| crisis*Spain | | | | | 1.185 | 1.52 |
| crisis*Portugal | | | | | 1.139 | 1.14 |
| crisis*Ireland | | | | | 0.567 | −4.98*** |
| crisis*Cyprus | | | | | 0.797 | −2.24* |
| crisis*Malta | | | | | 1.299 | 2.38* |

* = .05, ** = .01, *** = .001.

The second column of Table 6.2 demonstrates the dramatic reduction in support for EMU after the sovereign debt crisis hit in 2010 (with an odds ratio of 0.62).[13] In the third column of the table, interaction terms show that after

13 It might be thought that the course of the crisis would have an impact on attitudes, with its attenuation also attenuating negative views of EU or national government institutions. However,

the crisis, people in Ireland and Cyprus are much more negative about EMU, which is not that surprising. What is more surprising is that respondents in Spain, Portugal, and Greece are more positively inclined after the crisis than before. We return to this below.

But still throughout, the basic division between more highly educated and skilled, on the one hand, and less educated and skilled and the unemployed, on the other, remains very strong. Restricting the analysis to just Eurozone countries only strengthens these results. Support for monetary union has been seriously eroded by the crisis, with most of the erosion taking place in the Eurozone debtor nations, and especially among the more disadvantaged citizens of those nations.

The crisis has had more general, and even more disturbing, effects on attitudes toward European integration and, in particular, to both European and national political institutions. This comes through clearly in responses to questions about trust in the EU or national governments, and questions about satisfaction with democracy at the EU or national level. Because the results are so similar, I report only the 'trust' results.

Table 6.3 analyses responses to the question of whether respondents trust the EU, and their national governments. The impact of socio-economic factors remains substantial and strong: more disadvantaged groups have much less trust in both European and national political institutions than do others. The crisis has dramatically eroded trust in both the EU and national governments, especially in the most crisis-hit, debtor nations. It is interesting to note that respondents in Greece, Spain, and Cyprus appear to blame their national governments more directly than they blame the EU: the post-crisis collapse in confidence in these three national governments is much greater than the analogous loss of trust in the EU.

This more nuanced analysis of survey responses serves largely to confirm the impressions that emerge from even a cursory look at the descriptive statistics presented above. There are substantial differences among socio-economic groups in the evaluation of the value of European integration and monetary union, and in the degree of trust in the institutions of the EU and of national governments. The crisis has not appreciably reduced general support for European integration or EMU, but it has had a crushing impact on confidence in European and national political institutions. This impact has been close to universal in the most heavily affected debtor nations. While people in the less affected creditor nations in the Eurozone are somewhat disenchanted with both their own governments and the EU, in the debtor nations the fall in confidence is extraordinarily large, and quite general.

country year dummies from 2008 through 2014 show a continual decline in confidence. The decline seems continual and unresponsive to the specifics of crisis events.

**Table 6.3.** Odds of Trust in the EU and National Governments

| | EU Trust | | National Trust | |
|---|---|---|---|---|
| | Odds Ratio | Z-Statistic | Odds Ratio | Z-Statistic |
| aftersovcrisis | 0.480 | −10.39*** | 0.826 | −1.84 |
| age | 0.996 | −2.71** | 1.004 | 3.17** |
| gender | 0.949 | −3.32** | 0.947 | −2.79** |
| loweducation | 0.595 | −8.29*** | 0.733 | −4.72*** |
| higheducation | 0.739 | −5.26*** | 0.819 | −4.25*** |
| advancededucation | 1.160 | 4.46*** | 1.146 | 5.16*** |
| unskilled | 0.830 | −4.16*** | 0.858 | −3.49*** |
| unemployed | 0.748 | −5.13*** | 0.653 | −7*** |
| professional | 1.142 | 3.96*** | 1.075 | 1.9 |
| Belgium | 1.789 | 143.7*** | 1.879 | 104.27*** |
| Netherlands | 1.291 | 40.33*** | 2.486 | 180.43*** |
| Germany | 0.979 | −1.77 | 1.818 | 46.28*** |
| Italy | 1.168 | 49.39*** | 0.826 | −91.59*** |
| Austria | 1.052 | 4.31*** | 3.011 | 105.67*** |
| Luxembourg | 1.496 | 32.54*** | 5.005 | 97.01*** |
| Denmark | 1.305 | 15.57*** | 2.669 | 67.39*** |
| Ireland | 1.937 | 19.9*** | 1.426 | 7.52*** |
| UK | 0.525 | −64.12*** | 1.096 | 7.17*** |
| Greece | 1.469 | 11.43*** | 1.553 | 9.89*** |
| Spain | 1.799 | 19.03*** | 2.014 | 15.04*** |
| Portugal | 2.143 | 22.58*** | 1.324 | 5.85*** |
| Finland | 1.068 | 7.63*** | 3.746 | 216.18*** |
| Sweden | 0.878 | −11.07*** | 2.658 | 114.37*** |
| Cyprus | 2.106 | 19.96*** | 3.867 | 29.73*** |
| Czech Republic | 1.374 | 44.41*** | 0.828 | −16.75*** |
| Estonia | 2.238 | 81.67*** | 2.777 | 65.92*** |
| Hungary | 2.183 | 59.53*** | 1.361 | 24.37*** |
| Latvia | 1.190 | 17.62*** | 0.766 | −15.35*** |
| Lithuania | 2.412 | 225.14*** | 0.754 | −25.73*** |
| Malta | 2.131 | 16.94*** | 2.194 | 15.41*** |
| Poland | 1.830 | 61.02*** | 0.725 | −32.46*** |
| Slovakia | 2.065 | 94.86*** | 1.232 | 15.93*** |
| Slovenia | 1.568 | 62.19*** | 1.067 | 4.92*** |
| Bulgaria | 2.809 | 176.31*** | 0.971 | −3.5*** |
| Romania | 2.667 | 201.57*** | 0.863 | −20.16*** |
| crisisGreece | 0.431 | −11.24*** | 0.238 | −13.37*** |
| crisisSpain | 0.432 | −11.09*** | 0.242 | −13.21*** |
| crisisPortugal | 0.569 | −7.77*** | 0.542 | −5.76*** |
| crisisIreland | 0.564 | −7.55*** | 0.687 | −3.48*** |
| crisisCyprus | 0.445 | −10.37*** | 0.303 | −11.32*** |
| crisisMalta | 1.246 | 3.02** | 1.243 | 2.09* |

* = .05, ** = .01, *** = .001.

In some crisis-ridden countries, the EU takes much of the blame; in others, the national governments come in for more of the opprobrium. All in all, the implications for the future course of European integration, and of EMU, are hardly encouraging.

Clear messages come through from the analysis of these data. They are of direct relevance to the future of the EU, and of the euro, and they suggest a range of issues—and potential problems—that the EU and the euro will have to face going forward. I summarize them below.

1. Support for European integration remains high throughout the EU, and support for EMU remains high throughout the Eurozone.
2. There are substantial differences in the extent of this support among socio-economic groups. The differences across groups are large, and are quite similar among all member countries. Less skilled, less educated, and older citizens are more sceptical about European integration and the euro (as are women); by contrast, the more educated and professional classes are more positive, as are students.
3. The differences among countries in general support for integration and the euro are not as substantial as is sometimes assumed. To be sure, non-members of the Eurozone remain unenthusiastic about EMU. But within the Eurozone, support for the euro is quite strong among all member states. And positive views of European integration more generally are quite widely shared around the Union, with the exception of in the UK.
4. However, the crisis has had a massive, and massively negative, impact on attitudes toward the institutions of the EU and of the national governments within it. Perhaps surprisingly, the crisis has not had a major effect on overall support for integration and the euro, which remains high. However, the experience of the past eight years has deeply eroded trust in the institutions of the EU and the Eurozone. Europeans, in general, still want the EU to succeed and move forward; those in the Eurozone still want the euro. But they have lost almost all confidence in the ability of European leaders and national governments to manage the problems that have arisen in the past decade.
5. This loss of trust in European and national institutions is particularly concentrated, as might be expected, among those who have been hardest hit by the crisis. The loss of confidence has been almost complete in the most deeply affected countries, the Eurozone debtors. Across the EU, in general less skilled and less educated citizens, and those more likely to be unemployed, have come to hold strongly negative views about their own governments, and about the institutions of the EU. While our data do not allow inferences about a direct relationship between this and the increasing polarization of political positions in many European countries, it is almost certainly the case that the two phenomena are related.

What are the implications of these trends for the future of European integration, and monetary union, over the coming decade? Policymakers at both the national and European level can count on quite a deep well of support for European integration and for the euro: Europeans appear quite firmly committed to both the broad integration process and the EMU However, they have little confidence in the ability of existing political leaders to manage both the national and European economies in ways that respond to the concerns of European citizens. This dissatisfaction is particularly concentrated in the more crisis-ridden countries, especially the debtor nations of the Eurozone. Dissatisfaction is also concentrated in those social groups that have suffered most from the crisis: the less educated and less skilled, and the unemployed.

European integration, and EMU, cannot move forward without political support from the public. At this point, such support still exists in general, but there has been such an erosion of trust in policymakers that it is hard to believe that political backing for current policies will be forthcoming for much longer unless conditions improve markedly. And, given the striking differences among socio-economic groups—and especially the great and growing scepticism of the less advantaged among Europeans—it would seem that further progress will also depend on finding ways to include more Europeans in the gains from integration, and to shelter them from its costs.

*Acknowledgements*

The author thanks Francesco Caselli and Stefanie Walter for useful comments; and is especially grateful to Chase Foster, Dana Higgins, and Nicole Kiprilov for outstanding research assistance.

## 6.4. References

Anderson, C. J. and M. S. Reichert (1995), 'Economic Benefits and Support for Membership in the E.U.: A Cross-National Analysis', *Journal of Public Policy* 15(3): Sept.-Dec.), 231–49.

Banducci, S. A., J. A. Karp, and P. H. Loedel (2009), 'Economic interests and public support for the euro'. *Journal of European Public Policy*, 16(4), 564–81.

Duckenfield, M. (2006), *Business and the Euro: Business Groups and the Politics of EMU in Germany and the United Kingdom*, London: Palgrave.

Eglene, O. (2011), *Banking on Sterling: Britain's Independence from the Euro Zone*, Lanham, Md: Lexington Books.

Fernández-Albertos, J., A. Kuo, and L. Balcells (2013), 'Economic Crisis, Globalization, and Partisan Bias: Evidence from Spain'. *International Studies Quarterly*, 57(4), 804–16.

Frieden, J. (2002), 'Real sources of European currency policy: Sectoral interests and European monetary integration', *International Organization* 56(4) (Fall).

Frieden, J. (2015), *Currency Politics: The Political Economy of Exchange Rate Policy*, Princeton: Princeton University Press.

Gabel, M. (1998), 'Public Support for European Integration: An Empirical Test of Five Theories', *The Journal of Politics* 60(2) (May), 333–54.

Gabel, M. and H. D. Palmer. (1995), 'Understanding variation in public support for European integration', *European Journal of Political Research* 27, 3–19.

Gabel, M. (2001), 'Divided Opinion, Common Currency: The Political Economy of Public Support for EMU'. In Barry Eichengreen and Jeffry Frieden, (eds.). *The Political Economy of European Monetary Unification* Second edition. Boulder: Westview Press.

Guiso, L., P. Sapienza, and L. Zingales (2014), 'Monnet's Error?' Paper for Fall 2014 BPEA.

Hefeker, C. (1997), *Interest Groups and Monetary Integration: The Political Economy of Exchange Regime Choice*, Boulder, Colorado: Westview Press.

Jupille, J. and D. Leblang (2007), 'Voting for Change: Calculation, Community and Euro Referendums'. *International Organization* 61(4) (Fall), 763–82.

Kaltenthaler, K. C. and C. J. Anderson (2001), 'Europeans and their money: Explaining public support for the common European currency', *European Journal of Political Research*, 40(2), 139–70.

Magalhaes, P. C. (2012), 'Economy, Ideology, and the Elephant in the Room: A Research Note on the Elections of the Great Recession in Europe', *Available at SSRN.*

Moravcsik, A. (1998), *The Choice for Europe: Social Purpose and State Power from Messina to Maastricht*, Ithaca: Cornell University Press.

Moses, J. and A. Jenssen (1998), 'Nordic Accession: An Analysis of the EU Referendums', in Barry Eichengreen and Jeffry Frieden (eds.). *Forging an Integrated Europe.* Ann Arbor: University of Michigan Press.

Tucker, J. A., A. C. Pacek, and A. J. Berinsky (2002), 'Transitional Winners and Losers: Attitudes toward EU Membership in Post-Communist Countries', *American Journal of Political Science* 46(3), 557–71.

# 7

# The Challenge of European Inequality

*Francesco Caselli, Mário Centeno, Álvaro Novo, and José Tavares*

## 7.1. Introduction

In recent years there has been a resurgence of interest in the topic of inequality. Academics have devoted considerable effort to the task of uncovering the reasons for long-run changes in income inequality in most advanced (and many developing) countries. Public opinion has also become more aware of the large gaps between rich and poor. And, as a result of these trends, politicians and policymakers have increasingly been called on formulating a policy stance directed at inequality. As Europe looks forward to further integration, it will, too, have to take a stand on the issue.

But what is the inequality landscape in Europe *taken as a whole*? Much is known, of course, about inequality in individual countries, and on average across European countries. But if the European Union is to have a common stand on inequality, it is important to know what is the inequality situation in Europe when the member states are taken as a single unit, as opposed to as a collection of separate units. In this chapter, we offer a survey of the data, focusing on the distribution of income across European households. Most of the analysis is centred on eleven members of the Euro Area, that is all founding members plus Greece, and less Luxembourg, which is the group most likely to attempt further steps towards economic and political integration.[1] However, we also present some results for the broader EU. To have a benchmark against which to evaluate European inequality, we compare household income distribution in Europe and in the USA.[2]

[1] Luxembourg was excluded because in certain years it is not possible to compute income net of taxes and transfers.

[2] Henceforth, unless otherwise indicated, when we report results for 'Europe' we mean the Euro 11 countries listed herein.

We begin by examining market income defined as the sum of wages, self-employment, and property income and pensions, before taxes. The conventional wisdom, largely based on comparisons of individual countries, is that Europe is less unequal than the US. This is borne out in our data. In 2013, the Gini coefficient for household market income was 0.39 in Europe and 0.46 in the USA. It would be tempting to stop there and conclude that inequality is a comparatively minor issue in a unified Europe, that pressures for redistribution would be correspondingly moderate, and that a unified Europe can look forward to a relatively smooth path as it seeks to formulate a stance towards inequality. Yet, when compared with the USA, lower European inequality is associated with much greater levels of what may be called 'geographic clustering' of income levels: the fact that the relatively rich households and the relatively poor ones are geographically segregated.

Geographic clustering, in turn, is largely a result of the fact that average income in European countries has converged considerably less than among US regions. As a result, in Europe, country income distributions are clustered around very different means. While the typical US region is more unequal than the typical European country, US regional income distributions overlap much more than those of European countries. Households belonging to a certain percentile in their countries' income distribution are less likely to belong to the same percentile in the European distribution.

This finding has potentially wide-reaching implications for the prospect of achieving common ground on inequality in Europe. Consider a 'federal' policy redistributing from the ninetieth to the tenth percentile of the income distribution. In the USA, the person at the ninetieth percentile can expect her dollars to go to someone in the same region, and hence in a 'community' in which she has a certain stake. In Europe, they will almost certainly go to someone in another country.

Another potentially troubling difference lies in the cross-regional correlation between inequality and average disposable income. In the USA, the more unequal regions are also the richest regions, while in Europe it is the poorest countries that are the most unequal. Hence, one may conjecture that in America there will be greater awareness of the potential benefits of redistribution precisely in those regions more able to 'give.' In Europe, instead, the financial firepower is located precisely in those countries where people experience less inequality.

We next examine disposable income, namely market income after subtracting taxes and adding transfers. This takes stock of current redistribution practices. Once again, the common wisdom of a Europe that, on the whole, redistributes more than the USA is borne out: after taxes and transfers the Gini drops by 0.07 in Europe, and by 0.05 in the USA, widening the inequality gap between the two economies. But we also find a striking degree of heterogeneity in the extent of redistribution among European countries, which far exceeds that of US regions. In particular, richer countries redistribute considerably more than poor ones. As a result, paradoxically, redistribution may be pulling European households belonging to different countries further apart, rather than closer together, reinforcing the geographical clustering.

Over time, income convergence in Euro area members has brought down inequality and increased the level of overlap in individual incomes across nations; the Gini coefficient decreased from 0.41 in 1996 to 0.37 in 2007, but the process seems to have been interrupted during the economic and financial crisis, reaching 0.39 in 2013.

At present, redistribution in Europe is mainly a country issue. This raises doubts on the impact on inequality of the process of 'deepening' and 'widening' European integration. We analyse this issue by looking at the adoption of the euro and the Eastern enlargement. The EU28 is a much more unequal area and has a much smaller income overlap between countries. The Gini coefficient increases to 0.44 and 0.38, respectively, for market and disposable income. The stakes for integration are higher in this wider area.

There is a huge literature on income inequality in both the USA and Europe. For the USA, a comprehensive treatment is provided by Goldin and Katz (2008), with a particular focus on long-term trends. An influential volume by Atkinson (2008) deals with inequality in a large set of countries (see also Atkinson, 2015). International organizations have also dealt with the subject. The Organization for Economic Co-operation and Development (OECD) has produced several reports on inequality (e.g. OECD, 2011; OECD, 2015). Compared with the USA, there are only a few academic papers that treat Europe as a single economic entity. The exceptions are Atkinson (1996), Beblo and Knaus (2001), Boix (2004), Brandolini (2007), Hoffmeister (2009), Brandolini (2012). We contribute to this strand of the literature by treating Europe as a unity rather than a collection of countries (or their average).

There is also previous work comparing European approaches to redistribution to American ones. For example Alesina and Glaeser (2004) attribute the greater European proclivity towards redistribution to differences in its institutional setting, ethnic heterogeneity, and beliefs about the nature of poverty. But, once again, these analyses are based on redistribution policies within European countries. At a putative 'federal' level, as we show, the identity of the recipients, and their geographic position vis-à-vis the sources of redistributed resources, changes dramatically. The moot point is what will that do to European attitudes towards redistribution.

Given the differences in the current national stance vis-à-vis redistribution, Bertola (2010) argues that it will be more difficult to forge a common vision and pursue the integration process.

The rest of the chapter is organized as follows: Section 7.2 describes our data sources; Section 7.3 presents the analysis of inequality in market incomes; Section 7.4 reports on redistribution policies; Section 7.5 shows how inequality has changed over time; Section 7.6 summarizes the chapter.

## 7.2. Data

### 7.2.1. *European Data*

We use two sources of European data: the European Community Household Panel (ECHP), and its successor, the Survey of Income and Living Conditions (SILC). Combined, these two data sources cover the period from 1994 to 2012, with the exception of 2001 and 2002—the gap caused by the change from the ECHP to the SILC survey.

The ECHP is a harmonized annual survey that provides micro data on household income and living conditions. The ECHP ran from 1994 to 2001 in fourteen of the then fifteen member states. In 1994, a sample of some 60500 households were interviewed across Belgium, Denmark, Germany, Greece, Spain, France, Italy, Ireland, Luxembourg, Netherlands, Portugal, and the UK. Austria joined the ECHP in 1995, and Finland in 1996.

To solve some comparability and timeliness issues, and extend the data collection to the enlarged European Union, the ECHP was replaced by the EU-SILC from 2004 onwards. The 2004 EU-SILC includes information on thirteen member states and 116000 households. From 2005, Germany, Netherlands, and the UK joined, along with the rest of the new eight central and eastern EU countries. Since 2007, it represents all twenty-seven member states.

The income reference period is always the preceding calendar year, except for Ireland (twelve months prior to the interview) and in the UK (the period around the date of interview, with income totals converted later to annual equivalents).

As mentioned in Section 7.1, 'Europe' is a shorthand for a group of eleven Eurozone countries: Austria, Belgium, Finland, France, Germany, Greece, Ireland, Italy, Netherlands, Portugal, and Spain.

We will consider two definitions of income: market and disposable. Market income is the sum of employment income (wages, salaries, allowances, and bonuses); self-employment income (benefits or losses from self-employment, including royalties); pensions (old-age benefits); property or non-work income (income from rental of a property or land, interest, dividends, profits from investment in an unincorporated business and regular inter-household cash transfers). Disposable income is market income plus transfers (unemployment benefits, survivor's benefits, sickness benefits, disability benefits, education related allowances, family/children related allowance, social exclusion elsewhere classified, and housing allowances) minus taxes and contributions (inheritance taxes or taxes on gifts inter vivo and taxes assessed in holding of land or real estate, income, profits, and capital gains taxes, and social contributions).

Each household's income is adjusted to a per-adult-equivalent basis using the OECD equivalence scale. We express all income variables of ECHP/EU-SILC in 2010 euros, using as price deflator the Eurostat Harmonized Indices of Consumer Prices (HICP), all items. We used the Eurostat former euro area national currencies exchange rate to express in euros the income variables of the ECHP.

### 7.2.2. *American Data*

The American data come from the Panel Survey of Income Dynamics (PSID), run since 1969, although it does not cover all years in the more recent period. The PSID is a longitudinal study of US individuals and the family units in which they reside. The unit of analysis is the family unit, which is defined as all persons living together who are usually related by blood, adoption, or marriage. A household can be composed of more than one family. The PSID data files provide a wide range of information about families, in particular on income sources and amounts. The official statistics of household income are based on the CPS. However, research on the comparability of income estimates found that the PSID and the CPS track each other fairly closely (Gouskova et al., 2010). Overall the PSID is a better basis for comparison with the SILC.

To compare geographic patterns with Europe, we use the US Census divisions (East North Central, East South Central, Mid-Atlantic, Mountain, New England, Pacific, South Atlantic, West North Central, and West South Central), but we individualize the four largest states (California, Florida, New York, Texas).[3]

[3] The state composition of each resulting division is: (i) New England (Connecticut, Maine, Massachusetts, New Hampshire, Rhode Island, and Vermont); (ii) Mid-Atlantic (New Jersey and Pennsylvania); (iii) East North Central (Illinois, Indiana, Michigan, Ohio, and Wisconsin); (iv) West North Central (Iowa, Kansas, Minnesota, Missouri, Nebraska, North Dakota, and South Dakota); (v) South Atlantic (Delaware, Georgia, Maryland, North Carolina, South Carolina, Virginia, Washington DC, and West Virginia); (vi) East South Central (Alabama, Kentucky, Mississippi, and Tennessee) (vii) West South Central (Arkansas, Louisiana, and Oklahoma); (viii) Mountain (Arizona, Colorado, Idaho, Montana, Nevada, New Mexico, Utah, and Wyoming); (ix) Pacific (Alaska, Hawaii, Oregon, and Washington).

To conform the PSID income definition with the European surveys, we defined employment income as wages, salaries, bonuses, and overtime; self-employment income as the labour part of self-employment and farm income; pensions as annuities, private retirement income and other retirement income; property or non-work income as financial assets interest, dividends, rental income, trust funds, and the asset part of self-employment, alimony, child support from the head, help from relatives or friends, and miscellaneous transfers.

Transfers include payments from the Aid to Families with Dependent Children/Temporary Assistance for Needy Children programme (AFDC/TANF), social security benefits, unemployment benefits, worker's compensation, veterans' pensions, and other welfare income.

The total amount of taxes was estimated using the `Stata` marginal tax rate function (`mtr`). We express all incomes in 2006 dollars, using as price deflator the Bureau of Labor Statistics C.P.I.-U. series, all items. The incomes were also adjusted to a per-adult-equivalent using the OECD scale.

### 7.2.3. *Sample Characteristics*

Table 7.1 reports statistics on main demographic charactristics for the two surveys. The average age and education levels refer to the household's head or reference person. In the USA a larger share of heads of household has tertiary education. The fraction of households composed of a single adult with dependent children is two times higher in the USA than in Europe.

**Table 7.1.** Selected Demographic Characteristics in the EU-SILC and PSID 2013

| | EU-SILC | PSID |
|---|---|---|
| Age | 52.27 | 51.85 |
| Education (in %) | | |
| Tertiary | 26.50 | 37.82 |
| Secondary | 56.20 | 49.16 |
| Primary | 17.30 | 13.02 |
| Household size | 2.30 | 2.21 |
| Household composition (in %) | | |
| One adult | 32.73 | 38.02 |
| Two adults | 29.01 | 24.98 |
| One adult with children | 3.87 | 7.48 |
| Two adults with children | 26.27 | 19.72 |
| Others | 8.12 | 9.80 |
| Sample size | 106 598 | 9013 |

Demographic characteristics of the family head or household reference person. Tertiary education includes levels 5 and 6 of the I.S.C.E.D. classification; Secondary education includes levels 3 and 4; primary education levels 0 to 2.

## 7.3. Market Inequality in Europe and the USA

### 7.3.1. *Overall Inequality*

We measure inequality using the Gini coefficient, although we also report some results for other commonly used inequality measures such as the nintieth/fiftieth and fiftieth/tenth percentile ratios. Inequality as measured by the Gini coefficient can be interpreted as an income change expressed as a fraction of average income. A Gini coefficient of 0.4 means that the average tax or transfer required to obtain a perfectly equal society is equal to 40% of average income. The fiftieth to tenth percentile ratio is used to summarize lower-tail inequality, and similarly for the nintieth to fiftieth percentile ratio for upper-tail inequality.

The household market income distribution is more egalitarian in Europe than in the USA. This stylized fact is presented in Figure 7.1, with data for 2013. As we will show below, this difference is persistent across time. Brandolini (2007) reports results for 2000 with similar differences between the two economic areas. Europe shows a relative concentration of household

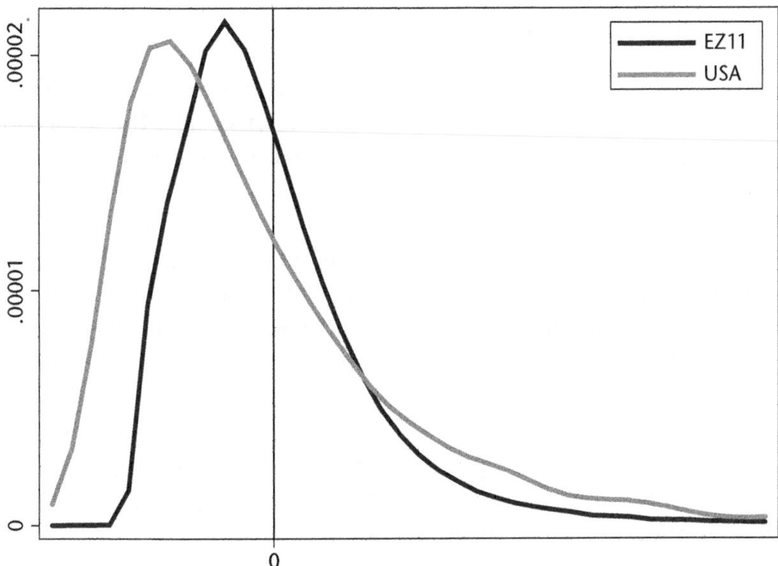


**Figure 7.1.** Household Market Income Distribution for Europe and the USA in 2013. EZ11 stands for the founding Eurozone members plus Greece less Luxembourg. For each economic area, we subtracted the average household income from each household's income. The vertical bar at zero represents the average household for both areas.
*Data sources*: SILC for Europe and PSID for the USA.

disposable income around its average (the vertical bar at zero for demeaned data), while the USA displays fatter lower- and upper-tails, that is, more of the very poor and more of the upper middle class to rich.

The higher income dispersion in the USA is reflected in different summary statistics that are commonly used to measure inequality. The Gini coefficient in the USA is 0.46, compared with 0.39 in Europe. This is an extremely large difference. The time series standard deviation of the Gini in Europe is 0.007; the difference between Europe and the USA is about ten standard deviations.

Although, both percentile ratios confirm the USA as a more unequal economic area, the differences at the lower tail are non-significant. The fiftieth/tenth percentiles ratio is 3.50 in Europe and 3.56 in the USA. While the upper-tail ratio is smaller in both economic areas, it is higher in the USA, 2.24 v. 2.72.

At first sight, lower market inequality in Europe makes for greater social cohesion and fewer social cleavages, and hence appears to bode well for further economic and political integration. But this simplistic analysis fails to take into account that high and low incomes in Europe are much more geographically segregated. We develop this point in greater detail in section 7.3.2.

### 7.3.2. *Geographic Income Clusters*

Economic and social integration of national economies promotes the convergence of income distributions over time. At this stage, the dispersion of income across European countries contrasts with a uniform picture across American regions.

There is a marked geographic clustering of poor/rich households in Europe. Figure 7.2 plots each European country's income distribution as well as the overall European income distribution. It is apparent that for some countries the overlap with the overall European distribution is limited. Greece, Portugal, and Spain have the bulk of the mass concentrated over the lower tail of the continental distribution. A remarkable fact is the almost perfect overlap between the German and European distributions. This is not a mechanical feature driven by Germany's large relative population. In Appendix 7.1 we show that the overlap is essentially unaffected when dropping Germany from the computation of the European distribution.

Income distributions for US regions, together with the overall US income distribution, are plotted in Figure 7.3. We immediately see that the income distributions of US regions overlap with each other (and with the overall distribution) much more closely than the European ones. This is true for wealthier regions such as Mountain, Pacific, and California, and for poorer

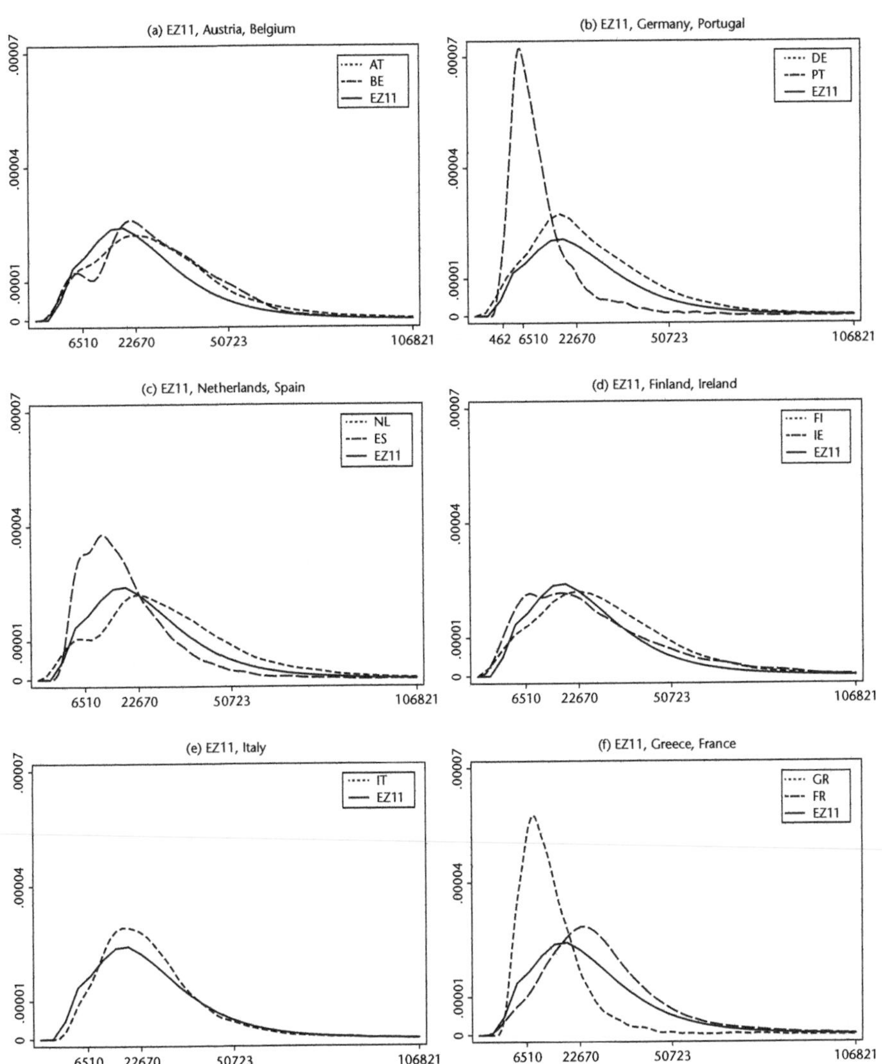


**Figure 7.2.** Equivalized Market Income Distribution for Eurozone11, 2013.

regions such as West South Central (WSC), East South Central (ESC), East North Central (ENC), and South Atlantic.

A more formal way to bring out the smaller European overlap between regional and area-wide income distributions is to compute the *rank correlation ratio*. Define $r_k(y)$ as the rank of income $y$ in country $k$, (e.g. twelfth percentile), and $r(y)$ the rank of the same income in the economic area

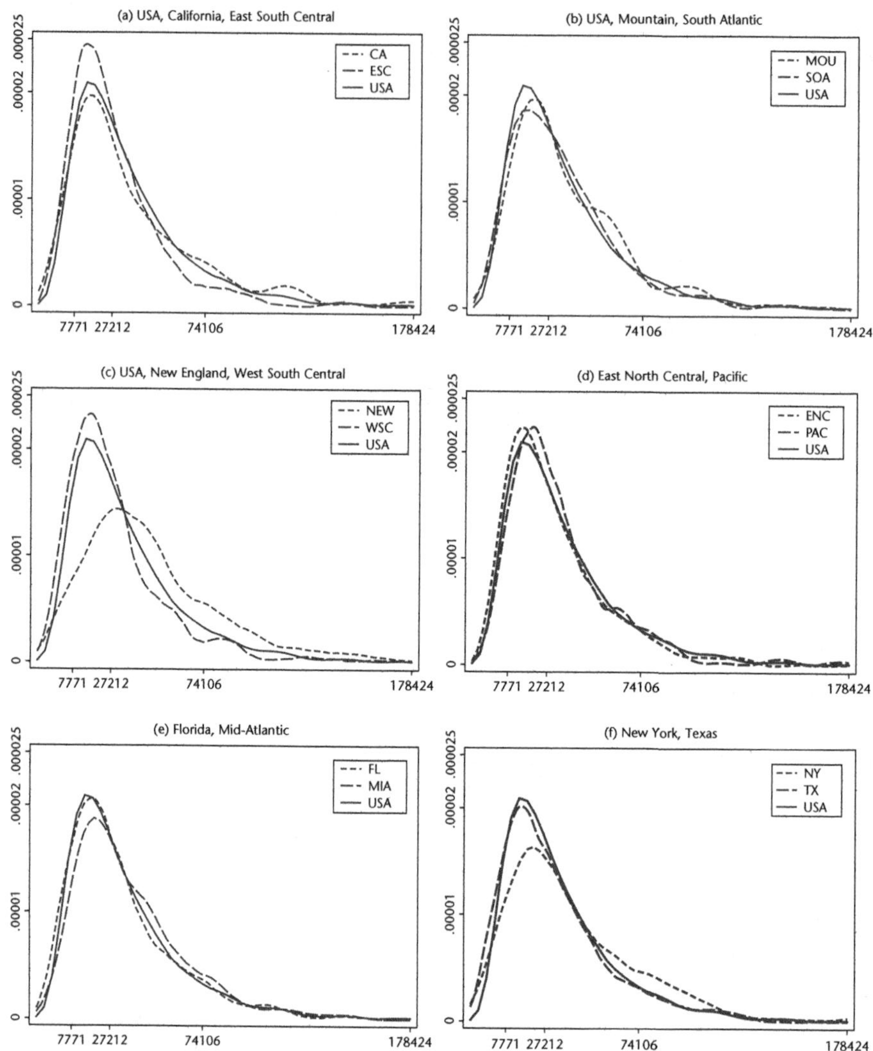


**Figure 7.3.** Equivalized Market Income Distribution for the USA, 2013.

distribution. Then, the rank correlation ratio is

$$R_k = \frac{cov[y, r(y)]}{cov[y, r_k(y)]}.$$

The rank correlation ratio is equal to one only if $r(y) = r_k(y)$, that is if each household income has the same rank domestically and in the continental distribution.

Rank correlation ratios for Europe and the USA are presented in Table 7.2. While in the USA these correlations are generally high, ranging from 0.35 to

**Table 7.2.** Rank Correlation of Country/Regions in Europe and the USA in 2013

| Eurozone11 | | USA | |
|---|---|---|---|
| Austria | 0.53 | California | 0.54 |
| Belgium | 0.50 | East North Central | 0.44 |
| Germany | 0.52 | East South Central | 0.35 |
| Spain | 0.14 | Florida | 0.41 |
| Finland | 0.53 | Mid Atlantic | 0.56 |
| France | 0.55 | Mountain | 0.49 |
| Greece | −0.11 | New England | 0.64 |
| Ireland | 0.51 | New York | 0.63 |
| Italy | 0.41 | Pacific | 0.43 |
| Netherlands | 0.57 | South Atlantic | 0.52 |
| Portugal | −0.13 | Texas | 0.55 |
| | | West North Central | 0.47 |
| | | West South Central | 0.35 |

0.64. In Europe, these correlations are smaller than in the USA, reaching at most 0.57 in the case of The Netherlands. There is a large dichotomy across countries, with Southern countries recording the lowest correlations; Portugal and Greece even have negative correlations, –0.13 and –0.11, respectively.

The rank correlation confirms the geographic segregation of incomes documented above. This blurs the picture of greater social cohesion evoked by the lower overall index of European inequality. From a political-economy perspective, this calls into question the level of tolerance for federal redistribution we can expect in a more integrated Europe.

### 7.3.3. *The Relation between Inequality and Average Income*

We have seen that European inequality, while lower overall, exhibits much sharper patterns of geographic income concentrations than American inequality. The geographic clustering of poor households may be seen as a serious potential challenge to the task of coining a common European stance towards inequality. In this section, we note a further difference between European and US patterns of inequality that could add a further dimension of difficulty.

Figure 7.4 plots country/regional average incomes against country/regional Gini coefficients. The striking difference is that poorer countries in Europe are generally more unequal than richer countries. In general, there seems to be a divide between 'northern' and 'southern' European countries, where the latter are not only poorer on average, but their distributions are also more unequal. In the USA, in contrast, with the exception of New England, richer regions are more unequal.[4]

[4] Nixon's remark about visiting a Socialist country before going to China seems to have withstood the test of time.

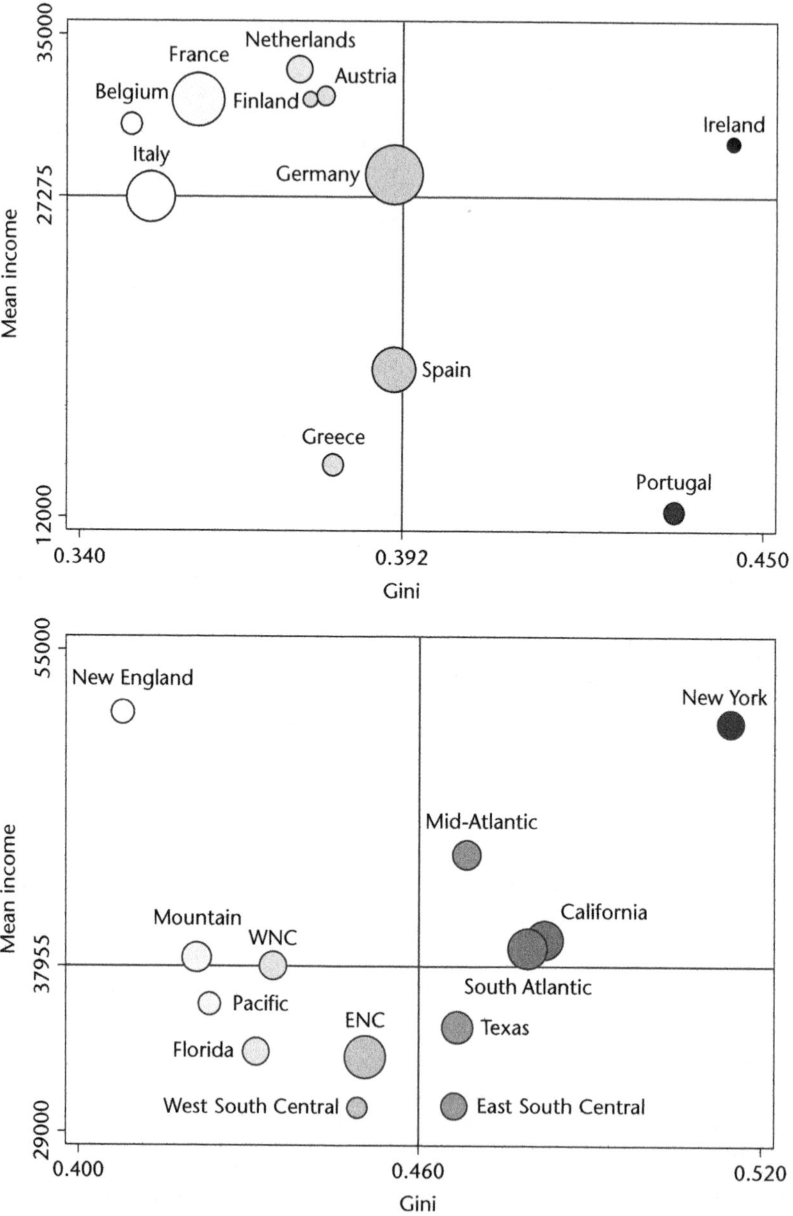


**Figure 7.4.** Average Income and Inequality (Gini Coefficient). Vertical and horizontal bars represent, respectively, area-wide inequality and mean income. Bubble size proportional to the population weight.

We may argue that the American states have the 'right' type of inequality, from the perspective of fostering a federal model of redistribution: as more unequal states are also relatively more wealthy, both the higher demand and the potential supply for redistribution are geographically located in the same places. In the Eurozone, we have the opposite relationship: those places where the resources for redistribution are concentrated are also the ones where local demand for redistribution will be most muted.

## 7.4. Redistribution

Disposable income (market income minus taxes plus transfers) is probably a more relevant indicator for individuals' well-being. However, the scope for redistribution depends on market outcomes, which are not independent of the tax and transfer systems in place. These systems are rather different in Europe and the USA. Federal mechanisms dominate in the USA, whereas national mechanisms prevail in Europe.

Figure 7.5 shows both market and disposable income distributions for Europe and the USA. It is apparent that Europe (or, rather, European countries) does considerably more redistribution through the tax and transfer systems than America. The Gini coefficient drops more in Europe than in the USA, even though it starts lower. Once again, it is tempting to be optimistic in light of this observation: Europe appears to be generally more willing to foster social cohesion through redistribution, which might seem to bode well for its prospects to deal with pressure for redistribution in a united entity. Yet it is crucial to bear in mind the results from the previous section: the current high redistribution in Europe is within country. In a federal Europe, it will be mostly across countries. And the ammunition for redistribution will have to come from the countries that—currently—have the lowest need for internal

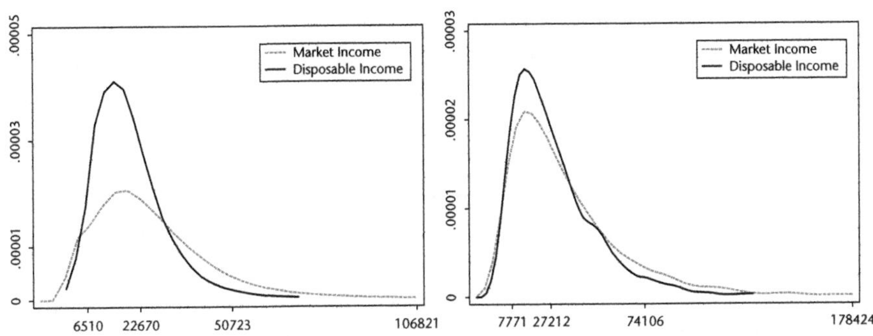


**Figure 7.5.** Gross and Disposable Income Distribution: Europe and the USA.

**Table 7.3.** Europe and the USA: Market Gini, Disposable Gini and its difference

| *Country* | *Gini market* | *Gini disposable* | *Difference* | *%Δ* |
|---|---|---|---|---|
| | | Europe | | |
| Italy | 0.3515 | 0.3216 | −0.03 | −8.5 |
| Greece | 0.3809 | 0.3307 | −0.05 | −13.2 |
| Spain | 0.3906 | 0.3306 | −0.06 | −15.4 |
| France | 0.3591 | 0.3007 | −0.06 | −16.3 |
| *Europe* | 0.3918 | 0.3247 | −0.07 | −17.1 |
| Portugal | 0.4357 | 0.3466 | −0.09 | −20.4 |
| Germany | 0.3906 | 0.3055 | −0.09 | −21.8 |
| Belgium | 0.3483 | 0.2659 | −0.08 | −23.7 |
| Austria | 0.3796 | 0.2824 | −0.10 | −25.6 |
| Finland | 0.3771 | 0.268 | −0.11 | −28.9 |
| Ireland | 0.4451 | 0.3157 | −0.13 | −29.1 |
| Netherlands | 0.3754 | 0.2602 | −0.12 | −30.7 |
| | | USA | | |
| Florida | 0.4314 | 0.3999 | −0.03 | −7.3 |
| California | 0.4821 | 0.4420 | −0.04 | −8.3 |
| Mountain | 0.4210 | 0.3848 | −0.04 | −8.6 |
| South Atlantic | 0.4791 | 0.4346 | −0.04 | −9.3 |
| East South Central | 0.4663 | 0.4209 | −0.05 | −9.7 |
| West South Central | 0.4493 | 0.4056 | −0.04 | −9.7 |
| Texas | 0.4668 | 0.4209 | −0.05 | −9.8 |
| *USA* | 0.4639 | 0.4181 | −0.05 | −9.9 |
| West North Central | 0.4344 | 0.3908 | −0.04 | −10.0 |
| East North Central | 0.4506 | 0.4039 | −0.05 | −10.4 |
| New England | 0.4078 | 0.3641 | −0.04 | −10.7 |
| New York | 0.5146 | 0.4578 | −0.06 | −11.0 |
| Pacific | 0.4232 | 0.3749 | −0.05 | −11.4 |
| Mid-Atlantic | 0.4684 | 0.4145 | −0.05 | −11.5 |

Countries/regions are sorted by decreasing order of percentage change.

redistribution. It is far from clear that attitudes towards redistribution will continue to be so positive in these very different circumstances.

Furthermore, the analysis of current redistribution reveals a further potential concern: redistribution is far from uniform among European countries. Table 7.3 lists market and disposable income Gini coefficients for each European country and each US region, as well as the difference between the two. The heterogeneity in the reduction in the Gini coefficient among European countries is striking. It varies from a minimum of 8.5% in Italy, to a maximum of 30.7% in the Netherlands. In comparison, redistribution in US regions is much more uniform, with a minimum of 7.3% in Florida and a maximum of 11.5% in the Mid-Atlantic region. There is nothing like a common European stance towards redistribution, so one will have to be forged from scratch. In light of the difficulties highlighted above, this is a tall order.

**Table 7.4.** Eurozone11 and the USA: Market and Disposable Income Percentile Ratios

| | 50th/10th | | | 90th/50th | | |
|---|---|---|---|---|---|---|
| | Market | Disposable | %Δ | Market | Disposable | %Δ |
| | | | Europe | | | |
| Ireland | 5.19 | 1.84 | −64.44 | 2.64 | 2.03 | −23.28 |
| Netherlands | 4.31 | 1.71 | −60.43 | 2.13 | 1.78 | −16.67 |
| Belgium | 4.23 | 1.84 | −56.57 | 2.00 | 1.75 | −12.75 |
| Finland | 3.69 | 1.80 | −51.16 | 2.11 | 1.77 | −16.09 |
| Austria | 3.85 | 2.00 | −47.88 | 2.14 | 1.80 | −15.93 |
| Germany | 3.42 | 2.08 | −39.07 | 2.26 | 1.92 | −15.16 |
| *Europe* | 3.50 | 2.22 | −36.41 | 2.24 | 1.95 | −12.71 |
| Spain | 3.60 | 2.34 | −35.05 | 2.32 | 2.08 | −10.43 |
| France | 2.52 | 1.80 | −28.83 | 2.04 | 1.89 | −7.62 |
| Portugal | 2.72 | 2.11 | −22.33 | 2.73 | 2.22 | −18.88 |
| Italy | 2.52 | 2.15 | −14.52 | 2.07 | 1.93 | −6.79 |
| Greece | 2.77 | 2.50 | −9.75 | 2.18 | 1.89 | −13.37 |
| | | | USA | | | |
| West South Central | 3.60 | 2.81 | −22.11 | 2.57 | 2.44 | −5.04 |
| California | 3.73 | 3.05 | −18.13 | 3.20 | 2.95 | −7.63 |
| East North Central | 3.63 | 2.98 | −17.87 | 2.73 | 2.42 | −11.61 |
| South Atlantic | 3.93 | 3.27 | −16.75 | 2.46 | 2.32 | −5.59 |
| *USA* | 3.56 | 3.07 | −13.95 | 2.72 | 2.44 | −10.31 |
| East South Central | 3.48 | 3.00 | −13.88 | 2.70 | 2.42 | −10.38 |
| West North Central | 3.28 | 2.85 | −13.24 | 2.42 | 2.26 | −6.60 |
| Texas | 3.83 | 3.32 | −13.20 | 2.92 | 2.55 | −12.81 |
| Mountain | 3.00 | 2.64 | −12.08 | 2.54 | 2.32 | −8.80 |
| Mid-Atlantic | 3.14 | 2.80 | −10.79 | 2.52 | 2.26 | −10.12 |
| Florida | 3.70 | 3.33 | −9.95 | 2.80 | 2.41 | −14.11 |
| New York | 3.41 | 3.09 | −9.58 | 2.94 | 2.47 | −16.04 |
| Pacific | 2.72 | 2.47 | −8.96 | 2.65 | 2.23 | −15.64 |
| New England | 3.14 | 2.92 | −7.21 | 2.57 | 2.27 | −11.58 |

Countries/regions are sorted by increasing order of the percentage change of the 50th/10th ratio.

The reduction in inequality in Europe comes about through a strong redistribution towards individuals with (very) low market income in high-income countries. Table 7.4 presents the fiftieth/tenth and ninetieth/fiftieth percentile ratios for market and disposable income in European countries and US regions. Finland, the Netherlands and Ireland go from the most unequal to the most egalitarian at the lower (and upper) tail. For instance, in the Netherlands the lower tail ratio falls from 4.3 to 1.7 (a reduction of 60%). At the opposite extreme, countries like Greece do not reduce lower-tail inequality by much, 2.8 versus 2.5 (a reduction of 10%). A lower and more uniform reduction in lower-tail inequality is achieved in the US regions.

The top two panels of Figure 7.6 constitute the most striking image we can produce to bring home the point that redistribution in Europe is highly asymmetric and benefits mostly individuals in high-income countries. It

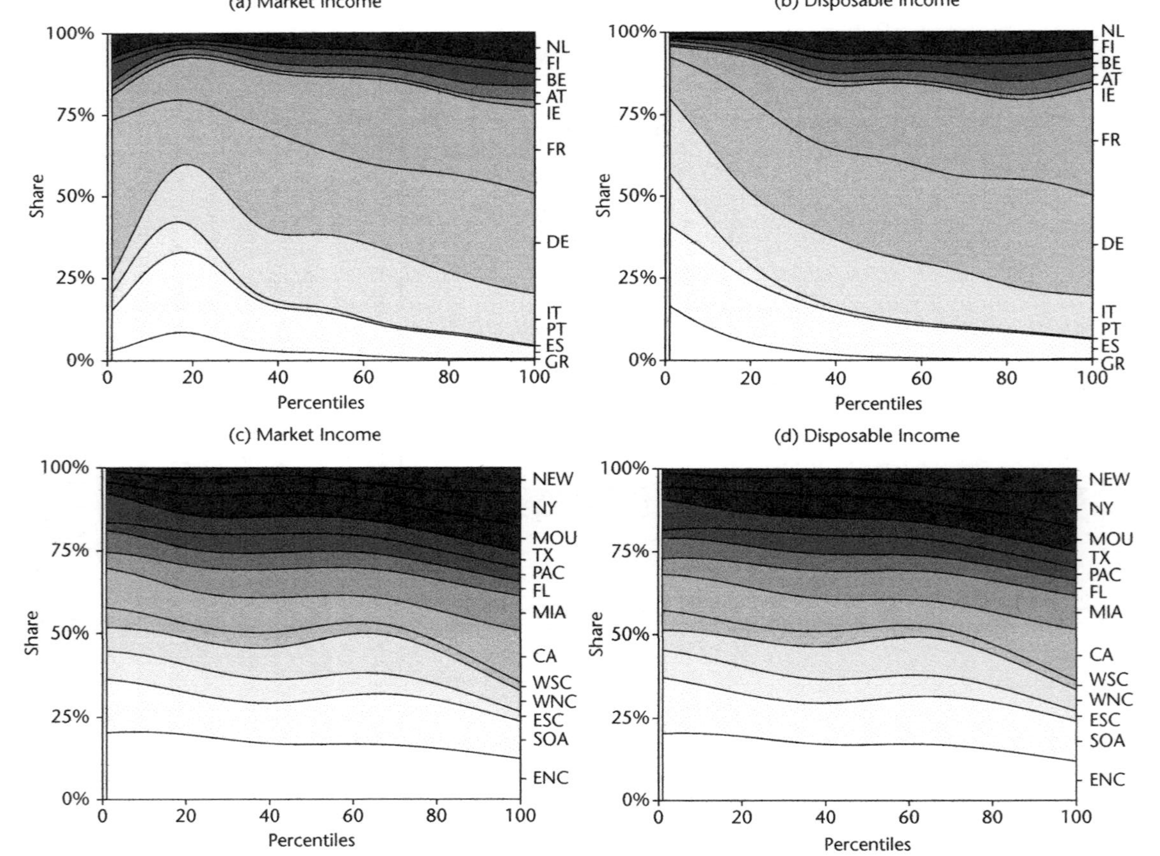


**Figure 7.6.** Share of Population per Region by Percentile of US Household Income. Share of Population per Region by Percentile of European Household Income.

depicts each country's share in the overall population of each percentile of the income distribution.

After (national) redistributive policies, the Southern countries gain a disproportionate share of the bottom percentile, while the Northern and core countries gain a disproportionate share of the top percentile. Spain, Greece, and Portugal, together, account for around 50% of the lowest disposable income decile, while their share of the population is only 21%. The likelihood of randomly drawing a citizen from one of these three countries in the bottom decile is 2.5 times higher than the probability of selecting a Spanish, Greek, or Portuguese citizen at random from the European population. Hence, in a unified Europe, any systematic policy of interpersonal income redistribution would amount to income redistribution across the original countries' boundaries.

The bottom row of Figure 7.6 shows that the situation is very different in the USA. The likelihood of selecting an individual from a US state or group of states is fairly constant across income percentiles, even at the tails of the distribution.

An additional observation about current European redistribution is that, almost by construction, it reduces the overlap among country distributions. Recall that we can think of the European market income distribution as a family of distributions clustered around different means. As each country is engaged (to a greater or lesser degree) into increasing the concentration of disposable income around its country-specific mean. Country-level redistribution means that the geographic clustering of disposable incomes is even greater than the geographic clustering of market incomes. In other words, country-level redistributive policies reduce inequality, but give rise to a more heterogeneous Union. This observation is potentially important for the design of redistribution in a putative federal Europe: if individual countries retain a significant role in (national) redistribution, the political feasibility of federal redistribution may be weakened. Will the attitudes towards federal redistribution be as positive as they are at the national level?

## 7.5. Changes Over Time

Economic integration and the establishment of a common currency may endogenously lead to income convergence across jurisdictions. The European economies examined here have deepened economic integration since the mid-1980s, adhering to the common currency of the Euro in 1999, and embracing enlargement to less developed Eastern European economies in the first decade of the 2000s.

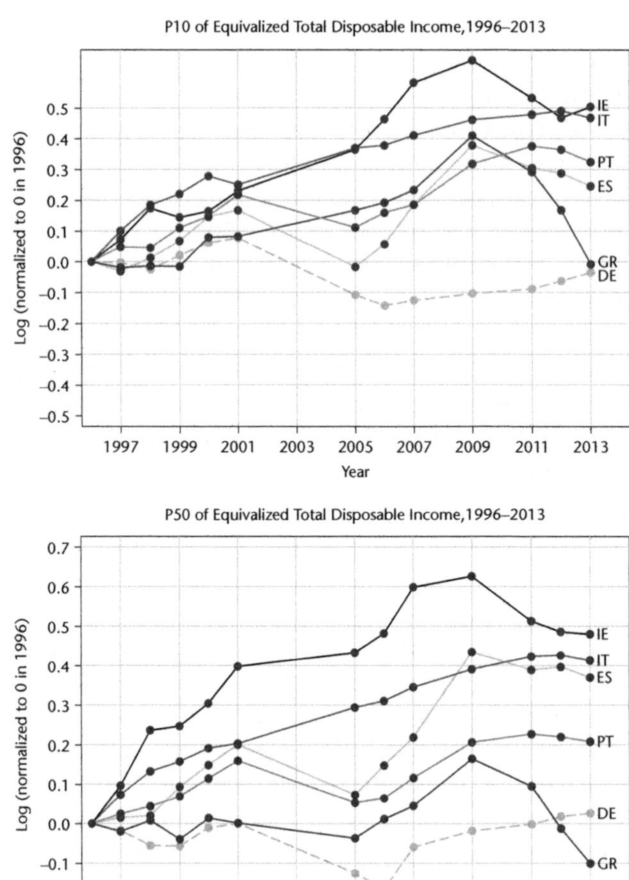


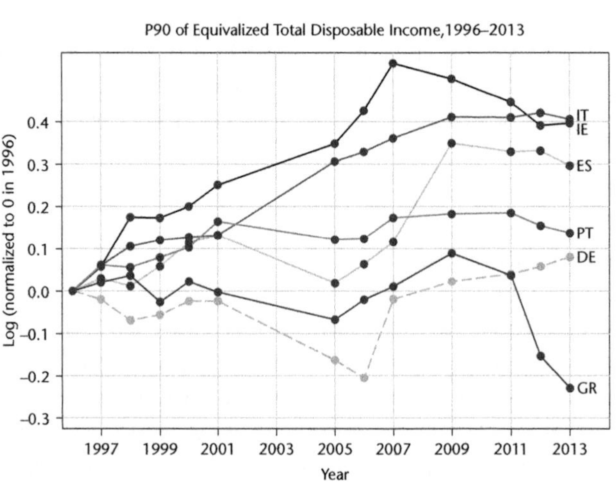


**Figure 7.7.** Income Percentiles Over Time for Germany, Greece, Italy, Ireland, Portugal, and Spain.

Figure 7.7 displays disposable income growth for the 1996–2013 period, for the tenth, fiftieth, and ninetieth percentiles for selected countries. Our indicators show convergence in income across European countries up until 2007. This convergence process results from faster growth in low-income countries than in high-income economies. The pattern of convergence between poorer and richer European countries becomes clear when we examine the evolution of income deciles. German households, at all levels of income, performed poorly up until 2011. The tenth and fiftieth income percentiles in Germany do not display positive income growth between 1996 and 2007. Germany's outlook improved only between 2007 and 2012, though not for the poorest German households, a fact that may be behind the recent policy decision to institute a national minimum wage in Germany. There have been similar evolutions in other high-income countries such as Belgium, Austria, and Finland, not shown in Figure 7.7. In sharp contrast, the tenth, fiftieth and ninetieth percentiles in Ireland, Italy, Spain, and Portugal display higher growth than their counterparts in Germany. Italy and Ireland were virtual champions of income growth, a process that slowed down only after the economic crisis. In Portugal and Spain, income growth was more modest, but still well above that experienced in the wealthier North. When it comes to Greece, the growth pattern is sharply different: dismal growth until the crisis, and a sharp decline after the crisis, especially in the fiftieth and ninetieth percentiles. The poorest Greece and in Germany end up with similar income growth at the end of the period, though following radically different intermediate paths: growth and decline in Greece, depression and, later on, recovery, in Germany.

Figure 7.8 displays the evolution of key percentiles for the income of European households as a whole, both for market and for disposable income. We witness a marked increase in market income in all income percentiles for the entire period, with two exceptions. First, there is a small decrease in income for the upper seventy-fifth and ninetieth percentiles, in the years up to 2001. The second, and most relevant exception, is the dramatic fall in market income for tenth lowest income percentile, in the wake of the 2009 economic crisis. Importantly, after we take into account government redistribution through taxes and transfers, the tenth poorest recover and their income path mimics closely the behaviour of the upper percentiles.

Hitherto, we focused our study on the Euro area countries. Because these countries built institutions to form a monetary union, they are expected to engage in a convergence process and be more homogeneous. Extending the definition of Europe to include non-Euro area countries results in higher inequality, 0.38 versus 0.325. This is the net effect of including Sweden, Denmark with high income and low inequality, the UK with both high income and inequality, Slovenia, Slovakia, Czech Republic, and Hungary with low

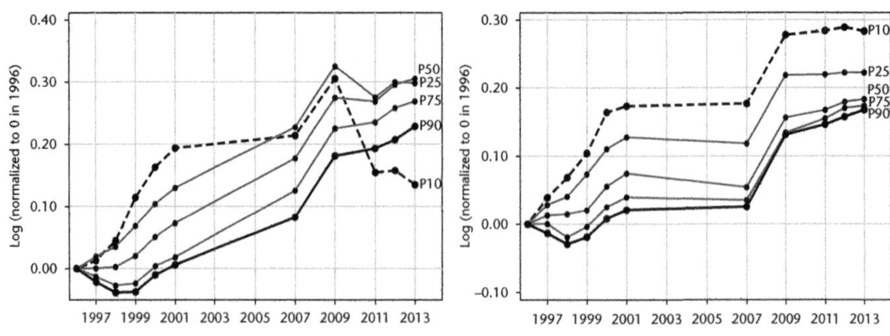


**Figure 7.8.** Market and Disposable Income Percentiles Over Time for Eurozone11.

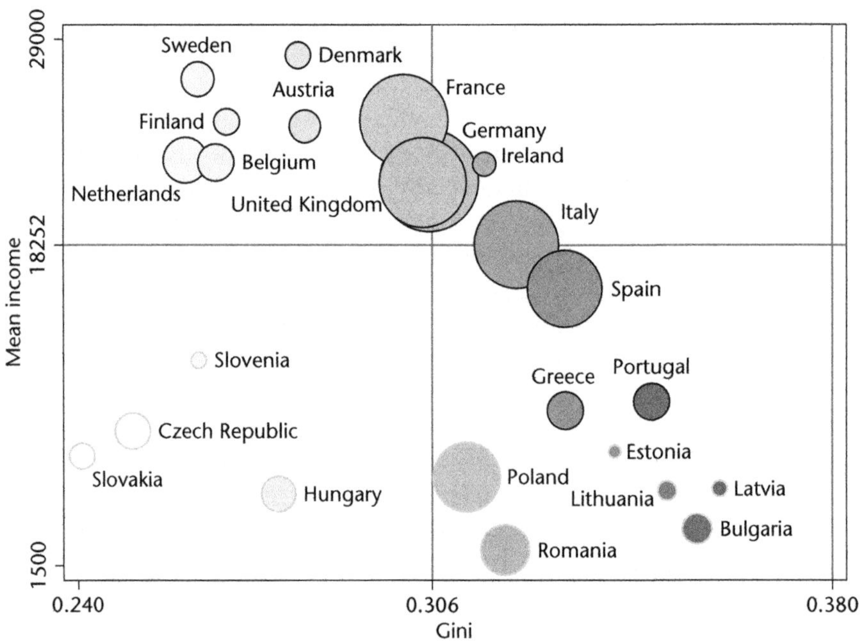


**Figure 7.9.** Average Income and Inequality, European Union 24, 2013.

inequality and low income, and, finally, low income, but high inequality countries, namely, Poland, Romania, Bulgaria, Estonia, Lithuania, and Latvia (Figure 7.9). The higher Gini results primarily from the between countries differences in average income, as most included countries have lower income. Remarkably, the Gini coefficient of EU28 as a single unit is larger than any individual country's Gini. A clear indicator of the lack of income overlap among these countries.

In a sense, the common vision of Europe as much more egalitarian than the USA is weakened (0.38 vs 0.42 in the USA). Furthermore, heterogeneity among European countries increases, reducing the overlap of countries' income distributions. These facts need to be taken into account in any policy discussion of European policymaking and its consequences.

## 7.6. Conclusions

We considered household income inequality in the Eurozone (the core of a putative United States of Europe) and in the USA. We take the Eurozone as a supranational economic entity similarly to the USA. We confirm that Europe, taken as a whole, is less unequal. The US household market income distribution is characterized by greater mass at the bottom and at the top.

But we also find that income distributions across US regions are more homogeneous than in Europe. European incomes are much more 'geographically clustered': the European poor concentrate in the poor European countries, and the rich in the rich countries. We also find that the rich European countries are less unequal than the poor ones. Finally, rich countries engage in much more redistribution than poor ones. As a consequence of national policies, the geographic clustering is reinforced.

We discuss how these features of European inequality might hinder the development of a common European understanding of what is an acceptable level of inequality, and the appropriate amount of redistribution. As we show with a broader definition of Europe, including among others the Eastern European countries, these issues become more pressing. Reaching such a common understanding is a critical step towards forging a closer union.

*Acknowledgements*

We thank David Neves for outstanding research assistance in the preparation and handling of the data. All views and errors are the authors' responsibility.

## 7.7. Appendix

The left panel of Figure A.7.1 shows the distribution of market income in Germany (the same appearing in Figure 7.2) as well as the overall income distribution of Europe after dropping all the observations from Germany. We can see that the remarkable overlap is not a mechanical feature. In the right panel, for disposable market, these features are more noticeable.

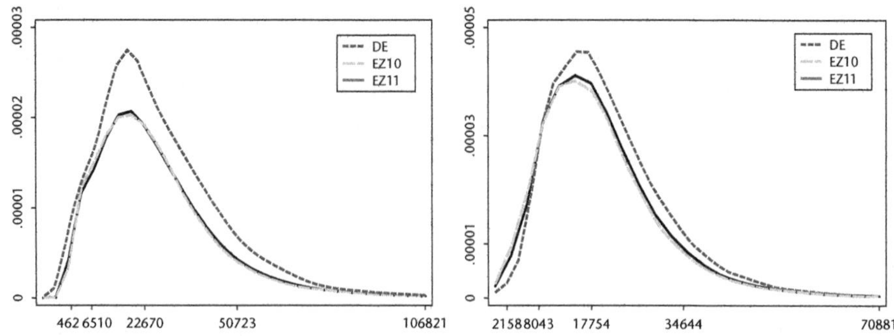


**Figure A.7.1.** Market and Disposable Income for Germany, Eurozone11, and Eurozone10, which excludes Germany.

## 7.8. References


Alesina, A. and E. L. Glaeser (2004), *Fighting poverty in the US and Europe: A world of difference*, Oxford University Press, Oxford.

Atkinson, A. B. (1996), 'Income distribution in Europe and the United States', *Oxford Review of Economic Policy* 12(1), 15–28.

Atkinson, A. B. (2008), *The changing distribution of earnings in OECD countries*, Oxford University Press, Oxford.

Atkinson, A. B. (2015), *Inequality: What Can Be Done?*, Harvard University Press, Cambridge, MA.

Beblo, M. and T. Knaus (2001), 'Measuring income inequality in Euroland', *Review of Income and Wealth* 47(3), 301–33.

Bertola, G. (2010), 'Inequality, integration, and policy: issues and evidence from EMU', *The Journal of Economic Inequality* 8(3), 345–65.

Boix, C. (2004), 'The institutional accommodation of an enlarged Europe', *Europäische Politik, Friedrich Ebert Stiftung* 6, 1–9.

Brandolini, A. (2007), 'Measurement of income distribution in supranational entities: the case of the European Union', in J. Micklewright and S. Jenkins, eds., 'Inequality and Poverty Re-examined', Oxford University Press, Oxford, pp. 62–83.

Brandolini, A., A. Rosolia, and R. Torrini (2012), 'The EU-wide earnings distribution', in J. A. Bishop and R. Salas, eds., 'Inequality, Mobility, and Segregation: Essays in Honor of Jacques Silber', Emerald Group Publishing, Bingley, pp. 205–35.

Goldin, C. and L. Katz (2008), *The race between education and technology*, Belknap Press.

Gouskova, E., P. Andreski, and R. F. Schoeni (2010), 'Comparing estimates of family income in the panel study of income dynamics and the march current population survey, 1968–2007', Technical Series Paper 10–01, Survey Research Center, Institute for Social Research, University of Michigan.

Hoffmeister, O. (2009), 'The spatial structure of income inequality in the enlarged EU', *Review of Income and Wealth* 55(1), 101–27.

Lerman, R. I. and S. Yitzhaki (1985), 'Income inequality effects by income source: a new approach and applications to the United States', *The review of economics and statistics* 67(1), 151–6.

OECD (2011), *Divided We Stand*, OECD, Paris.

OECD (2015), *In It Together: Why Less Inequality Benefits All*, OECD, Paris.

# Index

Tables and figures are indicated by an italic *t* and *f* following the page number.